SIKKIM

SIKKIM

A History of Intrigue and Alliance

PREET MOHAN SINGH MALIK

HarperCollins *Publishers* India

First published in hardback in India by
HarperCollins *Publishers* in 2021
A-75, Sector 57, Noida, Uttar Pradesh 201301, India
www.harpercollins.co.in

2 4 6 8 10 9 7 5 3 1

P-ISBN: 978-93-5422-643-4
E-ISBN: 978-93-5422-691-5

Typeset in 11.5/15.5 Bembo Std at
Manipal Technologies Limited, Manipal

Printed and bound at
Nutech Print Sertices - India

FSC
www.fsc.org
MIX
Paper from responsible sources
FSC® C143748

This book is Printed on FSC® certified paper
which ensure responsible forest management.

To

Late Ambassador N.B. Menon, whose manner of dealing with complex matters of foreign policy were an inspiration

'*But a nation can neglect geography only at its peril*'

—K.M. Panikkar, *Geographical Factors in Indian History*

CONTENTS

PART III: INDIA, TIBET AND SIKKIM

PROLOGUE

My posting to the political office for Sikkim and Bhutan took effect in October 1967 and was in a sense a continuation of my romance with the Himalayas. Born to a distinguished Sikh family of pre-Partition West Punjab, I spent my summers in Murree, a hill station—in the Rawalpindi district—like many others developed by the British to ease the effects of the hot summers of the plains upon their officials and families in India. Murree was within easy reach to those living in Rawalpindi. It was also en route to the Kashmir Valley that we often visited as my parents had connections there.

I was also fortunate to be sent to schools that had trekking in the Himalayas as part of their curriculum. Subsequently, I served in Switzerland as an officer of the Indian Foreign Service (IFS). These exposures made me aware of the difference in attitudes as well as the cultural mores that defined the peoples of the hills, the manner in which they approached nature and the tribulations they encountered living in difficult terrain, in contrast to how people in the plains interacted with nature. Nature itself set hills people apart from those residing in the plains. While recognizing this, I also arrived at the understanding that the people of the hills deeply valued their sense of independence and would sometimes use their unique setting to leverage advantage over interlocutors.

The appointment in Sikkim—my third posting as an officer of the IFS—was a reminder of the times before the partition of India when the hills of Murree had been an intimate part of my life. My time in Gangtok left a lasting impression on my mind of the strategic importance that the kingdom overlooking the Chumbi Valley in Tibet had for India.

The posting to Gangtok came about as a result of a request that I made to N.B. Menon when he had just accepted an appointment as a political officer in Sikkim covering India's treaty relations with both Sikkim and Bhutan and keeping an eye out, to the extent possible, on the political goings-on in Tibet.

The events leading to my seeking an appointment in Gangtok are worth recounting as they also throw some light on the manner in which the administration in the ministry of external affairs (MEA) appeared at times to close its eyes to inconvenient facts.

Surendra Singh Alirajpur came to hold the position of the first resident high commissioner of India to Singapore in July 1966. Coming from a feudal background, he was blessed with a feudal mindset and a degree of common sense, and often permitted emotion to overcome his intellect. Given the intellectual atmosphere prevailing among such people like Prime Minister Lee Kuan Yew and Foreign Minister S. Rajaratnam, he often came across as a square peg in a round hole.

I had been appointed as the second secretary at the high commission of India in Singapore, which I had assumed at the end of June 1966, and was the effective number two in the mission. The first hint I got of the difficulties in store for me was a letter from the joint secretary, holding charge of South East Asia, tasking me to send special reports on Singapore and its regional significance, in respect to the changing diplomatic relations among the countries of the region. This was a time when there were differences and uncertainties in South East Asia as a whole, particularly due to the backing that China was extending in both material and ideological terms to the communist movements in Malaysia and Indonesia. It was also a time when relations between the Maoist-friendly Sukarno and India's prime minister Jawaharlal Nehru were strained. The fact that the MEA expected that I would send these reports outside the knowledge of the high commissioner Surendra Singh Alirajpur not only put me in a professionally awkward position but such a breach in protocol could also destroy my career. I took care to send reports on regional developments at such times when Alirajpur was away from Singapore.

The second and more serious development occurred when the minister for external affairs M.C. Chagla made an official stopover at Singapore. It had been mutually decided among the countries, keeping in mind the brief period of the visit, that the bilateral meeting between the Indian and Singapore ministers would take place at the Paya Lebar airbase, at its VIP complex. The ministerial meeting was scheduled at 7.15 a.m. while the aircraft carrying Chagla and Secretary T.N. Kaul was to land at 6.30 a.m. I had informed Alirajpur at 5.15 a.m. that their flight was on schedule. He had responded with an intemperate explosion, making the unnecessary point that he was the high commissioner and needed no hand-holding.

He failed to arrive at the airport to receive the minister. What was worse was that he did not even turn up in time for the bilateral meeting. Secretary Kaul questioned me on the missing high commissioner to which, understandably, I was unable to respond with any convincing answer. A heavily perspiring Alirajpur turned up just a few minutes before the meeting came to an end. He was nervous and tried to throw the blame for his late appearance on me, which I vigorously refuted. Both Chagla and Kaul tore a strip off Alirajpur. Under normal circumstances, the high commissioner's indiscretion, that too in front of high-level Singapore government officials, would have been considered unacceptable behaviour, leading to his immediate replacement. However, this did not happen.

On the way back from the airport, N.B. Menon, then posted as deputy high commissioner at our mission in Kuala Lumpur, mentioned that he had accepted a posting as the political officer for Sikkim and Bhutan. On the spur of the moment, I asked him to consider me for a posting to the political office. He was kind enough to take this up with Delhi and secured my posting to Gangtok.

Gangtok provided me with an insight into India's position in an area of great strategic and security importance, the characteristics of the threats that the occupation of Tibet by the Chinese posed to our security and the manner in which China could leverage Tibet to gain advantage over India, including disrupting its relations with the Himalayan kingdoms of Sikkim, Nepal and Bhutan. A direct consequence of the Chinese occupation was the attempt by the rulers of Nepal and Sikkim to try and exploit the situation to serve their ambitions, ignoring in the process the negative diplomatic impact that this would have on their relations with India.

It is also worth recalling that the Sino-Indian War of 1962 broke out when I was in Mussoorie for my training after I was selected to the IFS. In trying to seek answers to all that had transpired leading up to that war, during those days in Mussoorie I spent time analysing Tibet's relations with India and China and what had brought things to a head between the two countries. Gangtok further provided me with an opportunity to look at things from close quarters and to understand the developments in both historico-cultural and strategic contexts.

During our initial days in Gangtok, N.B. Menon and his wife, Aneethi, mentored me and my wife. This was a rich learning process that in my case certainly resulted in a more rounded personality with an emphasis on patience that was not natural to the way I normally reacted. Watching Menon manoeuvre his way through the complexities of the relations between India and Sikkim, and India and Bhutan, with the Chinese game playing always on our minds, was a lesson in diplomatic dexterity that has forever remained with me. The manner in which both husband and wife managed to instil a family feeling among those in the mission was a lesson in people management that helped both me and my wife to bring a similar familial bonding in the missions that we later served at and headed.

INTRODUCTION

The geographical location of Sikkim makes it significant to the security of India, especially in the aftermath of the occupation of Tibet by the People's Republic of China (PRC) in 1950.

Historically,[1] Tibet had proffered no threat to the subcontinent and during the British Raj, it had effectively been cast in the role of a buffer state that ensured that neither the Chinese kingdom nor the Russian occupation of Central Asia posed a direct threat to India. The modelling of both Tibet and Afghanistan in the role of buffer states by Britain had helped in securing the western, northern and eastern frontiers of India.

This template was threatened in 1950 when a newly independent India was flanked on its northern frontiers by a Chinese-occupied Tibet that by implication threatened India's relations with the three Himalayan kingdoms of Nepal, Bhutan and Sikkim from a security perspective.

Of these three kingdoms, Sikkim was unique because it had, for all practical purposes been treated by the British as an Indian state—it was a member of the Chamber of Princes since 1922. In

1947, when India became independent and the process of merging the princely states with the Indian Union had been set in motion, the country was approached by a popularly led Sikkimese political leadership with the proposal that the kingdom of Sikkim also be merged with the Union of India. Prime Minister Nehru, who had taken over the responsibility for India's relations with the Himalayan states of Bhutan, Nepal and Sikkim, persuaded the delegation from Sikkim to not press the issue, promising that the popular demands for participative democracy would be accommodated within the functioning of the state. This promise remained largely unfulfilled till India acceded to the referendum for abolition of monarchy and for merger with India in 1975.

The British, first making inroads into India with the East India Company (EIC) and later, after the sepoy uprising of 1857, with the administration of India moving to the British Crown, had made several attempts to establish relations with Tibet. Their interest was primarily driven by colonial commercial gains, arising from the expectation that Tibet would provide a land bridge to trading with China from Calcutta, and by extension, London. It was here that Sikkim came to occupy a special place as it offered a direct and geographically secure route to Tibet's main cities, Shigatse and Lhasa. Sikkim's importance had surfaced when the Gorkha conquest of Nepal in 1768 resulted in the denial of the traditional trade routes that connected India's Benares to Tibet.

At first, a route through Bhutan had been adopted as an alternative to Nepal during the time of the governorship of Warren Hastings. This was the route that was used by the delegation that Hastings sent in 1774 under the leadership of George Bogle to Tashilhunpo. Eventually, the route through Sikkim via Chumbi Valley came to be preferred as it granted greater ease of connectivity and it was this route that was used by the Younghusband incursion into Tibet ending in Lhasa and the signing of the Anglo-Tibetan Treaty of 1904.

Relations with Nepal, Bhutan and Sikkim (a protectorate of India till its merger in 1975) were significantly tested, especially regarding security, with India needing to keep a close watch on Chinese actions after the 1962 Sino-Indian War and subsequently due to the threats issued by China on the Sikkim border during the 1965 and 1971 Indo-Pak wars.

The geographical location of the Chumbi Valley at the Sikkim border came to assume additional significance as it granted India's military with a major advantage—its posts overlooked the valley and the location of Chinese camps within it. This factor endowed our presence in Sikkim with added strategic and security significance. The Chinese tried to neutralize this advantage by adopting measures to drive India away from these heights resulting in the military clashes of 1967.

One of the consequences of Nehru taking over the responsibility of managing the relations with the Himalayan states was that Sikkim, despite having been part of the Chamber of Princes since 1922, was kept out of merger negotiations. It was only as China's aggressive intentions in Tibet became an established fact that Nehru finally decided that Sikkim would be retained as an Indian protectorate to meet India's strategic and security interests.

The underlying purpose of this book is to explore the strategic importance of Sikkim to the security of India and how this has been connected to Tibet's relations with India from the time of the East India Company. Examining the historical links that bound Tibet and India together leads to the geostrategic importance of Tibet to India with the overhang of these factors on the presence of China in Tibet. The value of the inherited extraterritorial rights for India and Nehru's failure to leverage this advantage to ensure that the Chinese occupation did not affect India's border ties with Tibet also needs to be considered.

The book looks at the realities of India's relations with Tibet and China, from British times, in some detail to establish that Nehru's approach to the issue of Tibet and its occupation by China failed to understand the import of the strategic and security impact that the appearance of China, as a neighbour, would have on India and its interests. The irony is that once the Chinese occupation of Tibet came to be an accomplished fact, it was Nehru who came up with the analogy of the Chumbi Valley being like 'a dagger pointed at the heart of India' threatening the 'chicken's neck'.[2]

Coverage on Sikkim and its merger with India has been outlined in three works of some seminal importance. The first is Sunanda K. Datta-Ray's book, *Smash and Grab: Annexation of Sikkim*,[3] which draws heavily on records made available to the author by the twelfth and last ruler of independent Sikkim, Palden Thondup Namgyal. As a consequence, the book ends up projecting his views on the merger. Datta-Ray was Palden Thondup's friend and is understandably sympathetic to his views. While Datta-Ray does describe the political events leading up to the merger, he does not grant sufficient weightage to the internal movement that arose against feudal rule from 1947 onwards. The movement was initiated by the Sikkim State Congress, reflecting the people's demands for a three-point agenda that included merger with India, popular representation and land reforms directed at ending the dominance of landlords. This political movement continued to raise its head from time to time. Palden Thondup's lack of experience and maturity, first as the Maharaja Kumar and subsequently as the Maharaja, failed to subdue this disquiet. The political differences between the people and the ruler, over time, resulted in several phases of unrest that eventually ended in the removal of the Chogyal, 'the righteous ruler' and the merger of Sikkim with India.

The next book, *Sikkim: Requiem for a Himalayan Kingdom*[4] by Andrew Duff, has drawn heavily on Datta-Ray's work and on letters written by two Scottish women who headed the Tashi Namgyal Girls' High School in Gangtok. Duff also had the advantage of drawing on classified documents released by London and Washington and therefore has a more comprehensive coverage of events. He does mention the strategic aspect but this is done more in passing and it does not get the detailed attention that it deserves. He, like Datta-Ray, portrays the merger as orchestrated by India, projecting his sympathy for the ruler's point of view and in the process diminishing the primary thrust for the merger—the people's wishes. Another determining factor was Prime Minister Indira Gandhi's loss of confidence in Palden Thondup, arising out of his and his sister Kukula's attempt to bring the Chinese into the India–Sikkim equation.

G.B.S. Sidhu's book, *Sikkim: The Dawn of Democracy*,[5] is a rather one-sided projection of the events that led to the merger of the state with India. He also, unfortunately, succeeds in granting substance to the claims of those who hold the opinion that the merger was an engineered event by India. Frankly, it's a book that should never have been written particularly by an intelligence operative who had only a limited view of the process of decision-making that was being handled in both Sikkim and India at levels beyond his reach or knowledge. There were many factors involved, and the decisions in Delhi were moved and influenced by the political and security events that were rapidly unfolding in Sikkim.

The overriding issue that ultimately resulted in the merger was the need to accept the popular will and to bring immediate peace to the state that was of primary strategic and security concern to India. China had on two occasions, when India was at war with Pakistan in 1965 and 1971, tried to pressurize India on Sikkim, threatening actions that showed clearly its aim at suborning India's relations and presence in the Himalayan kingdoms, and certainly conveyed a direct threat to the security of India. Sidhu grants too much credit to the efforts of the spymaster, R.N. Kao, as the plotter-in-chief of the merger; he fails to appreciate that the political establishment in Delhi had recognized the strategic importance of Sikkim to India, as Tibet came to be occupied by the People's Republic of China, and the essentiality of keeping Sikkim under India's direct control as far back as 1950.

Kao and the Research and Analysis Wing (R&AW) had only achieved operational competence from 1970 onwards, when the R&AW assumed operational responsibility to carry out cross-border intelligence from Gangtok. Its activities in Gangtok were, to an extent, constrained by the fact that its presence and purpose was known to the Chogyal and his underlings. In 1970, the Chogyal told me in Geneva that he was happy with the R&AW's presence in Gangtok as it granted credence to the legal argument that Sikkim was a foreign country in a special but limited relationship with India. I had at the time reported this fact to the foreign secretary T.N. Kaul.

The British interest in Tibet was mainly driven by two considerations. First was commercial, where Tibet was seen as a potential market for British goods, including tea and broadcloth, while also being a source of raw wool for Britain's consumption. The British also hoped to use Tibet as a land bridge for trade with imperial China's outlying provinces. The second consideration, and this was a subsequent development connected to the establishment of a frontier policy revolving around Russia and its Asian ambitions, was to establish Tibet as a buffer state between British India and Russian Central Asia.

It was Sikkim's geographical location and the ease of connectivity that it provided to Tibet that led the British to attach increasing importance to Sikkim. Eventually, the British ended up treating Sikkim as a 'federated princely state of India', encouraging its membership to the Indian Chamber of Princes in 1922. Nehru came to treat Sikkim as a state in a special relationship with India, turning down the demand of the popular movement that sought it to be treated on par with other Indian princely states.

The underlying objective of this book is to clarify and establish the primacy of strategic issues that lay behind India's decision to accept the demand that Sikkim be merged with India. The compelling security factors behind this merger included the presence of Indian troops at the commanding heights of Sikkim to neutralize the threat that the People's Liberation Army's (PLA's) occupation of the Chumbi Valley posed to the 'chicken's neck', the only land link that connects north-east India to the rest of the country.

The military exchanges between the Chinese and Indian forces in the autumn of 1967 along the Sikkim border with Tibet overlooking the Chumbi Valley, and more recently the standoff between the two forces at the Doklam plateau, once again reinforced the strategic importance of Sikkim, and its geographical location, to the defence of India, to counter any threat posed by China to the vulnerable Siliguri Corridor.

India's susceptibility due to the dominant Chinese presence in the Chumbi Valley also has a historical background. This was the route adopted by a combined Sino-Tibetan force to enter north India and defeat Arunasva, the Indian ruler who succeeded Harsha Vardhana in AD 649. It is the failure of the British to appreciate the strategic importance of the Chumbi Valley to India and, as a consequence, not insist on its retention as a part of the kingdom of Sikkim. In fact, John Claude White, the first political officer based in Gangtok, had pointed out to the North Bengal administration that the Chumbi Valley 'formed part of Sikkim'[6] and should be considered within the territory of Sikkim. The Tibet policy remained hostage to what London felt would be compatible with British interests in China. Accordingly, the Anglo-Chinese Convention of 1890 excised the Chumbi Valley from Sikkim by defining the Cho La range as the watershed delineating Sikkim's borders with Tibet and not the Himalayan range. Britain's commercial gains had trumped over the imperatives of Indian strategic interests.

Both London's actions during the 1904–06 period and Nehru's approach, subsequent to the 1950 occupation of Tibet, were guided by their outlook on relations with China failing to take into account, fully, the strategic importance of an independent Tibet to the security of India.

An important aim of this book is to grant clarity to the conflicting position that came to exist between London and Calcutta on India's relations with Tibet. Lord George Nathaniel Curzon as viceroy of India insisted that Russia's imperial interests in Central Asia posed a threat to India, not just to its north-western frontiers, but, by its moves on Tibet, to India's frontiers with Tibet. To spell this out in strategic terms, Curzon put forward the following two points for London's consideration:

First, that the security of the British interests in India was central to Britain's expanding colonial empire as India was the pivot around which Britain had built its empire.

Second, Britain could not ignore the imperative of securing India's frontiers by creating buffer states between Russian Central Asia and India in Afghanistan and Tibet.

However, motivated by its business and economic interests, Britain was reluctant to grant precedence to India's strategic interests in Tibet, maintaining that China's interests as the suzerain had to take precedence over India's interests and concerns in Tibet. Curzon's well-argued and pragmatic approach was ignored.

More importantly, by casting the tradition-bound relations that existed between China and Tibet within an unknown or only as understood within a European concept of suzerainty, Britain ended up depriving Tibet of its independence. This led to suzerainty being confused as sovereignty and enabled China to claim that Tibet was a part of China.

Nehru's 'Vision of Asia' policy was dominated by the idea of India and China becoming the pivots of a rising Asia, and resulted in his failure to attach an appropriate value to the extraterritorial rights that India had in Tibet. The mischief that China came to play, particularly in the Chumbi Valley, led to the exchanges of 1967 when the importance of retaining India's geostrategic positions in Sikkim was driven home to Delhi.

Notes

1. There were two invasions that had taken place in the seventh and ninth centuries that were exceptions and are dealt with later in the text with reference to the security threat that the Chumbi Valley of Tibet poses to independent India.
2. 'History of Sikkim', https://en.wikipedia.org/wiki/History_of_Sikkim.
3. *Smash and Grab: Annexation of Sikkim*, Sunanda K. Datta-Ray, Vikas Publications, 1984. Revised edition published in Westland India, 2013
4. *Sikkim: Requiem for a Himalayan Kingdom*, Andrew Duff, Random House India, 2015.
5. *Sikkim—Dawn of Democracy: The Truth behind the Merger with India*, G.B.S. Sidhu, Penguin Random House India, 2018.
6. *Sikhim and Bhutan: Twenty-One Years on the North-East Frontier 1887–1908*, J.C. White, p. 1; published in 1909 by Edward and Arnold, who were the publishers to the India Office.

PART I

BRITAIN, TIBET AND SIKKIM

1

SIKKIM AND CHUMBI VALLEY

To fully grasp why Sikkim has come to acquire such great importance to India's security and strategic considerations, a brief but pointed reference to its geographical features forms an important part of the narrative. The finest depiction of this can be found in a book compiled by the intelligence branch of the British Indian Army, published in 1907.

It states:[1] 'The territory known as Independent Sikkim, comprising an area of 3600 square miles, lies south of the main Himalayan range, and between two of its great southern offshoots; one, a range culminating in the great mass of Kanchinjunga and tailing down into what is known as the Singalela ridge; the other, the Cho [La] range.' This description makes the point that except for the south, Sikkim is entirely 'separated from its neighbours by a wall of giant mountains varying from 10,000 to 28,000 feet in height'. In actual fact, the entire territory of the state of Sikkim lies in the catchment area of the Teesta river.

Being an intelligence compilation, it grants credence to the claim that the Chumbi Valley was part of the kingdom of Sikkim till the

British desire to confine the reign of the Sikkim Maharaja within the Singalela and Cho La ranges excised the valley from Sikkim and ended up making it a part of Tibet. This view is confirmed in the statement of Sikkim's territorial limits: 'Westwards lies Nepal; on the north and east Tibet, Chumbi, and Bhutan; and to the south the British district of Darjeeling.' As is obvious, the reference to the valley as separate from Tibet recognizes that it lies south of the Himalayan watershed.

Elsewhere, the compilation, when describing events that had a degree of military content to them, is careful to make the distinction between the land of Tibet and that of the Chumbi Valley. The question remains, why did the British not have any interest in retaining Chumbi as a part of Sikkim? There is a partial answer suggesting that Chogyal Thutob Namgyal's pig-headed claim that he was answerable only to Lhasa was seen as one that he was adhering to because of his links to the Chumbi Valley.[2] It was felt that cutting off those links and forcing him to reside in Sikkim would place him under Britain's direct control. This confusion was caused by the incorrect belief that after 1792 the valley had become a part of Tibet. What was ignored was the fact that the Raja of Sikkim could not have placed his administrative headquarters in the Chumbi Valley if it did not belong to him as part of his kingdom. This had remained the situation till the signing of the Anglo-Sikkim Treaty of Tumlong (1861).

What was apparent was that the British were unaware of the historical fact that if any power that was inimical to India's interests came to exercise its hold on the Chumbi Valley, it could use the ease of connectivity that the valley provided to invade India. This had happened in the seventh and ninth centuries when a combined Tibetan and Chinese force invaded the Indian kingdom held by Harsha Vardhana's successors.

Interestingly, Sir Herbert Hope Risley does provide an insight into what lay behind the British thinking suggesting that the Raja's preference to live and operate out of Chumbi was a consequence of 'the Nepalese invasion of the country, [that] induced the Rajas to transfer the head-quarters of their Government to the Valley of Chumbi', describing this move as having 'the worst effect on the internal administration of the state'. Lepcha interests were neglected, and 'Chumbi became the Hanover' of Sikkim.[3]

The entire issue revolved around the British desire to have the ruler under their firm control and giving up the Chumbi Valley served to their administrative convenience, and it was a gesture that they felt would help create a more favourable environment for their proposals to open Tibet up to trade with them.

Arrival in Gangtok

I arrived in Gangtok towards the end of October 1967 to join the political office of India, which oversaw relations under the Indian treaties with Bhutan and Sikkim. The journey to Gangtok from Siliguri in my low-slung sports roadster that I had brought along with me from Singapore was quite an adventure. After we reached Gangtok, we had to spend a couple of days awaiting the arrival of our heavy baggage that was loaded at Siliguri on transport provided by the Sikkim State Transport Company.

Once we left Siliguri behind and moved on to the NH 31A, we were soon travelling along the western side of the narrow Sivak Gola gorge of the Teesta. The river flowed swiftly on its ways to debouch itself on the plains of Bengal for a short distance before entering what was then East Pakistan. We crossed the picturesque cantilevered concrete bridge built by the British over the Teesta, coming across a forked route, one road branching to Kalimpong and the other to Sikkim. This bridge, a historic landmark, was completely washed away during the monsoons of 1968, a victim to the fury of nature which we were to witness in Gangtok.

We entered Sikkim at the border crossing of Rangpo. At this stage we were still driving in the lower parts of the Teesta valley. As we gradually started to climb along a gentle slope, the west of the road fell away into the flood plains of the Teesta and the Greater Rungit. On both sides of the road there was a thick forest and lush vegetation that soon turned from deciduous to coniferous. A lot of this area, unfortunately, lost its tree cover due to the massive rain-induced floods of 1968.

A short distance later, we started our climb towards the town of Singtam and came to the famous landslide-prone 9th Mile area of Sikkim. Here we had to cross over a huge rocky mound that the landslides had created. The border roads personnel working on the road stood around to see how the low-slung car would cross this hurdle. Both my wife and brother had to be off-loaded and the car was manually helped across, where in some parts it was almost physically lifted and manoeuvred over the peak of the landslide. Once we had passed through Singtam, where we had our first taste of the famous Singtam mandarins, the next hurdle was the infamous 29th Milestone, where a landslide covered a longer part of the highway, but it was not as difficult to cross as the earlier 9th Mile portion. Thereafter we reached Gangtok, at that time a town of some 18,000, and the capital of Sikkim since the stationing of the first British political officer in 1861.

The road journey was part of my introduction to the strategic and security implications of the highway that was Sikkim's lifeline. It was the route over which almost all the supplies of goods and services to, and exports from, Sikkim were carried, but more important was its use in keeping the Indian Army supplied of all its requirements. The entire logistical planning of the two mountain divisions that were stationed to keep the Chinese in the Chumbi Valley honest was built around this highway.

I was aware that one of my responsibilities would be to keep track of the day-to-day relations between the 17th Mountain Division and the Sikkim secretariat headed by a chief secretary who was serving under the combined directions of the monarch and the Indian government's appointee, the principal administrative officer.

The India-Sikkim Treaty was signed in December 1950 to reflect the changed security perception forced on India with the Chinese occupation of Tibet, ending Tibet's role as a buffer state and bringing the Chinese to India's doorstep. Sikkim was reconfirmed as a state under the protection of India.

The first resident political officer at Gangtok was John Claude White, who served from 1889 to 1908. He would report to the colonial administration of North Bengal and was responsible for overseeing relations with Sikkim, Bhutan and Tibet. He was also the official who was placed in charge of coordinating the logistical and back-up support for the Younghusband expedition that led to war between the British colonial troops and the Tibetan forces. The war ended with the signing of the Anglo-Tibetan Treaty in 1904, a treaty that was subsequently amended and endorsed by the Anglo-Chinese Treaty of 1906.

The political officers appointed by the government of independent India continued to cover all three states till the end of Ambassador Appa Sahib Pant's stay as the political officer in Gangtok in 1961. Thereafter, till 1970, this office covered both Sikkim and Bhutan, till India established a full diplomatic office in Thimphu. The political office was disbanded with the merger of Sikkim with India in 1975. Ambassador N.B. Menon was the political officer at Gangtok when I joined the political office, a post that he held from 1967 to 1970.

White's selection of the location of the residence-cum-office of the political officer was in keeping with the typical British mindset. He placed it at one end of the saddle, with the other end connected to the Chogyal's palace. White ensured that the residency was located at a height that overshadowed the ruler's palace and symbolically conveyed the message that the political officer had greater authority than the king of the kingdom. The title of the ruler was similarly designated as Maharaja,[4] a title that was wholly Indian by definition, where, along lines similar in treatment to Indian princes, he was granted a fifteen-gun salute.

Within the first few days of my arrival in Gangtok, I called on Major General Sagat Singh, the commanding officer of the 17th Mountain Division. He was a clear-headed, no-nonsense officer and drew me a well-argued analysis of what had transpired and the manner in which the aggressive intent of the Chinese had been blunted and thwarted. What was of greater import was his spelling out the geostrategic importance of Sikkim to India's defence security, clearly defining the importance of occupying the mountain heights and high passes that overlooked the Chumbi Valley, significantly neutralizing the threat that the Chinese presence in Tibet posed to the Siliguri Corridor.

If anything, the events of 1967 had reinforced the importance of Sikkim to India's strategic and security interests threatened by China's occupation of Tibet. The Chinese attempt at forcing India out of the Nathu La and Jelep La sent a clear message that India could not afford to weaken its involvement in Sikkim.

The prevailing reality in Gangtok was that there were three centres of power: the Chogyal and his immediate entourage headed by Jigdal Densappa, the principal secretary to the ruler and an alumnus of Delhi's St Stephen's College; the Indian political officer who was the guardian of India's interests as spelt out under the Indo-Sikkim Treaty of 1950; and the commander of the 17th

Mountain Division, who along with his counterpart the commander of the 27th Mountain Division, based out of Kalimpong, held the responsibility for carrying out the provisions relating to defence under that treaty.

These two mountain divisions along with the 20th Mountain Division that was stationed in Binnaguri were part of the XXIII Corps based in Sukna and were involved in the overall defence structure, that included preserving the sanctity of the Siliguri Corridor and its surroundings. The XXIII Corps came under the purview of the Eastern Army Command that has the responsibility of defending the north-eastern and eastern borders of India from external threats to the integrity and sovereignty of the country.

In the autumn of 1967, there had been border skirmishes between Indian and Chinese armed forces at Nathu La and Cho La, including heavy artillery exchanges that led to casualties on both sides. The artillery equipment with the 17th Mountain Division had greater reach than what the Chinese possessed, and as the Indian forces held the higher ground, overlooking the Chumbi Valley, it helped them take on the Chinese and deliver a heavy blow, causing substantially higher casualties.

To the Chinese, despite all their rhetoric of visiting upon India a repeat of the debacles of the 1962 war, it would have come as a bolt out of the blue, that India was not only better prepared but, when confronted, were able to retaliate effectively.

While there was speculation on what lesson the Indian political establishment may have learnt from this attempted Chinese incursion, the ground reality was that Sikkim was vital to India's defence architecture against the threat of China.

The Chinese ultimatum during the course of the Indo-Pakistan War of 1965, asking India to vacate the Nathu La and Jelep La passes that were on the Sikkim–Tibet watershed—and clearly demarcated as Sikkimese territory under the Sino-British Convention of

1890—only brought home the danger that the Chinese occupation of Tibet posed to India. That this threat had arisen at a time when Pakistan had gone to war with India only confirmed the fact that India faced a two-pronged threat to its security and territorial integrity. That the Chinese were willing to violate provisions of treaties that they had signed and ratified proved right Sardar Patel's contention that they were deceitful and could not be trusted.

Sardar Vallabh Bhai Patel, deputy prime minister in Nehru's Cabinet, in his letter of 7 November 1950, pointed out the duplicitous nature of the PRC, suggesting that 'the Chinese Government have tried to delude us by professions of peaceful intentions'.[5] Patel was critical of the views and assessments of China put forward by K.M. Panikkar as India's ambassador to the PRC, claiming 'that at a crucial period they [the Chinese] managed to instil into our Ambassador a false sense of confidence in their so-called desire to settle the Tibetan problem by peaceful means'. Patel accurately described the Chinese occupation of Tibet as an act of 'perfidy' and pointed out that not only had they manipulated the Indian ambassador but also rejected Nehru's hand, extended in friendship, which indicated that 'even though we regard ourselves as friends of China, the Chinese do not regard us as their friends'.

The Chinese Stratagems

The Chinese attach considerable importance to the *Thirty-Six Stratagems* that are part of 'classic Chinese war theories'.[6] They are older than Sun Tzu's holdings on the art of war and play a vital role in China's daily endeavours. These stratagems are taught to each child in China and are a part of the cultural upbringing.

A reading of these stratagems confirms that the Chinese state applies them to gain its objectives, and that Mao and his able lieutenant Zhou Enlai used them effectively against Nehru while negotiating the occupation of Tibet and the consequences for India that followed.

The Chinese used deceit to lull the British while the former violated with impunity the Conventions of 1890, 1904 and 1906. To make it plain, the stratagems are 'gems that speak to the core of Chinese society', and have become part of their 'collective unconscious'. Rosalie Tung, a recognized Asian Scholar, puts it best, by stating that the Chinese approach is to engage 'in deception to gain a strategic advantage'.[7]

In their talks with India, the thirty-six stratagems that were employed to pull the wool over the eyes of Indian leadership are spelt out below and should be treated as lessons that any negotiator with the Chinese should keep in mind:[8]

'*Cross the sea under camouflage*' can be interpreted as 'the sight of common occurrences leads to slackened suspicion. Accordingly secret machinations are better concealed in the open than in the dark, and extreme public exposure often contains extreme secrecy.' In other words—hide your intent in the open.

'*Create something out of nothing*' translated into practice means 'design a counterfeit front to put the enemy off-guard'.

'*Conceal a dagger in a smile*' is perhaps the most compelling element of the strategies practised by the Chinese and is still a fundamental domestic and external policy tool. In its translated form it spells out both the philosophy and the strategy: 'You conceal your hostility by assuming outward friendliness. You ingratiate yourself with enemies, inducing them to trust you. When you have their confidence, you can move against them in secret.'

'*Lead away a goat in passing: pick up something on the sly.*' In translation, this makes it clear that the Chinese create situations that conceal the real intent by exploiting any lapses or weaknesses on the part of the opponent or rival. The intent behind this clause states that 'any negligence of the enemy must be turned into a benefit for you'. This is what they successfully employed to gain the confidence of the Indian ambassador, Sardar K.M. Panikkar, who was taken in by the charming blandishments expended on him by the Chinese leadership, in particular by Zhou Enlai, thus permitting them to lull him into the belief that they would not challenge the Indian position on the borders with Tibet.

'Toss out a glazed tile to draw a jade/Cast a brick to attract a gem.' This is perhaps an even more compelling principle of Chinese strategy that was successfully applied against India, lulling it into the 1954 Sino-Indian Agreement that ensured the unilateral revocation by India of its inherited rights in Tibet. The stratagem promotes 'presenting something superficial or of apparent value to induce another party to produce something of real worth'.

Here, India was manoeuvred into a position where it came to attach greater value to the idea of Panchsheel, the five principles of peaceful coexistence, over the reality of the rights that granted it both with a leverage and bargaining power to negotiate a deal that would be of real and lasting value to national interests. It is worth pointing out that the principles of Panchsheel were ones that Nehru believed in, and was sincere in his commitment to them, but for Zhou, they were a tool to establish relationships, with no emotional attachment to the sanctity of the principles. For instance, the Chinese were extending material and military support to the communist-led insurgency in Burma and continued to do so while promoting the Panchsheel principles with the Burmese prime minister, U Nu, as a guiding tenet of the relations between the two countries.

Both Mao Tse Tung and Zhou Enlai employed the stratagem *'remove the ladder after the ascent'*, that in substance suggests that 'you manoeuvre your enemies into a point of no return by baiting them with what looks like advantages and opportunities'.

Notes

1. *Frontiers and Overseas Expeditions from India*, p. 39, compiled in the Intelligence Branch, division of the chief of staff, Simla. Printed in 1907 at the Government Monotype Press.
2. He was citing the obligations that he had assumed by signing the Treaty of Galing in 1886 wherein it was declared that 'Sikkim was subject only to China and Tibet.'
3. *The Gazetteer of Sikhim,* H.H. Risley, Forgotten Books, London, 2018, page iii of the Introduction. First published in 1894 by the Bengal Secretariat Press.
4. Originally when the British came in touch with the ruler of Sikkim during the time of the East India Company, he was addressed by the Indian title of Raja. After the Treaty of Tumlong and with the then ruler agreeing to the stipulation of staying for at least nine months in the year in Sikkim, his title was revised to the higher title of Maharaja.
5. From the full text of Sardar Vallabhbhai's letter to Prime Minister Nehru dated 7 November 1950 in the compilation: *India–China Relations: 1947–2000*, Volume I, Avtar Singh Bhasin, Geetika Publishers (in cooperation with policy planning division, ministry of external affairs), New Delhi, 2018, pp. 441–447.
6. Taken from the *Book of Qi: A Biography of Wang Jingze*. Wang was a general who served the Southern Qi dynasty. The *Thirty-Six Stratagems* are attributed to have originated in both written and oral histories by many diverse writers. They are still in vogue in China.
7. The thirty-six Chinese strategies applied to negotiation described by Professor Rosalie Tung in: 'A Perspective on Cross-Cultural Negotiation and Dispute Resolution', *Pepperdine Dispute Resolution Law Journal* 403 (2008). Rosalie Tung teaches at the Beedie School of Business, Simon Fraser University.
8. *Ibid*.

2

LESSONS OF HISTORY

If anything, those who forget the lessons of history end up paying a price that at times can prove to be unsustainable. A historical fact was that the Chumbi Valley had in the past facilitated the invasion of north India. This was ignored by both the British during the entire period that they held India as a colony and subsequently by Nehru.

In the seventh century CE, a combined Chinese and Tibetan force invaded north India, entering the country through the Chumbi Valley. As John Keay in his history of China[1] puts it, there were three rulers at that time, heading three different kingdoms. They were Tang Taizong of China, Strong-brtsan-sgam-po of Tibet and Harsha Vardhana of Kanauj. Keay described them as 'a generation of Asian empire builders'. It was at this time that the Chinese Buddhist pilgrim, Xuanzang, visited India, delving into the depths of Buddhist literature and places of Buddhist learning. Harsha Vardhana extended a warm welcome to Xuanzang, who left behind a written record of the times and character of this great ruler of Kanauj.

Harsha Vardhana, who possessed a keen sense of history, established relations with the Chinese empire headed by Taizong. He sent emissaries on two occasions to the Chinese capital, Chang'an. In 643, Tang Taizong decided to reciprocate Harsha's gesture and sent a Tang mission headed by a military official, Wang Xuance. Wang travelled to Kanauj with an extensive entourage and a caravan load of tradeable goods. He was well received and was treated with the respect that was his due as an envoy from a fellow emperor. After a few years, Wang returned to China.

In 648 CE, he came to India with an even larger entourage but things had changed. Harsha had passed away the previous year and his kingdom was in chaos with rival factions in conflict. The Brahman faction had gained the upper hand and Buddhism was on its way out. Wang, a supporter of Buddhism, was attacked, his entourage massacred and his goods looted. He barely managed to escape with his life.

Desiring to avenge the disgrace to the Chinese imperial embassy, Wang Xuance demanded troops for a retaliatory attack and the Tibetan Emperor (Strong-brtsan-sgam-po, who was now in a relation of kinship with the Tang Emperor) obliged. A joint Sino-Tibetan force invaded India in 649 CE, 'probably by way of the Chumbi pass between Sikkim and Nepal [this is an error as the Chumbi lies between Sikkim on its west and Bhutan on its east and south], crossed the Great Himalaya and inflicted a very heavy defeat on Harsha's successors.' 'Thereupon,' says the standard Tang history, 'India was overawed.'[2] Keay goes on to record that Wang brought back as prisoner the usurper to the Tang court. The usurper's statue stands in permanent obeisance to Emperor Tai Taizong in front of his tomb.

A.L. Basham's history, *The Wonder That Was India*,[3] in a brief mention suggests that a joint force commanded by Wang defeated and captured the usurper, Arunasva, 'who was taken back to China to end his days in attendance on the Tang Emperor'. It is Keay who points out that, 'Indian tradition is blissfully ignorant of all of this.'

India was not only unaware of the mid-seventh century invasion but it was equally clueless that Tibetan Emperor Ral-pa-chan had held parts of India up to the northern banks of the river Ganga. Ral-pa-chan ruled Tibet in the ninth century and was the one who forced the Chinese to sign and abide by the treaty of AD 821.

Amnesia of these historical events conveys the degree to which India lacked an understanding that a strong power ruling Tibet could pose a serious threat to the security of India. Even more so when it was in the hands of a power inimical to India and its interests, as is the case today.

Clearly, it was a myth that China attacked India for the first time in 1962—it had happened before in the mid-seventh century.

Sikkim and Nepal

As the East India Company expanded its territories in India, controlling large areas, it came in contact with the mysterious land of Tibet. The first attempt to reach out to Lhasa to establish trade relations was made through Nepal in 1795. This was unsuccessful. In fact, relations between the Company and Nepal deteriorated to the point that the British finally went to war with Nepal. It was in this context that the British came to develop their first contact with the kingdom of Sikkim, leading to the signing of the Treaty of Titaliya in 1817.

The origins of the treaty lay in the undertaking by the British to contain the expansionist resolve of the Gurkha-led kingdom of Nepal. The Gurkha regime had invaded Sikkim, occupying its territory between the Teesta and the Mechi rivers. Nepal's actions against Sikkim coincided with Nepal raiding the Company's holdings along the Terai region. This resulted in the Company going to war with Nepal, for which it persuaded the ruler of Sikkim to ally with it.

Nepal suffered defeats at various fronts as the war progressed from 1814 to 1816. The British forces resorted to multi-pronged actions, with the Sikkimese force conducting joint operations with a British force led by a Captain Barre Latter, in the areas of Purnea and parts of western Sikkim that had been occupied by Nepal. At the time that the Anglo-Nepal Treaty was being negotiated, the joint forces had invested the Nagar Fort that was under Nepali occupation.

As the war ended with the signing of the Anglo-Nepal Treaty of Sugali in 1816, Captain Latter's force was located at the Sikkimese territory of Titaliya in the Terai, and it is here that the Anglo-Sikkim Treaty of Titaliya was signed in 1817. As part of this treaty, the British arranged for the return of a part of Sikkim's territory that had been annexed by Nepal. The rest, covering the Terai in the north Bihar area of Purnea and North Bengal, was retained by the Company as security against Nepal.

Sikkim had made common cause with the British against Nepal to regain its territories. An earlier alliance with the Sino-Tibetan forces had failed to achieve any return of territory. Nepal's advances on Sikkim's territories had coincided with its designs on Tibet, leading to the two Gurkha invasions of that country. The first took place in 1788, followed by a more ambitious invasion in 1790. The latter involved the sacking of the Great Monastery of Tashilhunpo (the seat of the Panchen Lama) and the occupation of the second-most important city of Tibet, Shigatse.

In 1788, a trade dispute between Lhasa and Kathmandu led to a confrontation between the two with the Nepalese invading Tibet, which led to the signing of a treaty that involved the payment of an annual tribute by Tibet to Nepal. Noteworthy in this case was that the Qinq court had not responded to an urgent Tibetan request for assistance. If China viewed Tibet as territorially aligned to it then the attack by Nepal should have resulted in an immediate military response. This did not happen as the Chinese did not have an inherent responsibility to come to the aid of Tibet, unless they felt that a military response was needed to preserve their own interests in Tibet.

The second invasion took place in 1790, when the Qianlong Emperor agreed to send a Chinese force to assist Tibet. The difference in response by the Chinese to the two invasions, where in each case Lhasa sought China's assistance, only goes to add substance to the argument that China dealt with Tibet more in the context of it being an alliance among equals grounded in kinship. Coming to Tibet's aid at the time of foreign attack was largely treated by imperial China on a case-by-case basis, depending on an assessment of what constituted a real threat to Buddhism and the Tibetan way of life. The trigger this time was the Nepalese acts of attacking Tashilhunpo and sacking the Panchen Lama's monastic holdings that were seen as attacks on Buddhism and the Tibetan way of life, making it clear that it was these two elements that underlay imperial China's relations with Buddhist Tibet.

The Chinese had met Lhasa's request on this occasion as it was made in the context of an act against Buddhism. It reconfirmed the basic tenets of relations between Tibet and China, confirming that it was always Tibetan Buddhism that remained central to the relations between the Dalai Lama and the Emperor. This owed its origin to the priest-emperor relationship that came to exist between Kublai Khan and the Sakya Lama from the time of the Yuan dynasty. This challenged the Maoist contention that Tibet had become a part of China since the Yuan period.[4]

Sikkim's ruler Tenzing Namgyal had made available a Sikkimese force to fight alongside the Sino-Tibetan forces and played a significant role in defeating the Nepalese. At the end of the war, the ruler expected that the treaty signed by the Chinese with Nepal, at Betrawati, would result in the return of Sikkim's occupied territories. This, unfortunately, did not happen and the ruler displayed his unhappiness over Sikkim's legitimate claims being rejected.

Having been let down by both the Chinese and the Tibetans, the king of Sikkim was understandably resentful towards them. He arrived at the conclusion that as Nepal continued to have a troubled relationship with the British, by making common cause with the British against Nepal, he might be better placed to regain his annexed territories. While he did succeed in getting back a fair amount of his territory, he also opened his state up to British machinations that ultimately led to the British extending their influence over Sikkim.

Notes

1. *China: A History*, John Keay, HarperPress, London, 2008, pp. 239–243.
2. *Ibid.*, p. 243.
3. *The Wonder That Was India*, A. L. Basham, Sidgwick & Jackson, London, third revised edition 1967.
4. The truth of the matter lies in the description of Chinese territories in the Great Ming Unification Record that clearly places Tibet in the section relating to 'Foreign Aliens' together with Japan, Mecca and Medina. Paper by Prof Han-Shing Lau, chair professor at the City University of Hong Kong, titled 'Tibet Was Never Part of China before 1950', published in *National Security*, Volume II, Issue I.

3

THE DARJEELING SAGA

With the Anglo-Sikkim Treaty of Titaliya, signed in 1817, the East India Company restored some 4000 square miles of territory between the Mechi and the Teesta rivers to Sikkim. It was then that British eyes fell upon what came to be known as 'Darjeeling', a distortion of the original Sikkimese name for the village of Dorje Ling.

O'Malley's *Darjeeling Gazetteer*[1] records that the East India Company first came into contact with the Dorje Ling tract at the beginning of the nineteenth century 'which now bears the name [Darjeeling]'. 'It then formed part of the dominions of the Raja of Sikkim, a petty ruler who had long been engaged in an unsuccessful struggle against the growing power of the warlike Gurkhas.' That this area was under the sway of Nepal is implied but not as categorically stated as in Risley's *The Gazetteer of Sikhim.*[2] The gazetteers on Darjeeling and Sikkim do agree that but for British interventions against Nepal, the whole state of Sikkim would have been occupied and become a part of Nepal.

Under the Treaty of Titaliya, the British colonial administration took upon itself the responsibility of maintaining peace in the region, thereby assuming overarching powers in Sikkim and conferring upon themselves the role of guarantors of the sanctity of the kingdom's frontiers against both Nepal and Bhutan.

At this stage, there was no attempt made to interfere in the internal affairs of Sikkim and the Namgyal rulers not only enjoyed complete autonomy but also continued to retain their hold on the Chumbi Valley, spending considerable periods of time administering their kingdom out of the valley. Apart from the ruler's estate in Old Chumbi, there were properties held by Sikkimese Bhutia nobles in the valley as well.

What lay behind the Company's moves on Sikkim was the long-held desire to establish commercial relations with Tibet. As Nepal refused to permit passage through its territories, the first governor-general of the Bengal Presidency, Warren Hastings, in 1774 had attempted to utilize Bhutan for the purpose. However, the terrain had proven difficult and the Company was looking for an alternative. What Hastings had in mind was quite ambitious—apart from trade with Tibet, he saw the possibility of Tibet being a gateway to trade with the more inaccessible parts of China.

The Bogle and the subsequent Turner delegations he sent through Bhutan in 1774 and 1783, respectively, did not proceed beyond Shigatse as Lhasa continued to close its doors to the British. The difficulty of Bhutan's terrain remained a primary obstacle that made its use for trade a challenging proposition.

After the Treaty of Titaliya, the British turned their attention to Sikkim and its geographical location that offered a more attractive means of not only establishing connections with Tibet but onwards to its neighbouring countries to the east and north. Rajiv Rai in his dissertation, *The State in the Colonial Periphery: A Study on Sikkim's*

Relations with Great Britain,[3] says, 'The small mountain kingdom of Sikkim had the economic blessing and military misfortune to be located on two of the most accessible natural routes between Tibet and India. The first route starts from Gyantse in southern Tibet, across Tibet's Chumbi valley, Sikkim's Jelep la to the Nathan valley, and onward to India. The second route began at Shigatse and continued south through Sikkim, and onward to the tea centre of Darjeeling and finally to Calcutta, the official heart of British India.' In all that Britain was aiming for, the location of Darjeeling became a crucial factor serving British intent on taking advantage of Sikkim's location.

Ceding 'Dorje Ling'

The next step was to take advantage of the goodwill that the return of Sikkim's territories had granted to the Company to seek the ceding of the village of Dorje Ling. The British were aware that the Raja was unhappy over those parts of his territory that the British had retained and decided to offer a return to him of some additional territory. Morung, lying between the rivers Mechi and Mahanadi, was handed back to Sikkim. Simultaneously, the demand for the grant of Dorje Ling and a tract of land around it was put forward.

The events that enabled the British[4] to extract this vital piece of territory from the ruler lay in the factional strife at the court. The battle lines were drawn between the Lepcha and Bhutia aristocrats, creating internal fissures that the British could play on and exploit at will. A serious falling-out between the two communities arose out of a rift between the king and his prime minister, Chandzok Bolek. Tsugphud Namgyal's mother was a Lepcha and Bolek was his maternal uncle. The Bhutia faction at the court did its best to poison Tsugphud's mind against Bolek. They convinced the Raja that Bolek had been intercepting the gifts and offerings made by the people of Sikkim to the ruler and only passing on a fraction of the offerings to the palace. They also successfully planted the thought in the Raja's mind that Bolek was conspiring to kill him. This led the Raja to devise a curious test to determine Bolek's loyalty. The muzzle of a gun was to be pointed at Bolek. If the gun went off, it would testify to his guilt and if it did not, his innocence would be established. Through this ploy, the Bhutia faction succeeded in assassinating Bolek, his wife and sons.

After the assassinations, many of Bolek's immediate relatives, accompanied by several hundred Lepchas, fled to eastern Nepal. Taking advantage of this situation, the Gorkhas encouraged the disaffected Lepchas to carry out a number of raids on Sikkim. The Raja now called on the East India Company, invoking the Treaties of Sugali and Titaliya, to mediate and resolve the dispute, which included the vacating of a hill overlooking the Mechi river that the Lepchas had occupied. Governor-General William Bentinck sent two representatives, Captain G.W.K. Lloyd, and an administrator, G.W. Griffith, to mediate and the issue was settled in favour of Sikkim.[5]

It was Lloyd, with the keen eye of a military strategist, who understood the tactical advantage of Dorje Ling to the British. From the surveillance aspect, he felt it would grant the British command over Sikkim while being ideally situated to become a staging point for the Company's trade with Tibet.[6] Lloyd added that its cool, bracing climate was ideal for the location of a sanatorium where expatriate British civilians and servicemen could find respite from the heat of the plains, and the ill and the wounded could seek rehabilitation and convalesce.

While mediating this dispute and settling it in favour of Sikkim, the Bengal administration asked the Raja to cede Dorje Ling along with some of its surrounding areas. After a period of hesitation, the

Raja agreed to cede the village,[7] with the condition that the British in return relinquish Debgong, an area that originally belonged to Sikkim. The Raja also demanded that the Pradhan of Morung be handed over to him along with the revenue accounts for two years that had not been paid after the area was transferred to Sikkim. As it turned out, though Morung was returned to the Raja, the land revenue derived from it continued to be deposited in the Company's treasury.

In an act of naiveté, while putting forward these conditions, the Raja had also drawn up the deed ceding Darjeeling to the British, and had handed it over to Lloyd. While doing so, it appears he did not mention that the deed would only become operational once his conditions had been met.

The *Bengal District Gazetteer* has recorded the text of this deed:[8]

> The Governor-General having expressed his desire for the possession of the hill of Darjeeling on account of its cool climate, for the purpose of enabling the servants of his Government, suffering from sickness, to avail themselves of its advantages, I, the Sikkimputtee Rajah, out of friendship for the said Governor-General, hereby, present Darjeeling to the East India Company, that is, all the land south of the Great Runjeet river, east of Balasur, Kahail and the Little Runjeet rivers, and west of the Rungno and Mahanuddi rivers.

O'Malley adds as an aside that 'this was an unconditional cession, of what was then a worthless uninhabited mountain'.[9]

The grant of Dorje Ling triggered a Tibetan reaction. Tibet had closed its doors to all non-Buddhist foreign visitors, a result of Chinese intrigue planting in Lhasa's ears that the British had not adhered to the understanding that they would not get embroiled in the battle of the joint Sino-Tibetan forces against Nepal. The Chinese had instilled in Tibetan minds that the British were an expansionist Christian power that posed a threat to the Tibetan way of life. This view was furthered by the Bhutanese who, having their own problems with the British, confirmed that the British were a threat. These developments led to Lhasa imposing a blanket ban on the entry of all foreigners to Tibet and Lhasa.

The amban, the Chinese resident commissioner in Lhasa, playing on these fears, drew Lhasa's attention to the grant of territory by Sikkim's ruler to the expansionist British, and questioned the ruler's loyalty to Tibet. It was only logical under those circumstances for Tibet to convey its displeasure to the ruler by denying him his right to visit Lhasa and depriving him of time-honoured grazing rights of cattle across the Tibet border. It was a right that the Raja and his predecessors had hitherto enjoyed without interruption.

Clearly, Tsugphud Namgyal was placed in the unenviable position of having to deal with two contesting masters. The Tibetans desired that the ruler adopt measures that would deny the British further entry into Sikkim, while the British were now intent on exercising the treaty options that had very evidently gained them the position of 'paramount power', claiming the right to control Sikkim's external relations. To complicate matters further, the British expected the ruler to use his good offices to help persuade Tibet to open its borders, thus permitting trade with India through Sikkim. Despite Lhasa's retaliatory actions, the deed had been done and Darjeeling had been taken over by the British.

Deteriorating Relations

Darjeeling developed rapidly under British administration and the innovative skills of its first superintendent, Dr Archibald Campbell. This also resulted in a rapid expansion of the tea industry and associated infrastructure, in direct contrast to the relatively primitive state of affairs in Sikkim, where the landholdings were in the hands of the combined Lepcha and Bhutia aristocracy—the Kazis.

The differing cultural and legal factors created misunderstandings that came to plague the relations between Darjeeling and Tumlong. The British, being the more powerful party, did not hesitate to take steps to impose their will, leading to localized clashes. A major complicating factor was the conflicting personalities of the two people helming the Darjeeling and Sikkim administrations—they were openly in opposition with each other. As often happens, circumstances can play an important part in deciding the turn that relations take. In the complex of factors that set the next stage of the British relationship with Sikkim, the personality clash between the two heading the Darjeeling and Tumlong administrations came to play a defining role.

Darjeeling had in Dr Campbell an enterprising official endowed with a spirit of adventure and sterling administrative skills. These very skills made him critical of any opposition offered to his demands by any native official. Campbell had been appointed the superintendent of Darjeeling in 1839. He displayed remarkable skill in bringing the tea bush to Darjeeling and lead by example by planting the first tea bush in his own garden, multiplying its growth and encouraging other planters to follow suit. His focus on infrastructure soon led to Darjeeling becoming a commercial centre. In the initial years, he was on good terms with the Sikkim durbar, finding in its dewan, the Lepcha Illam Singh, a kindred soul with whom he established a good working relationship. Problems arose when Dewan Illam Singh died in 1847 and was replaced by Tokhang Donyer Namgyal, generally known as Dewan Namgyal and also as 'Pagla Dewan', the mad prime minister. According to Campbell, Illam Singh's demise lead to his 'losing to … the Raja's

Counsels the only man of any honesty, or to be trusted in word or deed'.[10]

Dewan Tokhang Donyer Namgyal was a Bhutia, who was by beliefs closely aligned to Tibet. He, like Campbell, was an ambitious man, competent, 'with qualities which helped him play a significant role in the history of British relations with Sikkim'.[11] Dewan Namgyal manipulated his way to power by establishing a close relationship with the ruler's favourite concubine and marrying the daughter she had with the ruler. Campbell and Dewan Namgyal had crossed swords over the appointment of the replacement of Illam Singh, with Campbell favouring his trusted Lepcha candidate, Chebu Lama. Namgyal won and his conflict with Campbell created conditions that would end in Sikkim losing its independence.

A major contributing factor was that the Raja, Tsugphud Namgyal, was by now elderly, almost permanently living in the Chumbi Valley, devoting himself to religious matters and no longer spending time to govern his state or paying attention to its administration. Real power lay in the hands of the dewan. The fact that Dewan Namgyal was married to the ruler's illegitimate daughter with his favoured concubine and had the ruler's ear, granted him unchallenged power over the administration of Sikkim.

The Darjeeling Gazetteer said that the situation was 'far from satisfactory. The Raja, old and infirm, was a mere cipher in the hands of his minister Namgyal. Wrapt in religious contemplation, and abstracting himself from the consideration of earthly things, the Raja allowed the Dewan, a corrupt and ambitious official, to administer the State and enrich himself at its expense. The increasing importance of Darjeeling under free institutions was a source of early and constant jealousy and annoyance to the Dewan, who was himself the monopolist of all trade in Sikkim; and it was shared in by the Lamas and other notables, who lost their rights over slaves settling as British subjects in our territory.' The reference to 'our territory' was to Darjeeling.

As Darjeeling developed and its commercial interests grew along with its communication infrastructure, the demand for labour increased as well. This led people from the plains of Bengal and Gurkhas from Nepal to settle down in Darjeeling and its surrounding areas. Also, more and more Sikkimese came to settle there; among them were many who had escaped the bonds of slave labour that prevailed in Sikkim. This was due to a system of bonded labour that paralleled the rural landholding and agricultural practices in Tibet and had been granted legal sanction by the ruler of Sikkim. Given these circumstances, legal differences arose between the two authorities over the refusal by Darjeeling to repatriate escaped 'slave labour' to Sikkim.

The dewan of Sikkim, being himself vested in this practice, refused to accept the British position, proclaiming that by not handing back fugitives under Sikkimese legislation the British were in contempt of Sikkim's laws. To make matters worse, the Sikkimese refused to prevent the kidnapping of British Indian subjects who were later forced into slavery by their people. The main problem arose from a total lack of understanding on both sides of the differing cultural views, thinking and practices, and resulted in increasingly strained relations between the two administrations.

As Lamb explained,[12] Dewan Namgyal's failing was his 'consistent underestimation of the power of the British'. This was to have a telling impact. In 1848, Campbell sought the Sikkim ruler's permission, for an officially sanctioned visit, by the botanist Dr Joseph Hooker, to carry out a study of the flora and fauna of the Himalayan region, in Sikkim. Campbell addressed a letter to the Raja seeking permission for the visit. His request was turned down. Campbell was convinced that this was the result of the machinations of the dewan and with the concurrence of Calcutta proceeded to Tumlong to deal with the Raja directly. He was stopped on the banks of the Teesta river. The dewan put forward two reasons for denying access to the Raja. First, the Raja was engaged in spiritual pursuits and could not meet with him. Second, that Lhasa would object to such a meeting taking place. It was also mentioned that 'the protocol of such meetings demanded that they take at least two years to arrange'. Despite this formidable array of arguments, Campbell was able to meet the Raja and obtain his consent to Hooker's visit. The dewan however was not done yet. '[H]e now took the position that the presents brought by Campbell had to be presented to the ruler at a public ceremony granting to Campbell's visit the character of a tribute mission.'

Despite the melee, Dr Hooker was able to undertake his first visit to Sikkim. Subsequently, Chebu Lama, the Sikkim 'vakil', diplomatic agent, to Darjeeling through whom the Darjeeling administration dealt with Tumlong, was replaced by a confidante of the dewan. Campbell now sought a second visit to Tumlong. He also decided to join Hooker, who was on his second visit to Sikkim. Both were driven by a passionate desire to enter Tibet through the Chumbi Valley and get acquainted with that mysterious land. They were stopped on the outskirts of the Chumbi Valley by the *jongpen*, governor, of Phari. Once they crossed back they were arrested by the Sikkimese under the orders of the dewan, who treated Hooker with respect but out of vengeance decided to teach Campbell a lesson. Campbell was treated harshly and claimed he had been subjected to torture.

Hooker and Campbell were finally released in response to British protests and were escorted back to Darjeeling. According to a record of the events, it appears that when Hooker and Campbell crossed Cho La and were confronted by a Tibetan force, the dewan was at the Old Chumbi headquarters of the Sikkim administration and tried to encourage an encounter between the British party and the Tibetans. He had hoped this would result in Lhasa coming out in open support of his anti-British policy. Campbell apparently guessed what the dewan was up to and ensured that no incident took place.

The British, feeling that their prestige had been challenged by Campbell's imprisonment, stopped the annual payment of Rs 6000 to the Raja and, in addition, forced him to concede a further 640 square miles of Sikkimese territory in the Terai. This now enabled the linking of Darjeeling with the plains of Bengal.[13] Campbell wanted to see the end of Dewan Namgyal, but the ruler continued to depend on the dewan to conduct the state's affairs.

Treaty of Tumlong

In November 1860, having obtained the authority to occupy a portion of Sikkim's territory as punishment for the 'insults and injuries done to British subjects, and for violations of British territory', Campbell invaded Sikkim with an ill-equipped force that was roundly defeated by the dewan's army. Campbell had once again created a condition that impacted British prestige. To save face, a fully armed force led by Colonel J.C. Gawler and accompanied by Ashley Eden, the political officer, was sent a second time, which defeated the Sikkimese forces.[14] The Raja was forced to sign the Treaty of Tumlong in 1861.

Expectedly, the treaty had trade-related provisions at its centre to ensure that 'trade monopolies, restrictions on the movements of travellers, and duties on goods passing between Sikhim and British territory, are abolished'.[15] A second provision stated that 'on all goods passing into or out of Tibet, Bhootan or Nepal the Government of Sikkim may levy a duty of customs … that such duty shall, on no account, exceed 5 per cent …'

With this treaty, the British had now secured control over Sikkim's external relations, thus constraining any attempt by the ruler to bring Tibet into the equation. An important part of the agreement was the construction of a road connecting Darjeeling through Jelep La to the Chumbi Valley. The agreement clearly made the point that 'in the event of the British Government desiring to open out a road through Sikkim, with a view of encouraging trade, the Sikkim Government will raise no objection ...'[16] Darjeeling was now connected by road and a hill railway to the plains of Bengal and had turned into a bustling commercial centre. Sikkim, with its easy access to Tibet through the Chumbi Valley, enhanced its value as a British protectorate, setting the course that relations between British India and Tibet and subsequently China would take.

It was Ashley Eden who first suggested that the road that connected Darjeeling with the Teesta valley be extended up to Chumbi. This, to his mind, would create the conditions for active participation by Tibetan traders at the annual trade fair in Darjeeling, and result in 'persuading[17] the Thibetan authorities to repair the road between Phagri (Phari) and the Chola Pass. Noting that beyond Phari there is an excellent road to Lhasa and Jigutishar (Shigatse).' This approach, however, failed to take into consideration that since 1792, Tibet had adopted the policy that banned the entry of all non-Buddhist foreigners into Tibet.

In another important development around that time, Sidkeong Namgyal succeeded Tsugphud Namgyal as ruler of Sikkim. He agreed to spend nine months in Sikkim and only reside in Chumbi for a maximum of three months in a year. The British insisted on this arrangement based on the assumption that having the ruler at Gangtok for most of the year would grant them greater control over him and his court to serve British interests.[18]

From the security perspective, the British looked on the Himalayan state as sufficient buffer to deal with India's security interests. The driving force behind British actions in Sikkim and onwards with Tibet was centred on Darjeeling and their vision to turn it into a trade hub.

Ashley Eden explained this expectation suggesting that: 'A very considerable trade will spring up between Lassa … and Darjeeling. The Tibetans will only be too glad to exchange gold dust, musk, borax, wool and salt for English cloth, tobacco, drill etc.; and the people of Sikkim will gain as carriers of this trade, and their government will raise a considerable revenue from transit duties.'[19]

Notes

1. *Bengal District Gazetteers: Darjeeling District*, L.S.S. O'Malley. First published by the Bengal Secretariat Book Depot in 1907; re-published by Logos Press, New Delhi, 1985.
2. *The Gazetteer of Sikhim*, introduced by Herbert Hope Risley. First Published by the Bengal Secretariat Press in 1894. Re-published by Forgotten Books, London, 2018.
3. *The State in the Colonial Periphery: A Study on Sikkim's Relation with Great Britain*, a dissertation submitted to the department of international relations, Sikkim University. Published by the department of international relations, School of Social Sciences, Sikkim University, Gangtok, 2014.
4. *Ibid.*
5. The Treaty of Sugali in its Article VI states clearly that 'the Raja of Nepaul engages never to molest or disturb of his possession of his territories; but agrees, if any difference should arise between the State of Nepaul and the Raja of Sikkim. [sic] Or the subjects of either, that such differences shall be referred to the arbitration of the British Government by whose award the Raja of Nepaul engages to abide …' *Sikkim: A Short Political History*. Lal Bahadur Basnet, S. Chand & Co., New Delhi, 1974, pp. 28–29.

6. Llyod in his report to Governor-General William Bentineck 'pointed out its advantages as a center which would engross all trade of the country, and as a position of great strategical importance, commanding the entrance into Nepal and Bhutan.' Page 20 of *The Darjeeling Gazetteer* of 1907, quoting Llyod's report dated 18 June 1829.
7. '... the negotiation ended in the unconditional cession by the Maharaja of the Darjeeling tract under a Deed of Grant Dated February 1835.' Quoted from page 20 of *The Gazetteer of Sikhim*. The claim that it was unconditional is obviously disputed.
8. *Bengal District Gazetteers: Darjeeling District*. L.S.S. O'Malley. First published by the Bengal Secretariat Book Depot in 1907; re-published by Logos Press, New Delhi, 1985.
9. *The Darjeeling Gazetteer* was part of *The Bengal District Gazetteers* and was compiled by L.S.S. O'Malley who belonged to the Indian Civil Services.
10. *British India and Tibet: 1766–1910*, Alastair Lamb, Routledge and Kegan Paul, London and New York, 1960, p. 72.
11. *Ibid.*
12. *Ibid.*, p. 73.
13. 'This treachery was punished by the annexation of the entire Terai, and a large area of the middle hills bounded on the north by the Great Rungeet River. But Namguay, though ostensibly dismissed from office, continued to exercise great influence through his wife, an illegitimate daughter of the Raja.' Page iv of *The Gazetteer of Sikhim* from the introduction to it by H.H. Risley
14. Ashley Eden was a distinguished civil servant in the Bengal administration, he was posted to India in 1852, and held some prestigious positions such as governor of Burma 1871–77, lieutenant governor of Bengal 1877–1882, ending up as secretary of state's council for India 1882–87. Cited from '"A Difficult Country, a Hostile Chief, and a Still More Hostile Minister": The Anglo-Sikkim War of 1861' by Alex Mckay in the *Bulletin of Tibetology*, himalaya.socanth.cam.ac.uk.
15. The Anglo-Sikkim Treaty of Tumlong of 1861 made the provision that 'no duty or fees on import or export of British goods'.

16. *Ibid.*
17. *British India and Tibet: 1766–1910*, Alastair Lamb, Routledge and Kegan Paul, London and New York, 1960, p. 81.
18. *The Darjeeling Gazetteer* describes these events in some detail, setting out that Colonel Gawler 'at the head of a force of 2600 men … started from Darjeeling on the 1st February 1861 and reached Tumlong, the Sikkim capital, early in March 1861. The diwan fled, the British force dismantled the forts, the old Raja abdicated in favour of his son, and, on the 28th March, Sir Ashley Eden effected a treaty with the new Raja.'
19. *British India and Tibet: 1766–1910*, Alastair Lamb, Routledge and Kegan Paul, London and New York, 1960, p. 81.

4

SIKKIM AND TIBET

Little is known of Sikkim's early history. The Lepchas, considered the 'original' inhabitants, did not have any written record of the period before Tibetan migrants, known as Bhutias, settled in Sikkim. They entered the area through the Chumbi Valley. Legend has it that three leading lamas from the Drukpa Kagyu school of Tibetan Buddhism decided to consecrate Phuntsog Namgyal as the ruler in AD 1642, thereby establishing the Namgyal dynasty, that was of Bhutia origin, to rule over Sikkim. The Namgyal dynasty ruled for over 300 years, with its reign coming to an end with Sikkim's merger with India in 1975.

The Namgyal dynasty and its Bhutia subjects remained largely followers of the Drukpa Kagyu sect and after the Chinese occupation of Tibet, the head of the Drukpa sub-sect, the Karma Kagyu, the Galwya Karmapa, settled down at the monastery at Rumtek that is located on a hill opposite Gangtok. Most of Sikkim's rulers kept their links with Tibet alive by seeking their wives from among Tibetan aristocracy.

This tradition was broken by Chogyal Palden Thondup, who took for his second wife the American socialite Hope Cooke. Thondup's first wife, Samyo Kushoe Sandeki, was from Tibetan aristocracy; he had two sons and a daughter with her, before her demise in 1957.

The Bhutias mostly migrated from the eastern parts of Tibet. They were Buddhists, owing allegiance to the Nyingma sect, that represented an older school of Buddhism that had exercised power over Tibet, before its authority was replaced by the Mongol-supported Gelugpa.

As the Drukpa lost out, many of its followers left for the Chumbi Valley and onward to Sikkim, where they came to settle and set up monasteries and temples. Here, both legend and fact tend to merge. Vajrayana Buddhism in Sikkim, like in Tibet, is intimately related to the legend of Padmasambhava, also known as Guru Rinpoche, the eighth-century Indian master credited with establishing Vajrayana Buddhism in Tibet.

A Buddhist Dynasty

Guru Rinpoche is equally revered in Tibet, Bhutan and Sikkim, and is said to have visited Sikkim 'during his journeyings to Tibet and its western border-lands'. L. Austine Waddell, in his study of Lamaist Buddhism of Tibet, mentions that 'the introduction of Lamaism into Sikhim certainly dates from the time of Lha-tsun's (Gyalwa Lhatsun Chempo) arrival there about the middle of the seventeenth century'.[1]

A deeply revered figure in Sikkim, Lhatsun, more than anyone else, was responsible for the entrenching of the Lamaist form of Buddhism in Sikkim; he was also responsible for establishing the system of governance that followed, in principle, the prevailing customs in Tibet, shaping in a similar fashion the role that came to be played by the many Buddhist monasteries in Sikkim. The Bhutia Sikkimese followed Tibetan customs and language and sought to impose these on the mild-mannered Rong Pa or the Lepcha community.

Lama Lhatsun Namkha Jigme, also known in Sikkim as Lama Lhatsun Chempo, is associated with the founding of the monasteries in the late seventeenth to early eighteenth centuries of Dubde, Tashiding, Sangchelling, also known as Sanga Choelling, and Pemiongchi, also known as Pemayangtse, among others. The Pemayangtse monastery continued to play the main role in the consecration of the Namgyal Chogyals. It was the practice in Tibetan Buddhism that usually the second son of the ruler would be trained as a lama. For instance, the last Chogyal, Palden Thondup, was Maharaja Tashi Namgyal's second son and was considered a reincarnated Rinpoche. Paljor Namgyal, his elder brother, and crown prince, had joined the Royal Indian Air Force and died in a plane crash on 20 December 1941 while on manoeuvres in the North-West Frontier Province. Palden Thondup was then granted permission to be relieved of his duties as a lama to take up the position of the Maharaja Kumar of Sikkim. This was his official position at the time of India's independence.

Here, legend re-enters, claiming that the three Nyingma lamas responsible for introducing Vajrayana Buddhism, Lhatsun, the Kartokpa Lama and the Nadakpa Lama ('the Great Sage'), met at Yoksam around 1641 and decided to take the next step of appointing a ruler described by them as 'the dispenser of gifts' to 'rule the country on our behalf'.[2] Lhatsun settled the matter pointing to the 'prophesy' of Guru Padmasambhava, saying, 'It is written that four noble brothers shall meet in Sikhim and arrange for its government. We are three of these who have entered Sikkim from the north, west and south. Towards the east, it is written, that there is at this epoch a man named Pun-ts'ok, a descendant of the brave ancestors of Kham in Eastern Tibet. According, therefore, to the prophecy of the Guru we should invite him.'[3]

The three venerable lamas, having located Phuntsog (Pun-ts'ok of the prophecy) at the village of Gangtok, proceeded to crown him the Chogyal or Dharma Raja. The aim was that the monarchy thus established, with all the magic of the consecration that had made an impression on the Lepchas, would act as a bridge between the original inhabitants of Sikkim and the Bhutias, enabling the latter to consolidate their hold over Sikkim. To further secure this hold, the earlier rulers had taken in marriage wives from leading Lepcha families while subsequently marrying women from leading Tibetan families that helped grant greater strength to the Sikkim–Tibet relationship. Sikkim's ruler benefited from this link with Lhasa and extended Sikkim's cooperation whenever Lhasa needed it. This resulted in his being granted holdings in Tibet proper that extended his rule beyond Sikkim and the Chumbi Valley.

The romance of legend is attached to the Namgyal dynasty's rule over Sikkim. Phuntsog Namgyal, who was consecrated as the first ruler, claimed his descent from the legendry Khye Bumsa, purported to be the son of the ruler of the Kham kingdom of Minyak. Khye Bumsa married the Sakya Lama's daughter and settled in the Chumbi Valley. His wife having failed to conceive, Khye Bumsa was advised to seek the blessings of the Lepcha chief, Thekong Tek. A close relationship developed between them and professedly because of Thekong Tek's blessings, Khye Bumsa had three sons.

After Khye Bumsa's death, that took place in the Chumbi Valley, his three sons crossed into Sikkim. Phuntsog Namgyal was allegedly a descendant of Khye Bumsa through his youngest son. As part of the process of bringing the Lepcha and the Bhutia communities together within the embrace of Vajrayana Buddhism, Phuntsog Namgyal, symbolizing the union of the legendary Lepcha Thekong Tek and the Tibetan Khye Bumsa having sworn allegiance to each other as blood brothers, epitomized the union of the two communities that jointly formed the kingdom of Sikkim.

Sikkim–Tibet–China Triangulation

The Namgyal dynasty continued to govern Sikkim out of two capitals—one that was located in western Sikkim and the other at Old Chumbi in the Chumbi Valley. To help discharge the responsibility of governance, the ruler constituted a royal council that most of the time operated out of the valley, while in Sikkim proper, the lamas of important monasteries played a role in the governance of the kingdom adhering to Tibetan traditions of governance. The fact was that Tibet was Sikkim's proximate neighbour of influence. The connection between Tibet and imperial China revolving around the priest and royal disciple relationship (Cho Yan) also influenced Sikkim's ruler to call on the Chinese amban and Lhasa for settling disputes, or to seek advice in dealing with outside influences including, of course, the dealings with the British.

The problem that the ruler faced was his inability to understand that in his dealings with the British, his need to take Tibet into account carried no weight. For the British, Sikkim was under their control and its importance lay in the fact that it offered a convenient trade route with Tibet. Trade had been the motive that had driven Hastings to send the George Bogle trade delegation to Tibet, that had entered Tibet via the far more difficult route from Bhutan. After Bogle's demise in 1781, that attempt was followed by Samuel Turner in 1783, who had not proceeded beyond Shigatse. The Bhutan route had then been discarded for the one through Sikkim that was much better located for the purpose. The opposition that the British faced from the recluse Tsugphud Namgyal and his dewan, Donyer Namgyal, resulted in both suffering the whiplash of British wrath.

Tsugphud Namgyal was unsuited to deal with the complexities of the situation that he faced. Orthodox and conservative by nature, he had taken the spiritual route as he felt that the end of his earthly sojourn was upon him. He had all along considered Sikkim a dependency of Tibet, understandably tending to act keeping the relations with Tibet and China in mind. The Chinese, already wary of colonial designs exhibited by Britain in China, were keen to keep Britain out of Tibet. They called on Sikkim to raise barriers to British attempts at using its territory to establish relations with Tibet.

Prior to 1792, Tibet had not banned the entry of non-Buddhist foreigners within its territories. This ban came about with the Chinese deliberately misleading Lhasa, claiming that the British had ignored the Dalai Lama's request that they refrain from supporting Nepal in its war against the combined Tibeto-Chinese forces. Taking advantage of the limited worldview of the Tibetans, China was able to convince the Dalai Lama that Britain was an expansionist Christian power that threatened Buddhism and the Tibetan way of life. Separately, Lhasa had understood that the British were dependant on China to open the doors to Tibet's markets. They refused to deal with the British stating that they were prevented by the Chinese.

Lord Curzon's despatch to London[4] laid bare the folly of the policy adopted by Britain: 'We (Curzon) regard the so-called suzerainty of China over Tibet as a constitutional fiction—a political affectation which has only been maintained because of its convenience to both parties. China is always ready to break down the barriers of ignorance and obstruction and open Tibet to the civilizing influence of trade, but her pious wishes are defeated by the short-sighted stupidity of the Lamas. In the same way Tibet is only too anxious to meet our advances, but she is prevented from doing so by the despotic veto of the suzerain. This solemn farce has been re-enacted with a frequency that seems never to deprive it of its attractions or its power to impose.' Curzon was right in his observation that Lhasa only accepted China's advice when it suited its purposes, refuting any claim that the Chinese court or the Emperor could act on its behalf.

Lhasa was also, to a certain extent, influenced by representations that were being made by Kathmandu through the amban, seeking China's material and military help against the British. The Nepalis were being pressurized by the British to end their raids on Indian territory and there were a number of areas where differences between Kathmandu and India had reached a level where war between the two sides was an increasing possibility. Nepal, realizing that by itself and at its level of material and military resources it could not contain British advances, was using provisions of the Treaty of Betrawati to get China to intervene. Lhasa was also being fed by the Nepalese that the colonial authority in India, having defeated the Mughal empire, posed a threat to the independence of Nepal and Tibet. The Nepali messages were cleverly adding fire to existing apprehensions, entertained both in Beijing and Lhasa, of Britain as an expansionist Christian power intent on enforcing religious and cultural changes in Tibet.

Given this understanding of British intentions, it was logical for Tibet to view the British presence in Sikkim in negative terms and to oppose actions that they viewed as facilitating a British stranglehold over Sikkim, making it clear to the ruler and the

Sikkimese Royal Council that this was a development that was unacceptable. To drive home this point, Lhasa took action to discipline the ruler after he signed away the Darjeeling tract to the British. Tibet was acting within its understanding that both Bhutan and Sikkim, as its tributaries, were subservient to it and had to submit to its wishes and commands. Lhasa's actions were replicating the manner in which imperial China viewed its relations with countries considered as its tributaries.

Lepcha–Bhutia Rivalry

While the Tibetans were exerting pressure on the Raja of Sikkim to prevent the British from making encroachments in the kingdom, they were not privy to the internal rivalries and factionalism among the Lepchas and the Bhutias, as well as within the Bhutia community. These fissures within the kingdom helped create opportunities for the British, more particularly the Darjeeling authorities, to exploit the situation to serve their interests.

As was often their wont, the British held in contempt all those 'natives' who did not fall in line with their wishes. Not surprisingly, they came to consider the Bhutias, with some exceptions, as a particularly obdurate and untrustworthy lot. The British were more comfortable with the Lepcha faction at the Sikkim court as the Lepcha leaders were willing to promote closer relations with the British.

With the Bhutia faction, led by Dewan Namgyal, standing firmly in the way of British ambitions of establishing trade ties with Tibet, the desire to get rid of him had come to take precedence in the Company's dealings with Sikkim. The dewan, with the support of the ruler, took the position that it was Tibet that was the overlord of Sikkim and he had to carry out its wishes, which prohibited British presence in Sikkim.

The two opposing demands from Tibet and British India placed the Sikkimese ruler in an impossible position. Calcutta, driven by the pressures exerted by the tea traders of Darjeeling and British commercial interests in Calcutta and London, was bent on using Sikkim to set up its trade with Tibet. Opposing this was the demand made by the Dalai Lama asking the Sikkimese ruler to cut off relations with the British. The ruler, habituated to obey Lhasa's instructions, decided that he had no alternative but to act in accordance to what would restore him in the good books of Lhasa and, by extension, Beijing.

This led the British to strongly express their displeasure and the decision to severely restrict the Raja's stay at the Chumbi Valley. In addition, the annual subvention of Rs 6000 per annum was stopped. It was only after the events ending in the Treaty of Tumlong, with his successor Sidkeong Namgyal recognizing the ground realities and taking appropriate steps to placate the British, that the subvention was not only restored but increased to Rs 12,000 per annum.

Sidkeong Namgyal was appointed the ruler of Sikkim with his father, Tsugphud Namgyal, abdicating in his favour in 1863. Tsugphud Namgyal continued to reside in the Chumbi Valley and died later that year. Sidkeong, on his accession, agreed to abide by the British demand that the ruler remain a resident in Sikkim for nine months in the year and visit the Chumbi Valley with the permission of the British.

To bind the Sikkim ruler further to British India and to raise his status, it was decided to change his title from Raja, which implied a minor princeling, to the more richly protocolar title of Maharaja. This was the title by which all the subsequent Namgyal rulers were known till the time Palden Thondup took over as the thirteenth ruler of Sikkim and persuaded New Delhi to allow him to revert to using the Tibetan title of Chogyal. This change in title was agreed to even though it was clear that he was, by this change, making an effort to distance himself from India.

Tibet Opposes Jelep La Road

The next episode in the Sikkim–Tibet drama took place when the British, under the terms of the Treaty of Tumlong, commenced the construction of a road that would link Darjeeling to Jelep La, a pass in the Chola range of mountains that lay between the Sikkim land mass and the Chumbi Valley. The Tibetans expressed their hostility to the joint British-Sikkimese operation and as Basnet recounts it in his short political history of Sikkim,[5] 'the British hold over Sikkim and their manifest zeal in extending their trade northwards produced only hostile reactions in both Tibet and China'.

He goes on to explain this 'hostile reaction' by pointing out that 'the Tibetan ruling clique viewed the British endeavour with the greatest alarm since it posed a direct threat to the vested interest the clique had in the Tibet-China trade …' It was the Darjeeling interest in the export of tea to Tibet that created the strongest opposition to the opening of trade across the border through Sikkim. The road under construction was seen in this expansionist light and soon led to the next episode that ended in the British effectively establishing their administrative rule over Sikkim.

The negative position on British interests that Tsugphud Namgyal and his dewan held had been taken care of by the Treaty of Tumlong and the way forward became even smoother for the British, with the shrewder Sidkeong Namgyal taking over the reins of power in Sikkim. Sidkeong accepted the reality that Britain was the actual paramount power and that he and Sikkim had to deal with the British on their terms. He also agreed to use whatever good offices he possessed, arising allegedly out of the ruler's relations with Lhasa, to persuade Lhasa to open its doors to trade with Britain.

In 1873, the British, still unable to understand that Darjeeling and its tea industry were like a red rag to a raging bull for Tibet and, by extension, the imperial court in China, failed to take into account that the road linking Sikkim to Darjeeling would be viewed by the Tibetans—with the tacit support of the amban—as an additional affront.

At a time when opposition was brewing over the road, the British decided to depute J.W. Edgar, the deputy commissioner of Darjeeling, to visit 'Sikkim and the frontier with Tibet and to enquire into the condition and the prospects of trade with Tibet and the advisability of making a road through Sikhim to the Tibetan frontier'.[6] Edgar attempted to cross over to the Chumbi Valley. He was stopped by Tibetan officials but was allowed to discuss matters with the Phari jongpen, governor, who turned down his request that British subjects and traders be permitted to enter Tibet.

A disappointed Edgar returned to Darjeeling. According to Risley, Edgar discovered that 'the Tibetans were very jealous of our attempts to use the Sikhim Government and the country in our efforts to open up trade with Tibet, and that the Chinese "ampa" or Resident of Lhassa, had written to the Raja in the name of the Emperor of China, reminding him that he was bound to prevent the "Peling Sahibs" (Europeans) from crossing the frontier of Tibet, and warning him that if he continued to make roads for the sahibs through Sikhim, "it would not be well with him".'

In the meanwhile, efforts by the British representative in Beijing finally bore fruit. He obtained permission for a visit to Tibet by a British trade mission to be led by Colin Macaulay, who had earlier visited Khamba Jong that lies to the north of Sikkim, and held what he felt were worthwhile talks with the concerned Tibetan jongpen. Macaulay was an ambitious person and he was convinced that he could bribe the Tibetans, including the monks, into submission. His discussions with the Tibetans had left him with the impression that the real opposition to the opening up of the Indo-Tibetan trade relations was coming from China, with the support of the lamas of the main Tibetan monasteries.

The next scene in this theatre of contradictions arose as the Emperor of China finally, but with great reluctance, granted permission for the British trade mission that Macaulay, in anticipation of receiving the permission, had assembled in Darjeeling in 1885–86 to visit Lhasa. The Tibetan Tsongdu (Tibetan National Assembly) and the Kashag (Tibet's governing council), undoubtedly with the endorsement of the Dalai Lama, challenged the right of the Chinese Emperor to interfere in Tibet's matters. Denying that he had any rights over Tibet, they refused admission to the British mission. The Tibetan administration in all its relevant forums denied that the Emperor of China had any locus standi in Tibet's affairs or any right to grant permission to any outside power to enter or pass through Tibet.

This position made a mockery of the special provision relating to Tibet that had been included in the Anglo-Chinese Convention of Chefoo of 1876, also known as the Yantai Treaty.[7] The Tibetan refusal brought to the surface the reality of relations between China and Tibet, making clear that Lhasa only took into consideration those suggestions or pieces of advice that the Chinese court proposed that it found suitable.

To get a better understanding of the complexities that governed the British-Chinese relationship, a biography[8] based heavily on the diaries and papers belonging to Sir Henry Mortimer Durand, who was foreign secretary of British India from 1884 to 1894, provides a fascinating and very revealing account of what really transpired after the annexation of Burma by the British and how this also came to impact their relations with Tibet and Sikkim.

Sir Mortimer points out that from 'very early times, great empires have established their influence over a fringe of surrounding states, serving the same purpose that a glacis does to a fort. China was among the earliest to pursue this policy, and Tibet, Nepal, Sikkim and Burma, stage by stage, came within the sphere of influence of the Celestial Empire.' What is even more interesting is Sir Mortimer's conclusion that as 'the centuries passed and the British established themselves firmly in India, China gradually lost control of some of the buffer states, her place being taken by the British Empire so far as Nepal, Sikkim and Burma were concerned'.

Durand as foreign secretary of India, was making it clear that the position of Tibet was different from that of the other tributary states and that China continued to exercise direct control over Tibet. This was in spite of the fact that Tibet had shown ample evidence that it took its own lead on its relations with outside powers.

The next description of events is even more revealing. Sir Mortimer writes, 'In view of the former suzerainty of China over Burma, Nepal and Sikkim, the annexation of Burma by the British was a cause of active concern to the Tsungli Yamen, which had been accustomed to receive a Mission every ten years from the Lord of the White Elephant. The position was further complicated owing to hostilities that had occurred on the borders of Sikkim.'

Sir Mortimer refers to the 'reluctant consent to the dispatch of a Commercial Mission from India to Lhasa'. This is a reference to the Macaulay Mission which, as we have already noted, faced a hostile reception from Tibetan officials who refused to accept the instructions that the British had obtained from the Emperor of China. The Tibetans stated quite clearly that the Emperor had no right to interfere or instruct them on how they should conduct their relations with external parties. The interesting fact is that despite this clarity offered by Lhasa defining the reality of its relations with China, the British continued, as this suited them, to grant the Chinese a position on Tibet that Lhasa studiously repudiated.

Sir Mortimer, to grant substance to the argument that at that time the British were concerned more with getting China to accept their position on Burma than mending relations with Tibet, had this to say while commenting on the British Commercial Mission, 'Not only was the way barred by the Tibetans, but intense hostility was displayed. The question was referred back to Peking, and a solution to the difficulty was found. Great Britain on her part refrained from insisting upon the Mission carrying out its task, while China agreed to waive her shadowy rights over Burma.'

Clearly, the foreign secretary, who was carrying out the orders of the viceroy, Lord Dufferin, considered that Tibet and its rights were of low value, and they could be sacrificed in order to have China accept that it was Great Britain and no longer the Celestial Empire that held sway over Nepal, Bhutan, Burma or Sikkim.

The obvious discrepancy lay in the assumption by the British that a tributary status was akin to acceptance by that state that China was the suzerain power. This was based on a false premise and an act of sophistry on the part of the British, to better serve their interests both where the Himalayan kingdoms were concerned and in the case of establishing relations with Tibet—their main aim remained that the relations with China should not be impacted or imperilled. This was a very cynical approach in dealing with Tibet, that was forcibly cast into the mould of a country with compromised sovereignty, with the British pitching China in the role of the suzerain power over Tibet.

India–Tibet Border

The watershed principle is 'termed as such because rivers, tributaries, and entire water system for the area run down these mountain faces, and ownership up to the height of the peaks is a logical boundary, and it ensures that a nation will own the entirety of the water system, from the beginning to the end.' This is as spelt out by Evan Towt in his study, 'Border Conflict and Tibet'.[9]

The British in the nineteenth century were already taking steps to contain Russia's ambitions where almost the whole of Central Asia had become an integral part of the Russian empire and had come to pose a threat to the British Asian empire. It was in this context that the British were not just evolving a frontier policy that led, with the involvement of Sir Mortimer Durand, to the demarcation of the frontiers of Afghanistan with Russian Central Asia, but also the positioning of Afghanistan as a buffer between Russia and British India. Simultaneously, the British in India were also looking at India's frontier with Tibet and Tibet itself in the same context.

The Pamir Boundary Commission of 1895 was tasked to liaise with Britain's Russian and Afghan counterparts, to demarcate the frontier between Afghanistan and Russian Central Asia. The Commission placed an emphasis on the principle that 'geographically, politically and ethnographically watersheds … are the only true and stable boundaries …' To mark the importance of this point in the establishing of land frontiers, we have to understand that this was the principle that the British were relying on to get the Chinese to agree to the Himalayan watershed, that the Chola range, located on the geographical east of Sikkim, be used to define Sikkim's border with Tibet. In the process, as the Chumbi Valley lay on the eastern part of the Chola watershed, it was no longer treated as a part of Sikkim and was excised from it.

In the case of the India–Tibet border, the mighty Himalayan range along with its extensions forms a clear watershed between the two countries. This factor did play a role in the manner in which the British defined and determined relations between India and the Himalayan states. All that lay north of the Himalayan watershed was Tibet and all that lay south of it became part of the Himalayan and Indian princely states that were protected by India under treaties, with the rest of the territory being part of British India.

The issue that continues to face India is that the Chinese occupation of Tibet changed the entire dynamics of relations that had traditionally existed between India's northern states and Tibet. There had been peace between the two entities, with the exception of two occasions in the seventh and ninth centuries when the Chumbi Valley had been used to invade north India. Otherwise, there existed a history of largely peaceful religio-cultural exchanges between Tibet and India, with age-old routes connecting the two through passes.

These routes also enabled Tibetan and Indian pilgrims to visit places of religious interest in each other's countries. For Hindus, it was the holy complex of Kailash Manasarovar in Tibet, and for Tibetans, places connected to Lord Buddha and Buddhism in India. These were also the routes that facilitated trade and commerce between the two countries where the Indian state of Ladakh was one of the beneficiaries. The Himalayan mountain passes were contact points between the two geographies that permitted them to maintain mutually beneficial and peaceful contact. This was shattered by China's invasion of Tibet in 1950 and its refusal to abide by either the traditional or the watershed principles for demarcating borders between an independent India and an occupied Tibet, threatening peace between China and India.

The British did try and bring about a settled border between the Indian states and British India with Tibet and constituted border commissions for the purpose, but they invariably foundered on the British insistence to have China underwrite any agreement arrived at with Tibet. Certainly, whatever may have been the position earlier, by the mid nineteenth century, the Chinese were in no position to undertake such a role, with Lhasa denying them any such right.

Notes

1. *The Buddhism of Tibet or Lamaism*, L. Austine Waddell, first published in 1889; reprinted by Asian Educational Services New Delhi and Chennai 1991, p. 50.
2. *Ibid.*
3. *Ibid.*, p. 20.
4. Reference is in Dr P.L. Mehta's piece titled 'Lord Curzon's Despatch of January 8, 1903: Its Impact on His Tibetan Policy' published in Volume 21 (1958) on pages 536–542 of the *Proceedings of the India History Congress* by the Indian History Congress, www.J.Stor.org/stable/44145251.
5. *Sikkim: A Short Political History*, Lal Bahadur Basnett, S. Chand & Co., New Delhi, 1974.
6. Page v of Risley's introduction to *The Sikhim Gazetteer.*
7. The special provision on Tibet that was appended to the Anglo-Chinese Chefoo Convention stated as follows: 'Her Majesty's Government having it in contemplation to send a mission of exploration next year, by way of Peking, through Kanush and Kokonor, or by way of Szechuen to Thibet, and thence to India, the Tsungli Yamen, having due regard to the circumstances, will, when the time arrives, issue the necessary passports, and will address to the High Provincial authorities and the Residents in Thibet. If the Mission should not be sent by these routes but should be proceeding across the Indian frontier to Thibet, the Tsungli Yamen, on receipt of

a communication to that effect from the British Minister, will write to the Chinese Resident in Thibet, and the Resident, with due regard to the circumstances, will send officers to take care of the Mission, and passports for the Mission will be issued by the Tsungli Yamen, that its passage not be obstructed.'

8. *Sir Mortimer Durand: A Biography*, Brigadier-General Sir Percy Sykes, Cassell and Company, London, 1926.
9. *Border Conflict and Tibet: The Asian Giants and Their History of Power Struggle*, Evan Towt. Published as part of the Asian Studies Commons, and the Defence and Security Studies Commons, digfitalcollections. sit.edu/isp. Collection.

5

TREATIES AND NEGOTIATIONS

Thutob Namgyal succeeded his half-brother, Sidkeong Namgyal, as the Maharaja of Sikkim in 1874. Thutob was in his early teens when Sidkeong passed away. The British decided that Thutob should continue to reside in the Chumbi Valley to assist the Macaulay-led Commercial Mission to Lhasa. That visit was finally sacrificed by the British to secure their position with China on Burma. What the British failed to take into account was that Thutob had come under the influence of their bitter adversary, the ousted Dewan Namgyal and his Tibetan wife, both of whom played a central role in influencing the ruler's pro-Tibet views, claiming that Sikkim and he were subservient to Tibet and, by extension, to China.

Another fallout of the failed Macaulay Mission was the belief it created among Tibetan authorities that the British were 'afraid of the might of the Chinese Emperor', which led to their deciding to use force to put an end to the British-sponsored road connecting Darjeeling to Jelep La. The Tibetans crossed the pass and came to fortify their presence at the post of Lingtu, some sixteen miles within Sikkim. The first attempt to end the standoff was by a letter of protest to the Dalai Lama. It was summarily rejected by the Kashag, stating that 'there was no harm in protecting one's own territory and that the Tibetans were prepared to resist a British attack'.[1]

To complicate matters further, Maharaja Thutob Namgyal took the position that Lingtu and the area around it was actually a part of Tibet, which had graciously allowed its use by Sikkim, 'creating the false impression that it was part of Sikkim'. The Tibetans continued to strengthen their hold over Lingtu and its surrounding area. The Bengal authorities had concluded a formal agreement with China that would establish the boundary between Tibet and Sikkim. This required that the British develop a coordinated position with Sikkim, towards which end they invited Thutob Namgyal to visit Darjeeling for discussions. Realizing that he would have to clarify his stand, the ruler decided to defy the British summons, presuming that the Tibetans would be able to defend him and secure his hold on Sikkim.

Treaty of Galing

When pressed, and threatened with the stoppage of the annual payment made to him, Thutob claimed that he had signed a treaty that declared that Sikkim was 'subject only to China and Tibet; he was therefore unable to come to Darjeeling without the express permission of the Tibetan Government'.[2]

While this complication was developing, the British were, according to Risley, holding back in the expectation that the 'Chinese Government, moved partly by our (Britain's) diplomatic remonstrances, and partly by fear lest we should treat the Lingtu demonstration as a pretext for entering Tibet in force, would compel the Lhassa authorities to adjust their relations with Sikhim on a basis involving the recognition of our (British) predominance in the State.'[3]

An amusing aside was the fact that the Chinese, aware that their writ hardly ran in Lhasa, were hoping that a defeat of Tibetan forces would bring home a greater sense of the threat that the British posed to Tibet and would lead Lhasa to accept its dependence on China to bail it out. The irony was that the British, keeping in mind the importance of China as a market, were deliberately ignoring the real relationship between China and Tibet and were pushing China to exert its influence over Tibet, thus granting it an importance that in effect was against the security interests of India.

The so-called Treaty of Galing was signed by the Sikkim Maharaja and a Tibetan state secretary in 1886. According to Risley, a Tibetan secretary of state accompanied by 'a Chinese military officer' visited Paro in Bhutan to settle a dispute that led to the signing of an agreement in 1880. On his way back to Phari, he tried to extract a similar agreement from the then Maharaja of Sikkim but was refused. Six years later when, according to Risley, British influence had 'begun to wane', the subject was reopened, and a formal treaty was signed at Galing by the Maharaja.

The treaty is defined as being in the 'form of a petition to the two Chinese Residents (ambans) in Lhasa, setting forth that some Europeans, after petitioning the great officers of China, have to the detriment of the religion, got an order to enter Tibet for trade'. It goes on to claim, 'From the time of ... Penchoo Namguay all (our Rajahs ...) have obeyed the orders of China. You have ordered us ... to stop the passage of the Rishi river between Sikhim and British territory; but we are small ... (British Government) is great, and we may not succeed ... In such a crisis, if you, as our old friends, can make some arrangements, ... We all ... honestly promise to prevent persons from crossing the boundary.'[4]

What lay behind the treaty, or rather the 'petition' of Galing, was an acknowledgement that both China and Tibet had an equal interest in stopping the British and that Sikkim had to obey their orders. The fact that Lhasa was endorsing the petition that placed both Tibet and China on the same footing, thus acknowledging the right of the Chinese to interfere or impose or, at the very least, suggest the directions to be followed by Tibet, was in contradiction to the earlier expressed ire of the Kashag over the Chinese Emperor's attempt to interfere in Tibet's affairs.

The Tibetans, aware that the British had for their own reasons adopted the position of dealing with Tibet through China, used China as a convenient tool to keep the relations between Lhasa and Britain at bay. The Tibetans had, right from the time of Samuel Turner's visit to Shigatse, hidden behind the need to defer to China even on matters of trade, by conveying the impression that China was the one that would determine the relations that Tibet could have with an outside power, in this case, Britain. A similar strategy was adopted by the Chinese as well, as it continued to play the suzerain card that the British had dealt it, knowing clearly that it could not impose its will on Lhasa.

End of Occupation of Lingtu

One clear motive behind the 1861 Treaty of Tumlong was the British need to exercise fuller control over the Sikkim durbar and influence the manner in which the state was governed. It did this by insisting that the Raja and his council operate out of the state capital and not the Chumbi Valley. The intention was to undermine the relations that the ruler had with Tibet, which became paramount if he resided and operated out of the valley. By keeping him in Sikkim, the British concluded that they could control the ruler and manage him better. The treaty spells this out in its insistence that the Raja 'agrees to remove the seat of his Government from Tibet (the Chumbi Valley) to Sikhim, and to reside there for nine months in the year'.[5]

The British were trying to serve two objectives. First, they wanted China and Tibet to renounce any rights they may have over Sikkim and, as a sop, were letting Sikkim's Chumbi Valley become a territorial part of Tibet. Second, to ensure that China continued to grant primacy to British trade interests within its territories, the British acknowledged that Tibet lay in China's area of influence while expecting that in return, both China and Tibet would accept that in Sikkim, Britain was the paramount power.

To grant heft to the latter point, the Treaty of Tumlong spelt out that Sikkim was in effect a British protectorate. However, at this stage, there was still no attempt to situate a British officer in Sikkim to oversee British interests in the 'protectorate'. This occurred only after the complications that arose out of the Tibetan occupation of Lingtu and Thutob Namgyal's misstep in signing the Treaty of Galing.

The British finally used force to end the occupation of Lingtu. They first overpowered and forced the retreat of the Tibetan forces, pushing them beyond Jelep La and pursuing them into the Chumbi Valley. A second group of British forces took over Gangtok, along with the Maharaja's residence.

The movement of British forces into the valley created an opportunity for the Chinese amban, Shengtai, to assert his position by suggesting that a foreign force had invaded Tibet and the Chinese, as in the past, were coming to the rescue of Buddhist Tibet. This was not the time for a Chinese military force to come to the aid of Tibet, but it was an opportunity to use diplomatic means to help Tibet regain the valley. The Chinese move was not endorsed by Lhasa; in fact, the Kashag opposed it, but Shengtai ignored

Tibetan protests and made his way to Gnathong to negotiate with the British.

Shengtai's was a shrewd move as it granted credence to the British contention, despite all evidence to the contrary, that China was responsible for Tibet's external policies. The amban was acting in consonance with the British line that China should accept responsibility for Tibetan actions and was responding to the British insistence that they would only negotiate the terms of settlement to resolve issues arising from the Lingtu incident with the Chinese. The fact that the amban was making his moves in the face of opposition from Lhasa and had no Tibetan representative on his delegation, was not questioned by the British negotiators. The mandate set for them did not allow for such questioning of the amban or his credentials for conducting negotiations on behalf of Lhasa.

The main focus of the talks, as far as Shengtai was concerned, was to get the British to move out of the Chumbi Valley. To gain that objective and to prevent any possibility of a failure of the talks that might lead the British to deal with the Tibetans directly, he confirmed that he was willing to follow the British agenda in two matters:

1. Establish the boundary between Sikkim and Tibet based on the watershed principle
2. Establish trade relations between Britain and Tibet, including the situating of a suitable trade mart in the Chumbi Valley

Shengtai was aware that he did not really have the mandate to negotiate a settlement along these lines. By accepting the agenda, he was just playing for time.

Waning Influence of Imperial Court

Perhaps to set it in context, some clarity on the post of amban is required. The role he was expected to play on behalf of the Qing court at Lhasa, along with another amban who was chiefly involved with furthering Manchu interests in the barren wastes of the Kokonoor region of Tibet, was to both further the relations with Tibet and keep a watch on the Tibetan administration and its interactions with foreign elements. The decision for the appointment of ambans[6] as imperial residents in Lhasa and at Shigatse was a decision initially taken by Qinq Emperor Qianlong, in 1728. This also marked the end of a direct Mongol presence in Tibet and followed the events that had been set in motion after Emperor Kangxi's defeat of the Zungar Mongol presence in Tibet in 1720. It was the Zungar who had extended political support to the Gelug, bestowing the title of 'Dalai Lama' on the sect's head lama.

The Qing emperors were Manchu in origin. The Manchus, like the Yuan dynasty in the past, were a Mongol tribe that had established itself to rule over a predominantly Han China. The ambans that they appointed were also from among the Manchu hierarchy and were specifically non-Han in their attitude and behaviour. The Qing empire was at its peak during the reigns of the emperors Kangxi (1662–1722), Yongzheng (1723–35) and Qianlong (1736–95). Dahpon David Ho[7] makes the point, 'Since the early days of the dynasty, the Manchu court had endorsed Tibetan Buddhism and cultivated a patron-priest relationship with the Dalai Lama. The office of Amban (Imperial Resident in Tibet) was created by the Qing emperors to maintain contact with and at time even control over Tibetan affairs.'

After the passing away of Emperor Qianlong in 1799, the influence of the Manchu court had dwindled to the point where the amban had been reduced to a figurehead who carried little or no weight with the Tibetan administration. Amban Shengtai was acting on his own and was never able to get any support or endorsement by the Lhasa authorities to conduct negotiations with the British.

The initial discussions were held between the amban and A.W. Paul, who was acting as the political officer accompanying the British forces. This was soon followed by talks between the amban, who studiedly kept the Tibetans out, and British India's foreign secretary, Sir Henry Mortimer Durand. Sir Mortimer's thinking, as we had noted earlier, was to an extent influenced by the negotiations that he had held with the Chinese on Burma. As he put it in his diary about the Lingtu incident, 'There remains the unpleasant fact that the Tibetans are holding a piece of Sikkim. Tibet and China do *undoubtedly* exercise a certain influence in Bhutan, Sikkim and Nepal, but we do not want that influence *increased and solidified*. Sikkim stands in a very peculiar position. It is by treaty practically an *Indian feudatory state.* Nevertheless, Maharajah is much in the hands of the Tibetans. It will, I fear, be difficult to get them out of the country if they take a fancy of staying there and assert claims to suzerainty [emphasis added].'[8]

Lamb describes this best[9] when he states that in this period the Government of India 'right up to the 1880s tended to overestimate the Chinese strength in Tibet, just as it later on was disposed to ignore unduly the influence in Tibetan politics of the Amban'.

Sir Mortimer, despite his familiarity with the concept of established borders to safeguard India's security, failed to look at Tibet in the same context. He confined himself to the settlement of Sikkim's border with Tibet, intending to redefine Sikkim's relations with Tibet and, by extension, with China. What is even more baffling was Britain's failure to apply the same yardstick to the

Russian presence on Tibet's border that they had applied to Russia's presence on the Afghanistan border, making it obvious that both Calcutta and London were granting primacy to Britain's Chinese economic interests over India's strategic interests in Tibet.

The negotiations between Amban Shengtai and Foreign Secretary Sir Mortimer throw an interesting light on how the complex issues were handled and the extent of the power that the Chinese could actually exercise over Tibet. The amban intermittently admitted that he had no power to make the Tibetan authorities yield to any decision he might make on their behalf.

Sir Mortimer's talks with Amban Shengtai began on a sour note with the amban first refusing to admit that the Tibetans had committed any aggression. He held on to the logic that as Tibet was part of the 'Chinese empire', it could only act within the protocol that China permitted it to follow in the exercise of its rights and interests. He was not, of course, willing to put his claim to test as there was ample evidence to the contrary. He concluded that since Sikkim was a dependency of Tibet, any entry into its territory by Tibetan officials and forces could not be considered as an act of aggression.

He put forward the argument that as Sikkim was subservient to Tibet, it was also subordinate to China, and as such, the ruler was bound to follow the instructions that the suzerain power conveyed to him. Shengtai was clearly trying his best to deny that the British had the rights of a paramount power in Sikkim and in the process faulting British actions at Lingtu and their occupation of the Chumbi Valley. With the British denying that Tibet or China had any rights over Sikkim, the talks were headed towards a stalemate.

Again on the issue of trade, the positions of both parties were poles apart, with Shengtai categorically denying that the British had any right to insist on establishing trade relations with Tibet. The

Chinese were playing the game of deceit, with Shengtai maintaining that as the Chinese envoy he was in control of the situation and that Tibet could not oppose the decisions that he took on its behalf. When it came to negotiating the British demands on the Tibet–Sikkim borders and the acceptance of Britain's position as the paramount power in Sikkim, Shengtai quickly put forward the claim that he could not force his views or decisions on the authorities in Lhasa, whom he defined to Sir Mortimer as 'the real masters'. This kind of a double-faced approach was on display throughout the negotiations that the British carried out with the Chinese on Tibet. The Chinese would, however, come to agreements with the British whenever they had their backs to the wall, driven by the fear that the British may achieve an understanding with the Tibetans in keeping the Chinese out.

With both sides not budging from their original positions, the talks ended in a stalemate. Describing the situation that he had faced, Sir Mortimer in his diary mentions, 'Instead of showing any regret, or appreciation for our extreme forbearance, the Amban supported the action of the Tibetans and put forward on their account claims to suzerainty in Sikkim.' Sir Mortimer firmly refuted the amban's contentions by stating that the British were '... bound to stand upon the ground that the Tibetans opposed by force a Mission China had agreed to, that they had made war upon us, and that China did nothing effectual to stop or punish them. Therefore any rights that Tibet or China may have had in Sikkim, are necessarily forfeited and we will not discuss them.'

The amban at one stage tried to insert the Deb Raja of Bhutan, Ugyen Wangchuk, into the discussions, but as Sir Mortimer says, 'this typically Oriental attempt "to assert openly in our presence the influence of Tibet over Bhutan," was defeated and gradually the Chinese representative realized that his intrigues were doomed to failure'. As we shall see later, this was the negotiating style that confronted Nehru and other Indian negotiators who had to deal with China on the border issue from 1950 onwards.

Sir Mortimer, while calling off negotiations and packing up to leave, made the suggestion to the viceroy that the Chumbi Valley be occupied and remain with the British, both as a bargaining tool with the Tibetans to open up Tibet to trade with India and also as reparations to meet the costs of the Indo-Tibetan war. The remarkable commonality in Sir Mortimer's views with those of Curzon and Younghusband on the occupation of the Chumbi Valley as reparations for the 1904 Anglo-Tibetan war reflects that the Chumbi Valley was seen as a bargaining tool by the British to get their way with the Tibetans. They did not necessarily see it as important to the security of India or as a strategic factor for India's relations with Tibet and by extension with China. What was unfortunate was that when the time came for Nehru to exercise this option as Mao's PLA moved into Tibet, he too did not recognize the security implications of the Chumbi Valley falling into Chinese hands.[10]

Notes

1. *Tibet: A Political History*, Tsepon W. D. Shakabpa, cited by Lal Bahadur Basnett in his *Sikkim: A Short Political History*, S. Chand & Co., New Delhi, 1974.
2. *Ibid.*, p. 54.
3. Pages viii and ix of the introduction by H.H. Risley to *The Gazetteer of Sikhim*. Note the entire episode is related to the Lingtu incident where the Tibetan forces had transgressed the territory of Sikkim in order to prevent the completion of the road to Jelep La connecting it to Darjeeling.
4. *The Gazetteer of Sikhim*, H.H. Risley, Forgotten Books, London, 2018, page vii of the Introduction.

5. *British India and Tibet: 1766–1910*, Alastair Lamb, Routledge and Kegan Paul, London and New York, 1960, p. 81. Citing the Treaty of Tumlong, wherein the Raja undertook to not spend more than three months in any one year in Chumbi.
6. The first imperial amban was sent to Tibet in 1728 with the main task to monitor and provide support to the one-man rule at that time being conducted by Polhanas, a Tibetan aristocrat supported by the Qinq Emperor.
7. Article in *Modern China*, Volume 34, No.2, Sage Publications Inc., pp. 210–246.
8. *The Right Honourable: Sir Mortimer Durand, A Biography*, Brigadier-General Sir Percy Sykes, Cassel and Company Ltd, London, Toronto, Melbourne and Sydney. First published in 1926.
9. *British India and Tibet: 1766–1910*, Alastair Lamb, Routledge and Kegan Paul, London and New York, 1960.
10. Note: All the references to the negotiations between the then foreign secretary of India and the Chinese amban based in Lhasa that were carried out to settle the developments that had taken place over the Lingtu incident and the occupation by British troops of the Chumbi Valley are based on:

    1. *The Right Honourable: Sir Mortimer Durand, A Biography*, Brigadier-General Sir Percy Sykes, Cassel and Company Ltd, London, Toronto, Melbourne and Sydney. First published in 1926.
    2. *British India and Tibet: 1766–1910*, Alastair Lamb, Routledge and Kegan Paul, London and New York, 1960.
    3. Other papers and notes made by me while posted at the political office of India in Gangtok from 1967–70.

6

CHALLENGES TO BRITISH ADMINISTRATION OF SIKKIM

After the Lingtu incident, Sikkim was declared a British protectorate that was to be treated as an Indian princely state. The Bengal administration bearing A. W. Paul's recommendation in mind, appointed John Claude White as the first resident political officer based in Gangtok. This appointment took place in June 1889. Initially, he was designated as the assistant political officer and shortly afterwards re-designated as the political officer.

White's appointment was to send a clear signal to Tibet and to the Chinese amban that whatever may have been their earlier contention, of Sikkim being subservient to Tibet or China, this was no longer the case. Further, it also negated the concept, put forward by Tibet and China, of a triangular kinship relationship that bound Tibet, Bhutan and Sikkim together. According to this, the Chinese held that as Tibet was in a fraternal patron-priest relationship with China, all three states, including Tibet, owed allegiance to Peking.

A New Political Officer

White remained the political officer for the longest period in Gangtok, holding the position from 1889 to 1908. Unlike his successors who were all from the civil services, he was an engineer officer who had the experience of working in Darjeeling and Nepal before being stationed in Gangtok. In 1883, he had served at the British Residency in Nepal. He was no stranger to Sikkim, having accompanied Paul in 1887 when they visited Gangtok to 'induce the Maharaja to return from Chumbi, whither he had retreated some time before, and spend more time in his own country'.[1]

Paul had to return to Darjeeling but White remained behind, continuing the effort to get Maharaja Thutob Namgyal and Yeshey Dolma, his Tibetan wife, to come back to Gangtok. This was a futile effort as the Maharaja refused to leave Chumbi. However, White stayed on for another fortnight to get to know Sikkimese hierarchy and establish a firm relationship with the two brothers—Khangsa Dewan and Phodong Lama—who between them were running the administration of the country. White came to trust the two brothers who he found had progressive ideas on how Sikkim should be managed.

The brothers understood the benefits of a British presence, observing that it would bring a degree of prosperity to the state. Thutob Namgyal, a conservative at heart, disliked the two brothers and would have gladly replaced them. White also met the other members of the local aristocracy, some of whom were to assist him in administering the state after he took over as the political officer and they were appointed to the Royal Council to work with him.[2]

White was convinced that the Chumbi Valley should be retained as part of Sikkim. I saw in the archives of the political office in Gangtok a copy of the note that White had addressed to the commissioner of Rajshahi in northern Bengal, who was the authority that White reported to, stating that the Chumbi Valley was part of the kingdom and should be retained as such. This was not agreed to by Calcutta as it felt that such an action would be a challenge to China and could disturb the business end of Britain's relations with Peking. Instead, the British preferred the watershed provided by the Chola range of mountains to serve its interests in Sikkim.

White is credited with setting up a consolidated administrative and revenue system that was people- and user-friendly. Sikkim had hardly any road infrastructure. White used the marginal revenue surpluses that he was able to generate to construct roads and bridges that connected all parts of Sikkim to each other, making the movement of goods to markets a more efficient process. The demographic structure of Sikkim that included the original inhabitants, the Lepcha and some Limbus; and the migrant Tibetans, the Bhutias, was one that left large parts of arable land uncultivated.

Demographic Shift

To fulfil the requirements of construction and agriculture that White put in motion needed far more people, both as labour and to settle on land, than what the population of the kingdom could provide. He filled these two requirements by encouraging Nepalis to come and settle down in Sikkim. This was not a difficult task as the development of Darjeeling had already seen a migration from Nepal, of people looking to work as labourers in the tea gardens.

Risley puts in perspective the manner in which the demographic structure had come to change under White and his policy of attracting the Nepalis to settle in Sikkim. Dr Campbell had estimated that the population of Sikkim comprised 3000 Lepchas and 2000 'Bhotiyas'. White, who carried out a census in 1891, put the population of Sikkim roughly as:

Lepchas	5800
Bhotiyas	4700
Nepalis and others	19,500
The total being	30,000[3]

The Nepali settlers were being freely granted permanent residency amounting to citizenship. Apart from the interest that the British had in increasing the labour force to deal with the expanding needs of infrastructure development and maintenance, and the increase in revenue from taxing agriculture where new areas were now coming under cultivation, there was a political motive to encouraging the Nepali migration. The Darjeeling tea planters were eyeing western Sikkim as being ideal for cultivating tea and they eventually succeeded in getting their way. Here again, the demand for labour was largely met by migrant Nepalis contributing to the changed demographic structure of Sikkim.

Risley grants to the migrant issue a political dimension, suggesting that due to the hereditary enmity of Nepal and Tibet, the influx of Nepalis in Sikkim could be considered a guarantee against the revival of Tibetan influence. Here too religion played a leading part. The British were interested in neutralizing the demographic dominance of the Bhutias and thus containing the Tibetan influence in Sikkim. Risley concluded, 'Race and religion, the prime movers of the Asiatic world, will settle the Sikhim difficulty for us, in their own way.'[4]

White was implementing Calcutta's stated policy that included ensuring progress in agricultural development; a well-grounded forest preservation policy that permitted organized commercial exploitation of forest produce; and the expansion of infrastructure that would both meet the needs of a Sikkim now being administered by the British with local involvement and also the needs of conducting Indian trade along Sikkim's traditional trade with Tibet.

While the immigration policy was clearly motivated by both economic and political considerations, White was careful to keep in mind the central place that Buddhism had come to occupy in the minds not only of the Bhutias but also the Lepchas and, to some extent, among a minority of the Nepali migrants too. He did not attempt to destroy the political status that the Bhutia ruler or the local aristocracy enjoyed, nor did he or those who succeeded him as political officers take any measures to diminish the influence of Buddhism or of the lamas who headed various monasteries and *gompas* across Sikkim.

Chinese 'Policy of Delay'

White held the distinction of being the first political officer who had to deal with Sikkim, Bhutan and Yatung in the Chumbi Valley, tasked with the responsibility of ensuring the implementation of relevant provisions of the Anglo-Chinese Convention of 1890 and the Regulations of 1893 appended to it. This involved two clear actions. The first was the delimitation of the border between Sikkim and Tibet as provided for by the convention. The second was the setting up of the trade mart at Yatung in compliance with the provisions of the 1893 regulations. It was a job mired in difficulties and by detailing them we gain insight into the manner in which the complicated relationship that the Tibetans had with China created conditions for a British incursion into Tibet.

White stayed at Yatung for some months to get the trade mart on its feet. The Chinese had permitted the building of a wall across the narrow part of the valley that controlled access to Yatung. It was clear to White that the Chinese were intent on continuing with the policy of preventing, to the extent feasible, contact between British, Indian and Tibetan merchants by placing barriers in the way of trade. To this end, they were adopting policies to intercept any possibility for the traders to meet freely and exchange goods.

Every attempt by him to arrive at a suitable arrangement that would encourage trade was effectively thwarted, with a frustrated White observing, 'It was my first experience of the Chinese official, and I have since always found him of the same type, outwardly exceedingly polite and punctilious, but behind one's back deceitful and cunning, intent on the Chinese policy of delay, and most difficult to bring to the point in any negotiation.'[5]

White was able to observe first hand that the Tibetans openly defied the Chinese, refusing to accept the provisions of the Convention of 1890 that the Chinese 'had signed on their behalf'. This was a confirmation of what Sir Mortimer had recorded about negotiating with the Chinese at the abortive Gnathong talks.

White conveyed his views on the Chinese behaviour and the fact that the Tibetans would continue to oppose any decisions that the British had made over Tibet with China, to Calcutta with the recommendation that Britain revise its policy on the Chumbi Valley and take it over, at least to force both the Chinese and the Tibetans to fully implement the agreed provisions within the Convention of 1890 and the Regulations of 1893.

Notes

1. *Sikhim And Bhutan*, J. Claude White, first published in 1909; reprinted by AES, New Delhi and Chennai, 1995 and 2005.
2. The Royal Council had on it the Khangsa brothers, the Shoe Dewan, the Gangtok, Tashiding, Enchey and Rhenock Kazis and Lama Lari

Pemba of the Pemigonchi monastery. The lama was the only one who had the trust of the Maharaja.

3. Page xx of the Introduction by H.H. Risley *The Gazetteer of Sikhim,* Forgotten Books, London, 2018.
4. *Ibid.*
5. Note by J.C. White, political officer to the Bengal Administration cited from *British India and Tibet: 1766–1910,* Alastair Lamb, Routledge and Kegan Paul, London and New York, 1960.

PART II

BRITAIN AND ITS PERFIDIOUS DEALINGS WITH TIBET

7

GAME OF SHADOWS

According to the *Oxford English Reference Dictionary*,[1] 'perfidious' means 'treacherous'. The *Oxford Dictionary of Difficult Words*[2] defines it more clearly as 'deceitful and untrustworthy; capable of treachery'. I would use this particular adjective to describe the adoption of a cynical and indefensible policy by the British, out of choice and not out of compulsion, to push Tibet into a trap to safeguard its own relations with China. The British deliberately granted to the priest-patron relationship that bound China and Tibet together in a form of kinship the Westphalian connotation of suzerainty and at times used the term 'sovereignty'—concepts that were unknown to the two nations.

At other times, when it suited them politically, the British even used the term 'de facto independent'. This was while maintaining that they would agree to China having the powers of a suzerain as long as the Chinese accepted that their role in Tibet was nominal, with Tibet not only exercising full autonomy over its internal administration but also the full right to deal directly with Britain.

These contradictory policies were thrown about despite the expressed views of senior British officials in India, like Foreign Secretary Sir Mortimer and the viceroy, that the Manchu court did not exercise the powers of a suzerain over Tibet. The Tibetan response was pointed, clear and absolute in its opposition to a role being played by the Manchu Emperor to determine how Tibet should deal with or respond to demands made on it by an external power. The Macaulay Mission was in effect a test of the value that could be attached to the separate provision appended to the Chefoo Convention, a test that failed as Tibet refused successfully to be dictated to by the Chinese Emperor. Even more importantly, it called into question Britain's Tibet policy based on the role of China as the paramount power in Tibet.

To gain a proper understanding of the developments that took place in the post-1950 era, when the People's Republic of China came to occupy Tibet, and the issues that this created for India and the impact it had on India's Sikkim policy, we must understand the policies followed by Britain towards Tibet and China while it exercised its colonial hold over India. Britain formed its policy on Tibet guided by its commercial and political relations with Manchu China and subsequently with republican China, where the two world wars also came to play a role. India's concerns were taken into account as and when it suited London.

It was the demands of Britain's European policy and relations with Russia that drove Britain to keep alive the myth that China held suzerainty over Tibet. Different Cabinet bodies in England dealing with India, China and Russia failed to follow the line that George Nathaniel Curzon (as Britain's viceroy in India) put across to impress on Whitehall both on the place of India as central to the British empire and the importance of a frontier policy that kept India's security and strategic interests in mind. This was ignored largely because the powers-that-be in London were keen to grant primacy to Anglo-Chinese relations over all other intervening considerations that were in the immediate and future interests of India. It was only when it became clear that there was a possibility that the Chinese had come to an agreement with Russia over Tibet that London finally gave in to Curzon and the Younghusband expedition to bring the Tibetans to heel was granted the go-ahead.

Myth of Chinese Suzerainty

As we earlier noted, the British had obtained, in a backup to the special provision to the Chefoo Convention, the permission of the Chinese Emperor for the British Commercial Mission's visit to Lhasa. Lord Dufferin, viceroy of India, and Sir Mortimer Durand, his point man on India's foreign policy, were aware that the Chinese Emperor had granted his endorsement with the utmost reluctance and should have realized that China would find it difficult to impose its diktat on Lhasa.

The events that followed clearly showed that the Emperor's reluctance was well founded as the visit foundered on the rock of a clearly expressed Tibetan refusal to honour the Manchu Emperor's diktat. The statement issued by thc Kashag should have removed any doubt that Tibet was acting as an independent state. The Tibetans would listen to the advice that the Chinese Emperor extended, within the bounds of a religious kinship, but when and the extent to which they would follow this advice was determined on their own terms.

Lhasa sent a clear and pointed message to the British that China did not have any right, inherent or otherwise, to represent Tibet. If it did try to use its religious kinship relations to act on its behalf, such an act would be opposed in its entirety. Nothing could have made this clearer than the Chinese amban's report that Lhasa was completely opposed to the visit and had questioned the right of the Emperor to act in any way on behalf of Tibet.

Interestingly enough, Sir N. O'Connor the British charge d' affairs in Peking, in his despatches to London about his discussions with the Tsungli Yamen, had confirmed that the Chinese opposition to granting permission to the Macaulay Mission was based on the fact that the 'Tibetans would oppose it, probably by force of arms. Further stating that the officials in the Yamen had made it clear that the Chinese did not have the power to impose their wishes on the Government of the Dalai Lama'.[3]

The Chinese were taking advantage of the false opinion that Britain harboured of the Tibet–China relationship. They had originally strongly objected to the British definition that stated that 'Tibet was a dependency of China', by claiming that it was an 'integral part of the Chinese Empire'.[4] However, when the Tibetans categorically refused to honour the Chinese Emperor's permission for the British Commercial Mission to visit Tibet, the Tsungli Yamen admitted that China could not 'impose its wishes on the Dalai Lama'. The contradiction in Chinese policy statements was clear. While they were happy that the British saw them as the suzerain in Tibet and were willing to play along with this contention, in reality, they were aware that they had no real hold on Lhasa and its decisions.

Again, the bargain struck with the Chinese over Burma was based on the false notion that the tributary relationship that imperial Burma had with China granted the latter suzerain rights over Burma. The Chinese were aware that they had no such rights but they needed Tibet as a buffer against an expansionist Britain and played along and arrived at a bargain that they would agree to an immediate settlement on Burma, implying that they would accept the British terms, in exchange for 'permanent abandonment of the

Macaulay Mission'[5] to Tibet. O'Connor conveyed this proposal, suggesting its acceptance. Viceroy Dufferin gave it his instant approval, with the British accepting the palliative provision entitled 'relative to Burma and Thibet in the Anglo-Chinese Convention of 1886'. The text of this article is revealing:[6]

> Inasmuch as enquiry into the circumstances by the Chinese Government has shown the existence of many obstacles to the Mission of Thibet provided for in the Separate Article of the Chefoo Agreement, England consents to countermand the Mission forthwith. With regard to the desire of the British Government to consider arrangements for the further trade between India and Thibet, it will be the duty of the Chinese Government, after its careful enquiry into circumstances, to adopt measures to exhort and encourage the people with a view to the promotion and development of trade. Should it be practicable, the Chinese Government shall then proceed carefully to consider Trade Regulations; but if insuperable obstacles should be found to exist, the British Government will not press the matter unduly.

This article, when read along with what the Tsungli Yamen conveyed to O'Connor about China's inability to impose its will on the government of the Dalai Lama, can only cement the claim that British authorities both in London and in Calcutta, in full knowledge of the lack of power that China held over Lhasa, continued to maintain that China had control over Tibet. The inclusion of the term 'insuperable obstacles' meant that the Chinese had the option to put across that such an obstacle continued to prevail and Tibet could not be opened by it to trade with British India.

The next blow in this game of shadows was struck when the Lingtu incident occurred and the Tibetans quite clearly kept the Chinese out of their decision to forcibly contain British movement towards Tibet through Sikkim. After the British had ousted them from Lingtu by force, they kept up the charade of dealing with Tibet via China and the result was the Anglo-Chinese Convention of 1890. Lhasa continued to ignore it as it refused to grant China the right to act on its behalf. By adhering to the myth of Chinese control over Tibet, the British also ignored the fact that Tibet was of strategic importance to India.

Underplaying the Tibet–India Connection

The British could hardly have been unaware of the close ties of religion and, to an extent, culture that bound Tibet and India. In fact, it was one of their own, Laurence Austine Waddell,[7] who in his book published in 1889, had familiarized himself with works on Lamaist Buddhism by Emil Schlagintweit and C.F. Koppen and drew attention to the legend that lay behind the establishment of the monarchy in Tibet. The legend claimed that the first Tibetan monarch was a prince of Indian origin, the fifth son of Maharaja Prasenajit of Kosala, who because of certain physical deformities, was as an infant placed in a copper vessel by his frightened parents and set afloat on the holy Ganga. He was rescued by a farmer and brought up in his household.

On attaining manhood, Prince Prasenajit realized that he was born of a higher order and in his restlessness decided to set out, without any clear aim, to seek his fortune. In the course of his travels, he decided to cross the high 'snowy mountains of Lha-ri near the modern town of Tse-Thang in Tibet. Descending into the plains of Tsan-Than he was met by many natives of the country … asked him respectfully who he was and whence he came. Not knowing their language, the prince ... pointing up to top of Lha-ri wished them to understand that he had come from that direction. The Tibetans ... assumed he was a god descended from heaven, ... entreated him to become their king.' He was known as Nah-Thi-Tsanpo or the chair-borne king. This reference to the legend is also found in Risley's *The Gazetteer of Sikhim*.[8]

The *Gazetteer* also makes it clear that the British were aware of the influence Indian Buddhist pandits like Shantarakshita, Atisha, Dharmapala and the honoured Guru Padmasambhava had on the spread of Buddhism in Sikkim and Tibet. The influence of Pali and the script that the Tibetans had adopted from the Indian state of Kashmir had resulted in a degree of Indian cultural influence forming a part of the cultural mores of Tibet.

Historically imperial China, under the Mongol/Manchu influence, had established relations with Buddhist Tibet that granted it a degree of spiritual, cultural and political influence in Tibet. Indian influence, particularly in the spiritual and cultural spheres, had a more expansive role in Tibet and on Tibetan Buddhism. People like H.H. Risley, L. Austine Waddell and Thomas H. Holdich in their writings that had wide circulation among the British Indian ruling classes, made out that religious, intellectual and cultural links were responsible for a deep emotional and spiritual connection between India and Tibet. The colonial authorities could only shy away from the reality of Indian influence that prevailed in Tibet and place Tibet within the ambit of China, to meet their own selfish ends driven primarily by business and commercial interests.

While the Tibetans were opposed to having any direct dealings with the British on trade, they had put no barriers in the way of traditional trade that carried on being conducted by Indians with Tibet. Indian merchants, particularly from Ladakh, but also from other north Indian states, continued to cross over and trade with

Tibet, where in places like Lhasa, they even had clearly demarcated areas to live in as well as market their goods. These parallel facilities were extended to Nepalese traders too. Lhasa's problem lay with European entry into Tibet.

The British had decided to ignore that Manchu control over Tibet was more fiction than fact. Foreign Secretary Sir Mortimer arrived at the conclusion that the Chinese were not ready to put the claim of being the suzerain power in Tibet to the test as the Tibetans had shown clearly that Peking's writ in Lhasa was limited and would be ignored whenever it was not in consonance with Tibetan thinking on safeguarding their national interests. The British had ample evidence of the real nature of Manchu China's relations with Tibet. If they needed any additional confirmation, this was provided by Amban Shengtai at the Gnathong discussions. Shengtai maintained that he could not go back to Lhasa if he endorsed the British demands, as doing so would put his life in danger.

Sir Mortimer had held the point of view that Sikkim as a 'feudatory' state of India could not be permitted to pay homage to a foreign power. He was going by the principle that 'if we give way in respect of Sikkim, we must be prepared to do so, at some future time, not only with regard to Bhutan and Nepal, but with regard to Kashmir and her feudatories, such as Hunza and Nagar … We might even have China claiming suzerain rights over Darjeeling and the Bhutan Dooars, which we acquired from her so-called feudatories'.[9] Calcutta was clear where India's and Britain's interests lay—London had a different take on the situation.

Apart from what Sir Mortimer put across as the argument denying Chinese claims on the 'homage' that they expected the Sikkim ruler to continue to extend to Tibet and China, an important and telling element was his reference to Sikkim as a 'feudatory state of India'. This was also a point made by Sir Olaf

Caroe, who was foreign secretary during the Second World War. Immediately before India's independence, he put across in his note that 'Sikkim was an Indian State and was part of India'.[10]

To further fortify this contention, the Government of India Act of 1935 was applied to Sikkim and it was allotted a seat on the Council of State of the Federal Assembly. Later, Olaf Caroe while recalling his time as foreign secretary of India, a post that he held under the viceroys Linlithgow and Wavell, repeated that 'Sikkim was an Indian state' maintaining that the protectorate status to the state under the India–Sikkim Treaty of 1950 did not change the fact that it had been treated as an Indian princely state during the British period.

'This Protectorate status does not alter the fact that for decades prior to 1947 Sikkim had been a part of India, its external frontiers being a sector of India's frontiers,' Caroe wrote in an article on the merger of Sikkim with India in the British paper *Daily Telegraph* in its issue of 8 November 1975.

Anglo-Chinese Convention of 1890

Following the failure of the Gnathong talks, Calcutta took the position that there was no need for any further discussion. As far as the British were concerned, the position on Sikkim had been clarified and the action taken to force the hand of Maharaja Thutob Namgyal, by stopping his allowance and banishing him to Kurseong in Darjeeling district, had ended with him recognizing that he had no choice but to bend to the British. He had accordingly agreed to the proposal that his state be administered by a British political officer and a Royal Council constituted by the political officer. The main effort of the British at this point was to move the Maharaja out of the Chumbi Valley and force him to reside more or less permanently at Gangtok.

Sir Mortimer at one stage had even proposed that the British exercise the option of forcing the Tibetans to accept their terms, leaving China out of the equation. He had the viceroy's support for this policy, including getting the Tibetans to accept that they could no longer continue to exert any influence on Bhutan and Sikkim.

Calcutta appeared to have arrived at the conclusion that they could make a unilateral declaration about Sikkim after the Lingtu exchange, with the Tibetans and the Chinese giving the British the upper hand in dealing with the Himalayan states. There was satisfaction over the enforcement of the twin decisions of removing the Maharaja from the Chumbi Valley and placing him under the charge of a British Official. These two actions were thought to have diminished, if not ended, the influence that Tibet and China had over him. Calcutta assumed that they could, whenever the time was ripe, deal with Tibet directly on the trade issue without the intervention of Peking.

While Calcutta felt that there was no purpose served in continuing talks with the Chinese, London's attitude, governed by Britain's business interests, pressurized the British to restart the talks. Whitehall was obviously attaching greater priority to its relations with China, keeping in mind the importance of its power-sharing arrangements with other European powers in China. London was intent on seeing that China did not lose face over Tibet.

Meanwhile, the Chinese had come to realize that if they failed to arrive at an agreement, the British might drop the charade of Chinese suzerainty over Tibet and opt to deal directly with Lhasa. Ironically, the person advising the Chinese on the talks with the British was Sir Robert Hart, a British baronet employed by the Qing court as head of China's Imperial Custom Service. He held this position from 1863 to 1911. Sir Robert recommended that the follow-up to the failed Gnathong talks be conducted by his younger brother, James Hart. Viceroy Dufferin, in the meanwhile, had been replaced by Lord Henry Lansdowne, who supported Sir Mortimer's view that talks should be resumed only if the Chinese were to make a worthwhile offer.

Calcutta's views however were brushed aside, with London forcing the resumption of talks with China. The talks were resumed in Calcutta with Amban Shengtai, who had been mandated by China to follow the agenda set by the British. He was assisted by James Hart at the negotiations, while A.W. Paul consulted on behalf of Britain. The talks ended in the adoption of the Anglo-Chinese Convention on Sikkim and Tibet, signed in Calcutta on 17 March 1890.

Article I of the Convention[11] set the borders between Tibet and Sikkim as the 'crest of the mountain range separating the waters flowing from the Teesta and its affluents from the waters flowing into the Tibetan Mochu and northwards into the rivers of Tibet. The line commences at Mount Gipmochi on the Bhutan frontier, and follows the abovementioned water-parting to the point where it meets Nipal territory.'

Article II[12] effectively granted the Chinese endorsement of Sikkim being a British protectorate where the British government 'has direct and exclusive control over the internal administration and foreign relations of that State …'

Both governments guaranteed respect for the boundary thus established between Tibet and Sikkim and to 'prevent acts of aggression from their respective sides of the frontier'.

This was an interesting formulation that made Britain and China responsible for the security of the Sikkim–Tibet frontiers and implied that the border on the Tibetan side was actually the frontier with China, as the words used were 'their respective sides of the frontier'. This is important as the British were not apparently looking at Tibet as a buffer between India and China at this time. On the contrary, whether by intent or by a language misstep, they were granting China full control over Tibet.

The British were playing a game, where mercantile considerations had taken the upper hand and the interests of the British Indian empire were being subordinated to the gains that they were seeking in China. Tibet was the pawn and little, if any, regard was being granted to it by London over its fate or future.

Interestingly, the issues of trade, communication and so on were left to future discussions, ending in an agreement dated 13 December 1893 titled: 'Regulations of 1893 regarding Trade, Communications and Pasturage to Be Appended to the Sikkim–Tibet Convention of 1890'.

As per these regulations, a trade mart would be established at Yatung in the Chumbi Valley where British subjects would be free to travel, exchange goods and reside. The communications between India and Tibet were reduced to dispatches to be exchanged between the Government of India and the Chinese amban in Lhasa. This, in effect, took the Tibetan authorities out of the equation and in a most cynical manner continued to grant substance to the myth that it was the Chinese who were in control of the Tibetan administration. Tibet was reduced to the level of a Chinese protectorate.

The Regulations of 1893 had been hard-fought with the final version being adopted after a struggle of almost three years. As mentioned earlier, the two interlocutors were A.W. Paul for the British side and James Hart for the Chinese. The British were initially set on Phari, that lies on the Himalayan watershed and at the head of the Chumbi Valley, as the location for the trade mart. This was not acceptable to the Chinese as they were aware that at Phari they would not be in a position to control events in the face of open Tibetan opposition and defiance. They even feared for the lives of the Chinese officials supervising the trade mart. Their view prevailed and the British accepted Yatung, that lay just a short march away from Jelep La, as the location.

Initially, the British were hedging their bets because they thought Yatung would be a temporary location. What they did not take into account was the geographical location of Yatung, situated as it was at the narrow end of the valley through which passed the only road to Phari. That road could be blocked, as it was, with the Chinese building a wall across it that enabled them to control who entered the trade mart from the Tibetan side.

The British political officer in Gangtok was placed in charge of the Yatung trade mart as provided for under the Regulations of 1893. John Claude White took over this responsibility and as we have seen earlier, was confronted by an impossible situation where the actual trade operations were reduced to the level of a farce. This was despite the agreement of the British that a five-year moratorium be placed on the export of tea from India to Tibet. By this understanding, the British were recognizing that tea was a sensitive issue for both the Chinese and Tibetans, as it was the main source of revenue for the state of Sichuan, and for the leading lamas of Tibetan monasteries who held the monopoly over the China–Tibet tea trade.

The main outcome of both the Convention of 1890 and the appended Regulations of 1893 was that British India, under pressure from Whitehall, had accepted the directive that all of India's cross-border dealings with Tibet be conducted entirely with the Chinese. It was an outcome that set in motion the following situation. China, as the accepted channel for all things British relating to Tibet, was unable to deliver because Lhasa refused to cooperate with it. Britain had to reluctantly come to the conclusion that the reading that it had been getting on Sino-Tibetan relations from India was correct and that Peking would not be in a position to discharge the responsibilities that it had undertaken under the Convention of 1890.

Notes

1. *Oxford English Reference Dictionary*, Indian Edition, Oxford University Press, 2008, p. 1079.
2. *Oxford Dictionary of Difficult Words*, ed. Archie Hobson, Oxford University Press, 2004, p. 321.
3. *British India and Tibet: 1766–1910*, Alastair Lamb, Routledge and Kegan Paul, London and New York, 1960, p. 130.
4. *Ibid.* p. 127.
5. *Ibid.* p. 133.
6. Anglo-Chinese Convention on Burma of 1886; also known as the Chefoo Convention.
7. *The Buddhism of Tibet or Lamaism*, Laurence Austine Waddell, Cosimo, New York, 2007. First published in 1889.
8. *The Gazetteer of Sikhim*, H.H. Risley, Forgotten Books, London, 2018. First published in 1928.
9. *British India and Tibet: 1766–1910*, Alastair Lamb, Routledge and Kegan Paul, London and New York, 1960, p. 152.
10. Sir Olaf Caroe, foreign secretary of India till 1945, maintained that for decades prior to 1947, Sikkim had been a part of India. He was repeating a statement that he had made as foreign secretary in 1975 in an article that he published in the *Daily Telegraph* on 8 November 1975. This view was also reflected on page 140 of the book *The Future of the Great Game* by Peter John Brobst, University of Argon Press, 2005.
11. Convention between Great Britain and China Relating to Sikkim and Tibet, 1890. *Tibet Past and Present*, Charles Bell, Aes reprint, 1992, pp. 280–281.
12. *Ibid.*

8

HISTORY OF SINO-TIBETAN RELATIONS

There were three aspects that defined relations between Tibet and imperial China. Charles Bell,[1] who had an intimate knowledge of Tibet, its chronicles, its religious and cultural mores and its history, suggests that Tibetans comprised two strains. The first strain came from its north-east, thus making it of Mongolian stock, while the second strain came from Assam and Burma, that are located in Tibet's south-east. He mentions that 'philologically the Tibetans belong to the same linguistic family as the Chinese'.[2] One commonality between the Tibetan Buddhists' and the Indian Hindus' approach to history that cannot be argued against is, as Bell puts it, both 'lack the historical sense, as … is understood by Europeans, Chinese and Mohamedans'.

For the Tibetans, history made sense only if it was related to religion. This was an important factor as it was the underlying element that defined the relations that came to exist between imperial China and Tibet. What lay behind this was a complex relationship that came to exist between the Mongol tribes and Tibetan Buddhism where the Zungar tribe came to play a major role contributing to the Geluk-Pa gaining dominance over all other Tibetan Buddhist sects. The Mongol connection also resulted in the links between the Chinese emperors of Mongol origin, Yuan and the Manchu dynasties, entering into the priest-disciple (Cho Yan) relationship with the Tibetan chief lama. It was this relationship that the British came to incorrectly define as 'suzerainty.' A system totally foreign to the reality of the relations that had come to exist between Tibet and China.

Tibet's Monarchical Period

Tibetan history from the first to seventh century AD encompass a time when the land was divided among a number of clans and it was only after these clans came together and established a unified Tibet that in the seventh century a powerful ruler emerged, intent on expanding his kingdom. This was Emperor Song-tsen Gampo. He was a warrior who extended his kingdom to Upper Burma and Western China, Central Asia and Nepal. H.E. Richardson, another British Indian political officer in Gangtok, had established very close relations with the Tibetan hierarchy which helped him develop immense knowledge of both Tibet's past and its twentieth-century independent existence.

He grants insight[3] into the monarchical history of Tibet where China, under the Tang dynasty, was forced to sue for peace and sign a very revealing treaty with Tibet that remains in force, never having been revoked by either party. Bell's and Richardson's records of this period point to Tibet as a force that the Chinese could take on at their own peril.

The monarchical period of Tibetan history extended from the seventh to ninth century AD. At the time, both China and

Tibet were major powers who could be described as being on an equal footing. In fact, there is little doubt that Tibet was the more aggressive power and it was proving to be a major problem to the stability of the Middle Kingdom. The China forays of Song-tsen Gampo forced the Chinese Emperor to sue for peace and give his daughter as a wife to Song-tsen. She, along with his Nepali wife, ensured state support for a Buddhist Tibet and in this they had the involvement of the Emperor himself. The Emperor arranged for the acquisition of Buddhist scriptures from India. It was also in this period that the Tibetan alphabet was invented based on the Indian alphabet as then used in Kashmir.

The Chinese were under constant threat from frequent aggressions that were being committed against them by Tibet who, by this time, was holding vast Chinese territories. Kansu (later Gansu) was with Tibet and was being administered by Tibetans; a large part of Szechwan and Northern Yunnan was also under Tibetan rule. To 'win respite', the Chinese had to pay a yearly tribute of 50,000 rolls of silk as a peace offering. When this was withheld, the Tibetans occupied the Chinese capital of Chang'an (modern Xian), in AD 763.

When Ral-Pa Chan became the Tibetan Emperor (815–841), a treaty was signed between Tibet and China, ruled by Emperor Mu Tsung or Muzong of the Tang dynasty (reigned from AD 820 to 824). The treaty was to be held in perpetuity. Its violation by Chinese Communists in 1950 is one clear pointer to the manner in which Maoist China used deceit to mould a situation to suit its purpose. The pillar inscriptions present in Lhasa at the time of the Chinese occupation of Tibet in 1950, belonging to the Tang and the Manchu Chang dynasty periods, in clear terms set out the binding content of the Sino-Tibetan Treaty of 821–822.

The provisions of the treaty in translation states that it was signed by 'the Great King of Tibet' and 'the Great King of China,' in 'the relationship of nephew and uncle, have conferred together for the alliance of their kingdoms'.[4] It goes on to make the most earnest commitment by stating that 'they have made and ratified a great agreement. Gods and men all know it and bear witness so that *it may never be changed*; and an account of the agreement *has been engraved on the stone pillar to inform future ages and generations* [emphasis added].'

The portions emphasized by me are what stand out as the commitment made by both sides but was only violated by one side—the Chinese. The Sino-Tibetan Treaty of 821–822 categorically states, 'Tibet and China shall abide by the frontiers of which they are now in occupation. All to the east is the country of China; and all to the west is, without question the country of Great Tibet. Henceforth on neither side shall there be waging of war nor seizing of territory.'

In the chapeau to this treaty, the intent is clearly spelt out that the two rulers 'have made this great treaty in order to fulfil their decision to restore the former ancient friendship and mutual regard and the old relationship of friendly neighbourliness'. It sets out the inviolability of the borders or the territories of the two countries that are further described as an 'old relationship of friendly neighbourliness', obviously underlining that the treaty was between two sovereign states.

In a subsequent substantive paragraph, the treaty states, 'So that it may never be changed, the three precious jewels of Religion, the assembly of Saints, the Sun and Moon, Planets and Stars have been invoked as witnesses. An oath has been taken with solemn words and with the sacrifice of animals; and the agreement has been ratified.'

What it establishes is that this was a treaty signed among equals. The second inscription was also inscribed in Tibetan and Chinese in a pillar that was put in place in 1794 by the Chinese 'representative' in Lhasa, Ho Lin, which makes the statement that during the Tang and the Song dynasties 'there were friendly relations between China and Tibet but Tibet was not then numbered among the vassals of China'.[5]

The three most important Tibetan monarchs, Song-tsen Gampo, Ti-song De-tsen and Ral-pa-chan, were 'outstanding figures, both in war and peace among the kings of Tibet'. They were known as 'The Three Religious Kings, Men of Power'.[6] Of interest to us as Indians is a reference in one of 'the histories of western Tibet', covering the reign of Ti-song De-tsen that states that 'all the countries on the four frontiers were subdued. China in the east, India in the south, Baltistan and Gilgit in the west and Kashgar in the north were brought under this power.'[7]

The *Tibetan Chronicles*[8] describes the extent of the Tibetan empire under Ral-pa-chan: 'During the time of the King Ral-pa-chan, the lord of power, the frontiers held by the Kings of the four borders were as follows: The range of the Sro-long-shen mountains resembling a curtain of white silk, was the frontier with the Chinese King of Astrology; near the Great river, Ganges, there was an iron pillar, which was the frontier with the Indian King of Religion ...' This is translated and quoted by Charles Bell in his outstanding work on Tibet. The reference is to a Tibetan kingdom that not only contained parts of China but of north India as well, as it only goes to show that the assumption that the Himalayas posed an insuperable barrier to foreign invasion in the past is at best a myth and that recorded Indian history appears to have ignored this fact.

Ascendance of Buddhist Hierarchy

The monarchical period gave way to spiritual dominance where increasingly all temporal power came to be reposed in the hands of lamas. The well-armed and aggressive Tibet gradually disappeared. Tibet once again broke up into several states at loggerheads with each other. This decline of the Tibetan kingdom coincided with the decline of the Tang dynasty in China. However, the Tang were able to take advantage of the chaos that descended on Tibet and regain most of the Chinese territory that it had lost to Tibet. The end of the Tang dynasty in AD 905 resulted in a period when both China and Tibet remained physically apart with a no-man's land separating them. For the next three centuries, there was little contact between Tibet and China.

The next phase came about in the twelfth and thirteenth centuries when the Mongols, indulging in forays against both Tibet and China, re-established a connection between the two states. This period saw the 'first recorded invasion of Tibet' in 1239 by Godan, a grandson of Genghis Khan. It was Godan who established the pattern that eventually placed the Buddhist hierarchy at the head of both spiritual and temporal control of Tibet. He sent for the 'most eminent' lama of the time, the Sakya Pandita, 'and made him Vice-regent in Tibet'. This set in motion developments that led to the evolution and embedding of the Lamaist system of Tibetan Buddhism.

Godan and the Sakya Lama passed away in AD 1251. The next phase of interactions between Mongol leaders and Tibetan head lamas followed, with the connection being established by the Mongol leader Kublai Khan. Kublai, the great grandson of Genghis Khan, was the governor of regions of Mongolia located on the border of China and Tibet. To his court came a nephew of the Sakya Lama, Drogon Chogyal Phagpa, a charismatic individual with an imposing personality. Phagpa was also an inspirational religious teacher. He made a lasting impression on Kublai Khan and was appointed the vice-regent of Tibet, being granted the title '*tisri*' (or imperial preceptor) by Kublai Khan.[9]

There were three phases to the relations established between Kublai and Phagpa. First, as we have noted, Kublai appointed Phagpa the vice-regent of Tibet. His position consolidated further when Kublai became the ruler of Mongolia. The third phase occurred when Kublai Khan became the Emperor of China and established the Yuan dynasty. This was the firming up of the patron-priest relationship of 'a pronounced religious character' that had first been established between the Sakya Lamas of Tibet and the Mongols as overlords. This connection came to be a part of the process by which the Yuan court continued its relations with Tibet, with the lamas designated as Tisiris largely from the Sakya sect who spent much of their time at the Imperial court.

As the fortunes of the Yuan dynasty declined, there grew resentment in Tibet over the Sakya Lama receiving special treatment from the Mongol overlord. It was a time when consolidation of power in the hands of Chang-chub Gyaltsen, a prince of the Pagmotru family, was underway in Tibet. The Pagmotru family was closely connected to the Kagyu sect. A nominal link was maintained with the Yuan imperial court, but the entire temporal power in Tibet came once again in the hands of a Tibetan ruler. The relationship between the Yuan court and visiting Tibetan lamas continued but by 1358, the office of the tisri had 'ceased to exist'. The ending of the rule of the Yuan dynasty in China had no impact on Tibet as the relations between the two countries till then had been defined by the religious connection that was personal to the Mongol ruler. When the Mongol connection was ousted from China, the relationship also ended.

Richardson affirmed that at this point, 'a new dynasty in China meant nothing to the Tibetans', suggesting that, 'it may be seen that there is no substance to the claim of some Chinese writers that Tibet was in unbroken subordination to China from the time of the Yuan dynasty'. The fact was that the Mongol overlordship of Tibet was largely nominal in nature, particularly after AD 1350. With the Ming dynasty that replaced the Yuans, the religious connection continued in the form of visits to the Ming court by leading Tibetan lamas of different sects. These visits were undertaken at the invitation of the Ming emperors. This did not in any way impact the independent existence of Tibet as during the Ming dynasty period, temporal power was being exercised initially by the princes of the Pagmotru family, replaced around 1481 by the Rimpung family and from '1565 onwards by the Kings of Tsang'. The Ming court did not exercise any influence over the lay rulers of Tibet, nor did those rulers permit the Ming court to interfere in Tibetan affairs.

Ming Dynasty Records

Dawa Norbu in his seminal work, *China's Tibet Policy*,[10] sums up the conditions prevailing during the Ming period and the dynasty's relations with Tibet in two parts. His description of the period confirms the division of Tibet into 'Inner Tibet' and 'Outer Tibet'. Norbu challenges Tseton W.D. Shakabpa's contention that, 'Tibet gained its independence from the Mongols in the time of Changchub Gyaltsen (1302–64), and China gained hers in 1368 under the leadership of Chu Yuan-chang'.[11] Norbu claims that Shakabpa is only partially correct. Chang-chub Gyaltsen's Tibet included only U-Tsang and Nagari (Outer Tibet) and not Amdo and Kham. These two areas comprising eastern Tibet, and subsequently described as 'Inner Tibet' by the British, continued to have close relations with the Ming court.

The lamas of the Sakya sect continued to be connected with the Ming court and not only in a religious capacity. Their relations appear to have been a continuation of paying the ceremonial tribute to the Ming court, as it granted them permission to carry out profitable commercial relations with China. Whatever may have been the religious content of the relations, the lamas were also concerned with the worldly benefits that commerce granted them.

The nature of the relations between Tibet and the Ming dynasty highlight the duality that defined the relationship. As Norbu puts it, 'No other non-Lamaist regime in Tibet after the fall of the warrior kings had resisted Chinese diplomatic pressure as the Pagmotru, Rinpung and the Tsangpa rulers had done.' This is a period of over three hundred years when contact between Tibet and China was at a minimum and was largely conducted through the return of China to Confucian principles. While factional instability did prevail from time to time in the princely ruled Outer Tibet (Tibet Proper), it did not attract either Mongol or Chinese intervention.

One interesting reflection on this period is that the Ming rulers, who were passionately opposed to the Mongols, did at the same time relate to Buddhism of the kind that prevailed in Tibet and the relations with the Karmapa, the head of the Kagyu sect, replaced the primacy that the Sakya sect had enjoyed during the Yuan dynasty at the Ming court.

Another telling aspect of the relationship between the Ming Emperor and the Tibetan Buddhist lamas at the Ming court was that in the established tributary system that was patently hierarchical in its protocolar setting, where the kings of the tributary state were just placed below the Emperor in a descending order, the 'Grand lamas of Tibet ranked—and were often treated as being higher—than any wang [king] in east Asia'.[12]

During the Ming period, it can be argued that whatever may have been the nature of the political relationship between China and

Tibet, where despite the fact that at least in Outer Tibet the political connection was mainly confined to the diplomatic, and there was little contact between the two courts, the strong spiritual and, to an extent, cultural dimension continued to play a role based on the kinship principle. This has been described as an obvious result of Buddhism and Confucianism playing out at the Ming Court.

The clearest context of Tibet not being considered a part of China occurs where the Ming Emperor Ying Zong, in his preface to the *Great Ming Unification Maps*, specifies that what formed China in the Ming period were the listed thirteen provinces and, like Japan and Java, Tibet was an alien country, and it was shown on the Maps 1 and 2 of the Ming period as independent, while Burma was shown as a part of China.[13]

There is a clear demarcation of the territory of Tibet that also covers the eastern region of Kham as part of independent Tibet.

A detailed examination of the records carried out by eminent Chinese scholar Professor Hon-Shiang Lau at the City University of Hong Kong from where he retired in 2011, in his paper entitled 'Tibet Was Never Part of China before 1950: Examples of Authoritative pre-1949 Chinese Documents that Prove It' refutes the Maoist claim that Tibet was an integral part of China, stating, 'The claim "Tibet has been a part of China since antiquity" is crucial for the PRC to legitimize her annexation of Tibet in 1950. However, the vast amount of China's pre-1949 primary-source records consistently indicate that this claim is false. This paper presents a sample of these records from the Ming and the Qing dynasties to illustrate how they unequivocally contradict PRC's claim.'[14]

Professor Lau only confirms that all claims that were made by Yuan Shi Kai and Mao Tse Tung were based on a false reading of China's historical relations with Tibet. Mao's action to occupy Tibet should have been described as the colonization of Tibet by an expansionist China. Why did Nehru, with his claim to knowledge of China in civilizational terms, fail to see this? This is reflective of either a failure of intellect or indicative of his having ignored it due to his attachment to incorporating China in his 'Asia Vision'. What he did not anticipate was that China and its Middle Kingdom syndrome would never consider India as an equal in any partnership.

The 'Great Fifth'

The historical developments that led to the dominance in Tibet of the Gelug (so-called 'yellow hat' sect) and the battle that took place between them and the Kagyu ('red hat' sect) headed by the Karmapa, brings to centre stage the role that the Mongol tribal structure played in the Tibetan Buddhist system that had come to prevail throughout Tibet and Mongolia.

By the 1530s, there was a major power struggle between the Gelug[15] and the Kagyu sects where the former held sway in western Tibet and the latter in eastern Tibet. This struggle for dominance lasted almost a hundred years. To try and gain an upper hand, both the sects involved a Mongol tribal group to help them secure their cause. The Gelug appealed to a combination of Mongol tribal leaders belonging to the Qirat, Zunghar and the Char tribes, while the Karmapa appealed to the Chogthu Tribe.

Eventually, the strategic moves made by the Mongol leader, Gushri Khan, a strong believer in and follower of the Gelug creed, won the day by defeating anti-Gelug forces in Kham along with an army of the pro-Karmapa ruler of Tsang. It was Gushri Khan who 'conferred' on the then Dalai Lama 'supreme authority over all Tibet', thus inaugurating the era of the Dalai Lamas ruling Lhasa that lasted from 1642 to the escape of the fourteenth Dalai Lama in 1959.

With the Tibetan form of Buddhism being adopted by the Mongolians, religion became a major reason for the aligning of fortunes of Tibetans and Mongolian tribes. This brought about an affinity between 'the two races' that has prevailed to this day. This link was also responsible for the Chinese rulers adopting the priest-patron relationship with Tibetan lamas, including the Dalai Lamas, that came to define the dealings between imperial China and Tibet.

Before the fifth Dalai Lama assumed both temporal and spiritual power, the Mongol tribal head would exercise temporal power in Tibet. The fifth Dalai Lama, Ngawang Lobsang Gyatso, in effect promoted the belief that the Dalai Lama was an incarnation of Avalokitesvara, the 'bodhisattva of compassion'. He appointed his guru as the Grand Lama of Tashilhunpo and declared him the reincarnation of Amitabha, 'the Buddha of Infinite Light'.

The 'Great Fifth' as he came to be known, visited the Qinq capital of Peking and was given an unprecedented reception by the Manchu Emperor. It is recorded that to honour the Dalai Lama, the 'Emperor met him one day's journey from the capital'.[16] Then, in a startling deviation from protocol followed at the imperial court where any visiting monarch, for instance, had to kowtow several times before the Emperor's throne, the Emperor descended from the throne and walked a number of steps—according to some records he 'advanced eighteen yards'—to meet the Dalai Lama as he entered the throne room.

The Dalai Lama did not kowtow before the Emperor but merely bowed his leg. For all practical purposes, the Dalai Lama was treated as an 'independent sovereign'. According to one interpretation, the honour bestowed upon the Great Fifth was an acknowledgement of the importance the Emperor attached to the influence the Dalai Lama had over the Mongols. The intention here was obvious; the Chinese were placing hope in the alliance with the Dalai Lama in the belief that doing so would enable them to extend Manchu rule over Mongolia.

Priests and Patrons

The Manchu Emperor, K'ang-hsi or Kangxi, who reigned from 1661 to 1722, was a person of great diplomatic skill. He took advantage of the uncertainty created by Lhabzang Khan, the nominal Mongol king of Tibet, during the time of the sixth Dalai Lama, who was ousted with the approval of the Kangxi Emperor. This action met a popular demand in Lhasa and was taken at the behest of the Tibetans. What needs to be stressed is that imperial China's interventions were in support of Tibetan spiritual and temporal interests, with an acknowledgement of the supremacy of religion as the guiding force in Tibet's governance. All military interventions by the Manchu emperors, including against the Nepali invasions of Tibet in the latter part of the eighteenth century, were carried out at the invitation or behest of the Tibetan administration.

During the Manchu period, evidence points to the importance attached by both parties to the priest-patron (Cho Yan) relationship. Even the Chinese resident commissioners, the ambans, were seen mainly as the Emperor's representatives who were to keep the Manchu court informed of developments in Tibet. It was to serve this purpose that the ambans were primarily positioned at Tashilhunpo and Lhasa. The fact that Peking had to post a military escort to ensure the safety of the Chinese ambans was in itself an acknowledgement that the Tibetans were averse to any interference by the amban in Tibet's affairs. There had been occasions when the very life of an amban had been in jeopardy; in at least one case, it had ended in the killing of an amban.

Unfortunately, the British hierarchy failed to appreciate that it was the Cho Yan factor that governed China's relations with

Tibet. Instead, they tried to place the relationship within a Western construct, defining it as suzerainty; this ended up muddying the waters that in turn enabled China to exploit the situation to its advantage. Even after the imperial system in China ended, Britain remained unwilling to acknowledge that Tibet was an independent country. Instead, they persisted in their formulaic approach of describing Tibet as an autonomous state where China had a kind of nebulous control over Tibet's external relations.

The reality was that once Buddhism became the dominant factor in Tibet, it moderated the Tibetan penchant for aggression that had caused so much distress to China. Thereafter, the relationship moved into its triangular format where Tibet's religious propensities influenced its relations with the Mongols and the Chinese. With the conquest of China by the Mongol forces of Kublai Khan and his founding of the Yuan dynasty in the thirteenth century, the patron-priest arrangement came to govern the relations.

The main political implication of this relationship was that the Chinese Emperor as the patron held himself responsible for the security of Buddhist Tibet, which now lived within a psychology of limited defence. The Chinese interventions were carried out in response to Lhasa seeking protection and there is ample evidence that Tibetan armed forces took part in what were joint operations headed by their respective commanders. There is also evidence that there were moments when the Chinese presence in Lhasa could be intrusive where the Chinese resident was able to exercise some control over the internal administration of Tibet. To further such control, the Chinese did not hesitate to use the classic employ of setting one power base, represented by the Dalai Lama, against the other power centre, represented by the Tashi Lama, the presiding lama of Tashilhunpo.

Tea trade was the other factor that was used to establish control, where the Tibetan market for Chinese tea was handled by the leading monasteries. This created an important lobby in Tibet that China exploited to retain its influence at Lhasa. Another important feature of the Sino-Tibetan relations was the Mongol factor. Richardson[17] placed the relationship in its proper perspective, describing it as 'a nominal expression of allegiance by the ruler of Tibet to the person of the Mongol Emperor'.

The relevance of this assessment is confirmed by the fact that 'a diplomatic connection with the Mongols was kept up even after the fall of the Yuan dynasty and its eviction from China'. It was this Tibetan-Mongol equation that defined the relations between the Yuan Emperor and the head Tibetan lama.

When the Ming dynasty replaced the Yuan dynasty, they continued with the practice of maintaining a connection with the leading lamas of Tibet, a relationship that was entirely spiritual in nature. During that period, the lay leadership assumed the temporal reins, with the controls remaining in princely hands for the next three hundred years. Clearly, this was in contrast to the Chinese claim, that 'Tibet was in an unbroken subordination to China from the time of the Yuan dynasty'.

An Intelligence Report on Tibet

While the tribulations over the implementation of the Convention of 1890 and the negotiations resulting in the adoption of the Regulations of 1893 were underway, a British military intelligence officer, Captain H. Bower, managed to enter Tibet. His report on 'Tibetan Affairs' was forwarded to the Government of India on 2 February 1893 by the office of the quartermaster general, intelligence branch, of the British Indian Army.

Bower visited central and eastern Tibet, meeting a host of Tibetans from various walks of life. His report provided a realistic assessment of the nature and form of government in Tibet, the makeup of its population and the prevailing market preferences, particularly with regard to the tea trade. He provided a useful insight into the ground realities prevailing in Tibet in the late nineteenth century.

The most important part of Bower's observations concerned the presence of China in Tibet and the error of London's pro-China stance. Bower questioned the assumption that Tibet was under the control of China, including in regard to its external affairs. According to Bower, Tibetan authorities in Lhasa made a public show of 'servility' to the Chinese amban, but 'in reality, he [the amban] has no authority and lives in continual dread of the powerful Priesthood. Even in "Chinese Tibet," a country [is] in no way to be confused with Independent Tibet, the Chinese power is merely nominal.' Within Tibet proper, or as he puts it, 'Independent Tibet', the popularly held view, including by those in authority, placed relations with China firmly within the realm of 'friendship' with the presence of the amban 'testifying to that friendship'. Bower, like White, pointed out that 'any claims the celestials may have over "Tibet Proper" are of *the most shadowy description* [emphasis added]'.[18]

In 1893, a British official tasked by the British Indian authorities to carry out a deep examination of ground realities, ended up making a clear distinction between the two regions that comprised Tibet by using the terms 'Chinese Tibet' for the eastern Tibetan region, which he placed within the 'nominal control' of China and 'Independent Tibet' where the relations with China were confined to that of friendship and where, he observed, China was not in any position to overrule Lhasa's decisions.

Another striking observation by Bower was that the Chinese expatriate community, and this did not exclude official Chinese representatives, were not permitted to bring along their wives. Apparently, Lhasa did not permit Chinese women to visit Tibet. Bower suggested that this very fact was 'enough to show that how shadowy are any claims the Chinese may have to supreme sovereignty'.

Particularizing the difference between 'Chinese Tibet' and 'Tibet Proper', he described the chaos that prevailed in Chinese Tibet. He outlined the laxity of local authorities and the inability of the Chinese to maintain law and order in that part of Tibet. In contrast, he finds that in Tibet Proper, there was responsible governance, an atmosphere of peace with a better government in place that ensured law and order.

Commenting on the commercial and market system, Bower observed that the Tibetan had a natural bent to trading and of making use of any opportunity to 'make money'. As the tea traders of Darjeeling were a pressure group, who, along with other commercial and business interests of Britain and India, were pressing the British government to open the trade doors to Tibet, Bower observed that the Chinese and Tibetan monastic interests held the common position to keep Indian tea out of Tibet. While both quality and logistics would favour Indian tea over Chinese tea, vested interests were set to deny entry to Darjeeling tea in Tibet.

Placing the issue in context, Bower said, 'If we insist on tea being admitted, the Chinese may sign the treaty, and then go in for passive resistance in which they are past masters that annuls all treaties, and will do all in their power to induce the Lhasa people to levy unauthorized duties and discourage or forbid its sale, sheltering themselves all the while behind protestations of friendliness mixed with regrets at their weakness.' Bower's observations, in a sense, justified the conclusions that Curzon was to arrive at as viceroy—that China's hold on Tibet was a 'constitutional myth'.

The final part of his report ended up questioning the British policy of remaining on good terms with China in the hope that it would be an ally. According to Bower, the Chinese 'hate all foreigners and will always hate them'. It is only when they are in fear of their opponent that they take the other party seriously, and that is the only way by which the Sino-British relations can be maintained 'on a satisfactory basis'.

Apparently, a lot of Britain's actions vis-à-vis China were influenced by reports carried in the *Peking Gazette*, an official bulletin. The *Peking Gazette* tended to exaggerate the strengths of China as an ally, as it papered over its weaknesses and projecting it as a military power over the neighbouring states of Mongolia, Chinese Turkestan and Tibet. Bower argued that all of this was based on myth-making. He questioned the reliance that the British had come to attach to its reportage, likening it to Aesop's fables. He was astute enough to point out that the policy being followed by Britain was permitting the Chinese, and to a matching extent, the Tibetans, to pull the wool over British eyes. Common sense dictated that Britain follow a line that stayed within the logic of the circumstance where the Tibetan hierarchy refused to accept any role by China. Bower ended up questioning the decision to give China 'any say in Tibetan affairs'.

Bower's classified report was important not only in its content but in its timely warning that the Chinese were quite happy procrastinating on the talks on trade to delay an agreement, as they were aware that they would not be in a position to deliver on the commitments that they undertook on behalf of Lhasa. He warned the Government of India that any agreement arrived at would ring hollow as the Tibetans would prevent its implementation. Bower's report, because it went against the grain of the policy that Calcutta under pressure from London had been tasked to follow, was ignored. As he had predicted, Chinese commitments on behalf of Tibet were rejected by Lhasa.

Notes

1. *Tibet: Past and Present,* Charles Bell, Motilal Banarsidass, New Delhi, 2000. Bell was the British political officer in Gangtok who had also administered the Chumbi Valley for the three years that Britain held it in terms of the Convention of 1904. He became very close to the XIIIth Dalai Lama and had an intimate knowledge of the Tibetan language and of Tibet.
2. *Ibid.*, page 21.
3. *A Short History of Tibet*, H.E. Richardson, E.P. Duton & Co., 1962.
4. Text taken from the treaty between China and Tibet during the first half of the eighth century as recorded on the western face of the stone pillar near the Temple of Lhasa.
5. *A Short History of Tibet*, H.E. Richardson, E.P. Duton & Co., 1962, p. 30.
6. *Tibet: Past and Present,* Charles Bell, Motilal Banarsidass, New Delhi, 2000.
7. *Ibid.*, p. 28.
8. *Ibid.* p. 21.
9. Drogon Chogyal Phagpa (AD 1235–1280) was the fifth leader of the Sakya School of Tibetan Buddhism. Phagpa was appointed as the first imperial preceptor in Kublai Khan's court and to the Yuan dynasty that Kublai established to rule China. Phagpa was the one who introduced Kublai Khan to Tibetan Buddhism. His position at court lay between the Emperor and the crown prince, making him the second most important person in the Chinese imperial court. This was the commencement of the Cho Yan (priest-disciple) relationship between imperial China and Tibet.
10. *China's Tibet Policy,* Dawa Norbu, Routledge, New Delhi, 2001.
11. *Ibid.*

12. *Ibid.*, p. 61
13. 'Tibet Was Never Part of China before 1950: Examples of Authoritative pre-1959 Chinese Documents that Prove It', Hon-Shiang Lau, *National Security*, Vol. II, Issue I.
14. *Ibid.*
15. The founder of the Gelug Pa sect was Tsong Kapa, who was a noted reformer of Lamaist Buddhism, instituting a very strict code of morals. Born in Amdo in 1358, he established the three leading monasteries of Ganden, Sera and Drepung that became the three most powerful religious bodies in Tibet. His successor, Ganden Truppa, established the monastery of Tashi-lhunpo that came to house the Tashi Lama, the second most powerful religious leader after the Dalai Lama. It was Truppa who fashioned the system of reincarnation that spread throughout Tibet.
16. *Tibet: Past and Present,* Charles Bell, Motilal Banarsidass, New Delhi, 2000, p. 36.
17. *A Short History of Tibet*, H.E. Richardson, E.P. Duton & Co., 1962.
18. Some notes on Tibetan affairs by Captain H. Bower from the Intelligence Branch dairy No. 10 of 1893/Tibet.

9

CURZON'S FRONTIER POLICY

With British insistence that China remain the interlocutor through which they would deal with Lhasa, the mistakes continued to multiply. The Convention of 1890 and the Regulations of 1893 appended to it were soon to be breached by the Chinese who were unable to enforce Tibetan compliance to the provisions. The person who was confronted by the Chinese failures was John Claude White who, as political officer in Sikkim, was the British point person placed in charge of both the Yatung trade mart and the management of the border between Tibet and Sikkim.

White was soon faced with the Chinese amban's failure to implement the agreement he had arrived at with White on the demarcation of the borders between Sikkim and Tibet. The amban had readily agreed to the establishment of a tripartite arrangement to carry out the survey of the border and its demarcation by stone markers. It was soon evident that the amban's orders were treated with contempt by the Tibetans. Eventually, White was authorized to carry out the exercise on a unilateral basis and he demarcated the eastern border between Sikkim and the Chumbi Valley up to the Himalayan watershed. He put in place stone markers that were pulled down and destroyed by the Tibetans.

A further problem was the presence of Tibetans south of the northern borders of Sikkim, around the area of Giagong. Here, two issues arose. One was to get the intruding Tibetan herdsmen to leave Giagong, the other was the demarcation of the North Sikkim border with Tibet. The amban once again promised that a joint Chinese-Tibetan official group would participate with White to deal with both these issues. Here, too, the amban failed. Lhasa did not send out an official mandate to settle matters and the meetings ended in total failure.

'The True Fulcrum of Asiatic Dominion'

It was in this scenario that in 1899, the new British viceroy to India, George Nathaniel Curzon, stepped in. He replaced Lord Elgin, who had been particularly reluctant to push the Chinese or to unilaterally enforce the provisions of the Convention of 1890.

Curzon was young (forty years old when he arrived as viceroy) and had travelled widely over almost all of Asia, including Central Asia, China, Japan and Persia. He had a deep knowledge of India that he had not only acquired through earlier visits to the subcontinent but also as the under-secretary of state for India in 1891. According to his own reckoning, based on the insights that he had gained by observing Asia first hand, 'the true fulcrum of Asiatic dominion' lay increasingly in the empire of Hindustan.[1]

Curzon brought a refreshing strategic outlook to India and its environs and granted primacy to India's frontier policy, particularly to preserving the security of the Indian empire by establishing buffer states that would help curb and contain Russia's Asian ambitions in Central Asia. As Lovat Fraser puts it in his admirable study of Curzon, India was emerging from a period of 'partial isolation' as 'the encircling sea, and the mighty Himalayas, no longer served to shield her from the world without'. This was a factor that Curzon, with his knowledge of India's political geography, was particularly equipped to take into account. He told his fellow Old Etonians at a dinner hosted by them to honour him on his appointment as viceroy that he had gladly accepted the office because he loved India, 'its people, its history, its government, the absorbing mysteries of its civilisation and its life'.

Curzon had prepared himself by visiting the subcontinent four times before he took up his charge as viceroy. He was convinced that Russia posed a major threat to Britain's Indian empire and hence favoured a frontier policy to contain Russia's Asian ambitions. He further reinforced his approach by insisting on the importance to India's security, that both Afghanistan and Tibet serve as buffer states to safeguard India's frontiers.

To buttress his frontier policy, he drew attention to the fact that India was the 'fulcrum' around which the expansion of the British empire had taken place, covering East Africa and the western and eastern reaches of Asia. It remained in Britain's interest to adopt policies that safeguarded India's maritime and land frontiers. In putting this across, Curzon was reminding London that the expansion of Britain's empire had behind it the primacy of the security of the Indian empire. It was within the logic of this argument that Curzon insisted that Britain look on Tibet as being of great strategic interest to India. He was questioning the priority that Whitehall continued to attach to China's relations with Tibet, mentioning that it was a policy that was not serving India's interests.

Attitude towards Tibet

Curzon addressed a note dated 8 January 1903 to the India Office, detailing the objectives of his Tibet policy and the process by which he hoped to achieve them. The main thrust of the note was an analysis of China's inability to persuade the Tibetans to carry out the commitments that the Chinese Emperor had made on their behalf. Curzon used all the tools at his command to force London's hand to permit him to carry out his forward policy on Tibet, motivated by his desire to establish it as a buffer state. He detailed in the note the developments in Lhasa, drawing attention to the effort that the thirteenth Dalai Lama was making to cosy up to the Russians and the steps he had taken to establish contact with Russia. Curzon warned that as the Manchu hold on China was weakening, there was a danger that Tibet would come under the protection of tsarist Russia and argued that Russia acquiring any exclusive influence on Tibet would be detrimental to British interests.

Before looking at Curzon's despatch, the events on the ground that formed the basis of the despatch need to be set out. All the efforts that White had made, both on the trade-mart front and the demarcation of the Sikkim border with Tibet, had created an impasse that Curzon as viceroy decided to confront head on. This was a policy decision that in a very clear and direct manner set aside the earlier reluctance to adopt the radical approach that White had proposed to deal with the ground realities that confronted the British.

White observed that while the lay Tibetan was friendly and keen to trade with India, the opposition to Anglo-Tibetan relations was being raised by the lamas of the three leading monasteries of Sera, Drepung and Ganden. Given that these three monasteries dominated politics in Tibet, any lack of determination shown by Britain in forcing its way would only strengthen them in their resolve to keep the British away and, more importantly, to continue to interfere in the affairs of Sikkim and Bhutan.

Among White's proposed actions to send a forceful message was the occupation of the Chumbi Valley. Both the commissioner of the Rajshahi division to whom White reported and the lieutenant governor of Bengal, Sir Charles Elliot, supported White's approach. Elliot in his demarche to Lord Elgin made the point that if it were not 'to pay some regard to China he would have no hesitation in advising Lord Elgin to make it plain to the amban *that unless demarcation was speedily carried out the Chumbi valley would be occupied by British troops'*. Elliot, keeping in mind that London preferred to keep India out of its relations with China, offered the palliative that the occupation of the Chumbi Valley would help China reassert its authority over Lhasa. Elliot's suggestion was that Peking be 'pressed to permit the temporary occupation of Chumbi'. It was a typical play at placating all parties while furthering what he determined was in British India's interest.

Lord Elgin did not endorse the suggestion. Throughout the period that Elgin was viceroy, his policy remained within the bounds of 'conciliation' and to keep the trade mart at Yatung in play as the trade that was taking place, although not satisfactory, was enough to keep the British commercial bodies happy. In fact, he made the trade issue his priority and went to the extent of proposing to the amban that in exchange for a British concession on the Tibetan claims to Giagong, a greater opening be granted to British trade interests at Yatung.

This policy of conciliation was one that Curzon almost immediately put to rest, granting a fresh look at the suggestions White had made in 1889:

1. If Lord Elgin's proposal on Giagong were to be implemented and it were to be handed over to Tibet in exchange for greater facilitation of trade, then the British should insist that the trade mart be shifted to Phari from Yatung.

2. The Tibetans should agree to sign an extradition treaty to cover the return of criminals who had escaped from British territory to Tibet.
3. The British should negotiate directly with the Tibetan authorities in Lhasa as it was clear that neither the amban nor Peking was in a position to assert any authority on Lhasa.

White's informing Calcutta of the progress that the Russians were making in establishing their influence in Tibet was what possibly clinched the approval. Curzon endorsed the main suggestions made by White and decided to adopt two of them: shifting the trade mart to Phari and dispensing with the mediation of the Chinese while dealing with Lhasa.

Curzon was making it clear that the previous policy of dealing with Tibet only through China had failed as Lhasa had categorically refused to accept the principle that China could act on behalf of Lhasa. In any arrangement, Curzon now insisted that the Tibetans had to be fully involved. The new policy went into operation in the form of two interlocked approaches.

The first was the settlement of the Giagong issue. It was clear that as the watershed principle was to be the guiding element in deciding the border. Despite the claims and counter-claims that Alistair Lamb set out so assiduously in his book, *British India and Tibet*,[2] in which he questioned White's handling of the issue, Lamb agreed that Giagong actually lay within the Teesta basin as it was located south of the Himalayan watershed. The second was related to the review of the Regulations of 1893. The British position had come to focus on Yatung as having ill-served the trade relations, and it was to be replaced with Phari as the location of the trade mart.

The Tibetans refused to attach any sanctity to the convention or the regulations resulting in infructuous talks on both the issues of trade and the demarcation of the border. The Chinese amban, You Tai, brother of the earlier amban with whom the Convention had been negotiated, showed himself willing to assist the British but it was clear that his word carried no weight with the thirteenth Dalai Lama.

Curzon had authorized White, accompanied by Sir Francis Younghusband, to once again try and arrive at a settlement on the North Sikkim border issue with Tibet. These talks failed once more, with the Tibetans refuting the argument that the Chinese had any right to represent them or sign any treaty that they had no involvement with.

Thwarted Attempts

As a result of the developments outlined above, Lord Curzon decided to establish a direct system of communication with Lhasa. A contributing factor to the decision was the coming of age of the thirteenth Dalai Lama. He, unlike his predecessors, had managed to survive all attempts made on his life and emerged as a powerful figure who could and did make decisions on his own behalf.

As Lamb puts it, 'In 1895 the Tibetans acquired a focal point for their aspirations of independence in the person of an adult Dalai Lama.'[3] The policy now adopted by the British was tactical in nature. While the myth of Chinese control would be adhered to nominally, recognizing that the Chinese were not in a position to influence the Tibetans, the British would open communications with the Dalai Lama and deal with him directly.

Curzon first attempted to reach the Dalai Lama through Ugyen Kazi, the Bhutan vakil in Darjeeling who had established links with

Lhasa on behalf of the Tongsa Penlop. He agreed to act on behalf of the British Bengal administration during a business visit to Phari. He was told to address a letter to the Dalai Lama conveying that the British were willing to discuss matters directly with a senior Tibetan official on matters of mutual interest. This attempt failed, although Ugyen Kazi mentioned that the Dalai Lama was not uninterested but was being cautious as his interest lay in keeping the Chinese at bay and he possibly did not want to complicate that relationship with a British connection.

The Bengal administration decided that another attempt would be made by Ugyen Kazi. This time, they conveyed a more direct proposal referring to the setting up of the trade mart at Phari and holding out the threat that it was not in the Dalai Lama's interests to ignore the British Indian request for dealing with Lhasa on matters of mutual interest. The letter also mentioned that a positive approach would ensure that Tibet's interests were protected and attempts by Russia or China to exert their influence on Tibet would be neutralized by the British connection.

Ugyen Kazi's letter of December 1899 received a response in March 1900 from the Dalai Lama. It did not convey any agreement to deal with the British directly. It did, however, address the Russia issue, mentioning that 'on no account will we let them in ... They have repeatedly, with the orders of China, wished to come within our boundary ... We will not allow them on any occasion to come, and on this we are united, both lamas and laymen.'[4]

In the meanwhile, a search for another agent who would be in a position to carry conviction with Lhasa continued. Attempts to find someone in Nepal were ruled out on the advice of the British resident in Kathmandu. The Burmese advisor on Chinese affairs to the Government of Burma, Taw Sein Ko, was rejected as 'unsuitable' on the advice of Rangoon. Finally, a Ladakh connection was identified—Captain R.L. Kennion, assistant to the British resident to Kashmir and Leh. Kennion crossed over the border between Ladakh and Tibet with the intention to deliver Viceroy Curzon's letter to the Garpons of Gartok for onwards transmission to the Dalai Lama.

The letter was a politely worded offer for establishing a friendly discourse between the two countries and trade for mutual benefit. The letter made it clear that the British had no territorial designs on Tibet. Kennion, a young officer imbued with a spirit of adventure and ruled by the emotion of the greatness of Britain, pushed his way into Tibet despite attempts by the Tibetan border guards to prevent him. Eventually, well short of Gartok, he was stopped and was visited by representatives of the Garpons 'who were very friendly' and took charge of the viceroy's letter. In March 1901, the Garpons of Gartok returned the viceroy's letter unopened with the comment that the 'Tibetan Government saw no need for any communication with the British'.[5]

Ugyen Kazi was now called upon to make a third attempt, being tasked to present a letter from Lord Curzon directly into the hands of the Dalai Lama. This letter, unlike the one that Kennion had carried, was strongly worded and carried the threat that if the Tibetans did not commence negotiations with the British in the 'near future' then 'my Government must reserve the right to take such steps as may seem to them necessary and proper to enforce the terms of the Treaty, and to ensure that the Trade Regulations are observed'.[6] This, for all intents, was an ultimatum that not only put the Tibetans in a bind but also the British home government. The latter had not been consulted on the content of this letter and it was clear that some action would have to be taken if the Tibetans refused to act or react to the viceregal letter. London's hands were being forced.

In keeping with the attitude that the Dalai Lama had consistently maintained, he refused to accept the letter that was returned unopened with its seal intact by Ugyen Kazi in October 1901. The Dalai Lama had told him that he could not accept any letter that came in the way of the understanding that 'forbade him from having any dealing with a foreigner except in consultation with the Amban'. Making a further point that there was nothing to negotiate about with the British as 'there was nothing at fault with [the] present state of Anglo-Tibetan relations'.[7] It later appeared that Ugyen Kazi may have never met the Dalai Lama but was persuaded by the Khalons, whom he had consulted, that he would only refer to the letter when and if he met the Dalai Lama.

While all efforts made by Curzon to enter into a dialogue with the Dalai Lama had failed, there was increasing evidence that the Dalai Lama was extending a hand of friendship towards the Russian Tsar. This was being done at the prompting of a Russian subject, the Buryat Buddhist lama, Agvan Lobsan Dorzhiev. This duality of purpose being shown by the Dalai Lama could hardly have been ignored by the British and soon enough, matters came to a head, leading to the next set of actions that would have a major bearing on the direction of Indo-Tibetan relations.

Notes

1. *India under Curzon and After,* Lovat Fraser, Forgotten Books, London, 2016, p. 12. Originally published by William Heinemann, 1911.
2. *British India and Tibet: 1766–1910*, Alastair Lamb, Routledge and Kegan Paul, London and New York, 1960.
3. *Ibid*. p. 183.
4. *Ibid*. p. 197.
5. *Ibid*. p. 201.
6. *Ibid*. p. 202.
7. *Ibid*. pp. 202–203.

10

EMPIRE VERSUS EMPIRE

The events in the first few years of the twentieth century saw major changes that had a lasting impact on Tibet and its relations with India. Deliberations on all the issues that were central to the relations with Tibet, as per British India's perspective, had reached a dead end. The Tibetan position on the Convention of 1890 and the Regulations of 1893 remained that they had no obligation to enable the implementation of agreements that Britain had entered into with the Chinese. Lhasa refused to grant any credence to the demands made by Calcutta.

The proposed solution to the Giagong standoff carried no conviction with Lhasa. The contradictory position adopted by the Dalai Lama on refusing Curzon's letters on the grounds that he was duty bound to deal with such external messages only with the approval of the amban, while at the same time permitting exchanges with the Russian Tsar, projected a position of confrontation that the British could not afford to ignore.

By the time Curzon forwarded his comprehensive note on the policy towards Tibet on 8 January 1903, there was growing unease in British India over Tibet's closeness to Russia, which was strengthened by a perception that there was a Chinese arrangement also with Russia on Tibet. A power vacuum had emerged in Tibet that needed to be urgently filled, otherwise the Russians would gain long-term advantage in an area that was of strategic importance to India. Curzon's note, in a sense, also served notice to Whitehall, hinting that 'he would defy the Home authorities, if the interests of the Government of India were imperilled seriously'.[1]

The issues raised in the despatch covered:

- Following through the gains made by John Claude White on issues of border demarcation and trade.
- Confronting a possible Russian-Chinese deal on Tibet that would pose a serious security problem to India.
- Agreeing to a conference with the Chinese but on a triangular basis, involving representatives of Britain, China and Tibet. The venue for this conference would have to be Lhasa.[2]

Curzon insisted that the exchanges between the three representatives would have to cover not only the implementation of the provisions of the 1890 Convention and the Regulations of 1893, 'but the entire gambit, of "our future political relations" with Tibet (and China) and the degree to which influence of another great Power (Czarist Russia) could be allowed, "for the first time," in the affairs of Imperial India's weak, insignificant and lama-ridden neighbour'.[3]

Curzon had a perceptive understanding of Russia's imperial designs on the Eurasian landmass. He was convinced that its ultimate ambition was the domination of Asia, which would make it come up against British interests in Asia. The 'Great Game', as it came to be called, was afoot and it was played out by British India in its quest to contain Russia's ambition in Eurasia.

Tibet in 'Russian Sphere of Influence'

London at first was sceptical of Curzon's claim that Russia's presence had reached a position that created a necessity for British intervention. It took time for the home office in England to accept that the Russian presence was likely to reach a level that would bring it literally to the doorsteps of the British Indian empire. There was a view at that time that Curzon was basing himself on rumour rather than the specifics of evidence. Material that has since become available from released Russian archives confirms that there was both political and military content to a relationship that Russia appeared ready to establish with Lhasa.[4]

Lama Agvan Lobsan Dorzhiev, designated as the 'thirteenth Dalai Lama's emissary', had succeeded in establishing 'political relations' between Moscow and Lhasa. Alexandre Andreyev, in his contribution to the Alex McKay edited *Tibet and Her Neighbours*[5] details Dorzhiev's efforts to 'draw Tibet into the Russian sphere of influence', an effort that was 'viewed positively by the Tibetan leader'.

Alexandre Andreyev's essay is based on access to the Russian foreign office and other classified papers and correspondence. He explains how Dorzhiev was able to influence the Dalai Lama to look upon the Russian Tsar as a saviour who could protect Tibet's interests, threatened by an aggressive and expansionist Britain, that an enfeebled China under the declining Qing dynasty was unable to secure.

Dorzhiev made three visits to St Petersburg—in 1898, 1900 and 1901. He was received at court as the Dalai Lama's special envoy, but his attempt to secure a treaty or a formal agreement that would in effect place Tibet under the protection of Russia failed. The Russian Tsar did not want to add to the already 'antagonistic relations' with Britain. Russia was also unwilling to create a situation that could lead to the partitioning of China among European powers.

Another factor was the threat that Russia was facing from Japan in its Far Eastern region. The Russian foreign office did, however, agree to establish a consulate at Tajchienlu that remained in place for a year before it was dismantled and closed. While there was no formal Russian-Tibetan military agreement, Russian records show that there was an active dialogue with Dorzhiev on military aid and a certain amount of military equipment along with a training detachment were provided to Lhasa.

Dorzhiev had several meetings with the Russian war minister A.N. Kuropatkin where these arrangements were discussed. An interesting insight is provided by a somewhat cryptic message that the Dalai Lama sent to the war minister:

> To the Tibetan state, remaining in the lap of Buddhist teachings, the English foreigners are enemies and oppressors. For this reason we, trying to eradicate the bane of our people, dispatched these two emissaries, having given them precise and secret instructions. Please report kindly of these circumstances to His Majesty so as to promote our mutual well-being.[6]

This is a message that grants a clear insight into how the thirteenth Dalai Lama at that stage had come to view Britain as a threat to Tibet.

Evidence now available shows that at least the Russian military leadership, at the level of the war minister, was at one stage seriously considering some kind of intervention to contain the British Indian presence in Tibet, but the Russo-Japanese war that broke out in 1904 put an end to this Russian venture.

What also added to the unease in both Calcutta and London were media reports of a Russian-Chinese agreement on Tibet becoming a Russian protectorate where China's interests and Tibetan Buddhism would be preserved.

To complicate matters further, the Government of Nepal conveyed its apprehension that if Tibet was on the road to becoming a Russian protectorate this could result in an increase in the military threat to Nepal, projecting a possible Tibetan vengeance mission, as Tibet acquired military equipment and material support from Russia. Nepal's view that a Russian effort was on in Tibet helped add further content to Curzon's projections to Whitehall of the growing threat that Russia had come to pose.

In what was an absurd development in mid 1902, Whitehall suggested that the Nepalese be encouraged to send a force into Tibet and demand 'from Tibet an assurance' that it would not permit any Russian troops to enter 'its country'.[7] This suggestion did not carry weight with the British defence administration and was dropped. The British war office expressed the need to oppose any Russian military presence in Tibet as it would threaten both India and Nepal.

That the Dorzhiev missions and meetings with the Tsar had no political implications did not satisfy either the British government or the Government of India. Added to this was the fact that a feeling was now gathering momentum that Chinese suzerainty over Tibet was 'constitutional fiction'. It was a convenience whose time had expired and the resulting power vacuum in Tibet needed to be swiftly filled and Russia kept out. Diplomacy had failed; it was time to move into the next phase, of direct action.

Younghusband's Expedition

Following the impasse that the Anglo-Tibetan relations had reached, including the insult to the viceroy in the Dalai Lama's refusal to accept any communication from him, Whitehall gave permission for an expedition led by Sir Francis Younghusband to cross over into Tibet via the Chumbi Valley to force the Tibetans to talk to the British. With the expedition continuing to face opposition, including having to fight its way to Gyantse after subduing Phari, it was finally decided that it must push on to Lhasa. This caused considerable loss of life among Tibetans, who were ill-prepared to confront Younghusband's well-equipped force.

Younghusband spelt out the purpose of his expedition, given that Tibet sat on the 'frontiers of India', it was 'indispensable that British influence should be recognised at Lhasa in such a manner as to render impossible for any other Power to exercise a pressure on the Tibetan Government inconsistent with the interests of British India.'[8] To Curzon, nothing short of an Anglo-Tibetan treaty, negotiated and signed in Lhasa, was the answer. The treaty was also expected to put an end to Russian intrigues in Lhasa.

A Russian presence in Tibet was not welcome and Russia's denials about such sights did not carry conviction. Within the logic of these circumstances, the British Expeditionary Mission commenced its operations, set on its purpose to achieve a settlement that would keep all foreign powers out of Tibet, except the Chinese, with a clear commitment that Tibet would become a buffer state between the British and Russian empires.

As Younghusband's march towards Lhasa commenced, the Dalai Lama accompanied by Dorzhiev went into exile, leaving the Tri Rinpoche of Ganden monastery as the regent. When Younghusband entered Lhasa, he was welcomed by the Chinese amban You Tai. It soon became apparent that the amban held little influence with the Tibetan authorities. It was the regent, having obtained the endorsement of the Tsongdu, who entered into negotiations with Younghusband that resulted in the signing of the Anglo-Tibetan Convention of 1904.

The 1904 convention, in its nine articles, was comprehensive in its coverage to satisfy what Curzon had set out to achieve. It addressed the issues of the Sikkim–Tibet border, including its demarcation with border pillars.[9] It took action on trade issues, including the addition of trade marts to the already existing one at Yatung. It was decided that new trade marts would be established at Gartok and Gyantse with British agents stationed at both the new marts, in addition to Yatung. There was a provision for the opening of other trade marts, if and when found necessary. Trade regulations that would encourage exchanges between the two countries, including the need to maintain and ensure logistical support, were to be put in place. The sensitive issue of tea and tariff was left to subsequent deliberations.

Article IX of the convention specified the exclusion of all other foreign powers from exercising influence in Tibet, where in its chapeau and the first provisions to the article stated that:

The Government of Thibet engages that, without the previous consent of the British Government:

1. No portion of Thibetan territory shall be ceded, sold, leased, mortgaged or otherwise given occupation, to any Foreign Power;
2. No such Power shall be permitted to intervene in Thibetan Affairs.

This Article also ensured that Lhasa could not permit the entry of any agent or representative of a foreign power without permission from the British government. There was, however, no reference to any restriction on this account being extended to the existing agents of China and Nepal, nor for that matter was there any reference to China and its so-called suzerainty over Tibet.

The convention, in keeping with what Curzon had in mind, was implicit in assuring the continuance of Britain's influence in Tibet. To achieve this, in the face of London's objection to any permanent British presence in Lhasa, a separate agreement was reached that mentioned that the British agent at Gyantse could visit Lhasa in order to discuss matters relating to the provisions of the convention, as and when he deemed it fit to do so.

The other, and from the Indian point of view important, provision in the convention related to the holding of the Chumbi Valley as security for the payment of the indemnity of Rs 75 lakhs in annual instalments of Rs 1 lakh a year. This would have kept the Chumbi Valley under the control of the Government of India for a period of seventy-five years and in 1950, when the Chinese intention to occupy Tibet had commenced, India could have used it to hold on to the valley.

London's intervention, again in direct opposition to India's interest, forced changes on both the issues of indemnity and the visit to Lhasa by the British agent in Gyantse. The British home office, in particular the secretary of state for India, accused Younghusband of having exceeded his brief. The main concern in London was that the convention would ruffle feathers in Moscow, particularly, as the retention of Tibetan territory for a period of seventy-five years could be considered as the annexation of it. This would be counter to any British assurances that they had no desire or intention to annex any part of Tibet.

One of the main factors behind these differences were the political divergences that had[10] come to infect the relationship between William St John Brodrick, head of the India Office, and Curzon. Brodrick and Lord Oliver Ampthill, acting viceroy from 30 April to 13 December 1904 while Curzon was away in England, considered Articles VI (the indemnity/Chumbi Valley clause) and IX as well as the note dealing with the visit by the Gyantse agent to Lhasa, as problematic.

Alastair Lamb concluded that there were 'at least three Tibetan policies' that were in play simultaneously. Brodrick was looking at the Younghusband march into Lhasa as a 'demonstration of British might'. In his letter of 4 July 1904 to Ampthill, he makes his thinking quite clear, mentioning that 'our main point is to re-establish our prestige, and to make it clear to Russia that we will not surrender predominance in Tibet to her'[11]. According to him, a show of force was all that was needed and he attached little importance to any treaty being signed at Lhasa.

To Curzon, and this was what Younghusband was obviously trying to achieve, it was essential to have representation in place in Lhasa, as a means of asserting British influence and to keep Russia out. The British government, particularly the foreign secretary, was more interested in playing the Younghusband presence within Tibet as a bargaining chip with Russia to get an acceptance by it 'of the principles of the recent Anglo-French agreement over Egypt'.[12]

Changes to 1904 Treaty

The outcome of the compact between Brodrick and Ampthill was the change to the indemnity clause in Article VI and the adoption of a declaration dated 11 November 1904, endorsed by both, that Britain 'is pleased to direct as an act of peace that the sum of money which the Tibetan Government have bound themselves to … pay to His Majesty's Government as an indemnity … be reduced from Rs 75,00,000 to Rs 25,00,000'. The period was drastically reduced from seventy-five years to three years 'after the due payment of three annual instalments of the said indemnity … provided, … that the trade marts … shall have been effectively opened for three years …; and … the Tibetans shall have faithfully complied with the terms of the said Convention in all other aspects.'

With this amendment to Article VI, London effectively moved the Chumbi Valley back into the possession of Tibet. The Lhasa Convention, in its unamended entirety, would have served India's long-term strategic and security concerns. The retention of the Chumbi Valley would prevent the ease of passage it provided to any power inimical to India's interests coming to occupy Tibet. Curzon was clearly committed to securing India's security and strategic interests. This aspect, unfortunately, carried little weight with the British government, as it attached greater primacy to its relations with Russia within the European context. This act on the part of Brodrick certainly did not serve India's interests but worked against the logic of British moves in Tibet having an Indian security element behind it.

The British could have got around any Russian opposition to the retention of the Chumbi Valley by advancing the argument that the valley was actually a part of the kingdom of Sikkim. It had wrongly been excised from the kingdom by employing an incompletely thought out application of the watershed principle to determine the borders between Sikkim and Tibet. This argument was not advanced by either the British Indian administration or by the secretary of state for India who was responsible for serving India's interests in the British Cabinet.

Another feature of the Convention of 1904 was that while Amban You Tai had been consulted by Younghusband with all aspects of the negotiations and was present at its signing, he was not asked to append his signature to the convention. Younghusband's account of the signature ceremony which was carried out in the presence of the amban, and was signed in all three languages—Tibetan, English and Chinese—does not make any reference to the amban having been asked to append his signature to the convention. However, in his address on that occasion, Younghusband stated that 'we were not interfering in the smallest degree with their religion, we were annexing no part of their territory, we were not interfering in their internal affairs and we were fully recognizing the continued suzerainty of the Chinese Government'.[13]

The fact that the convention was signed between the British and the Tibetans with no reference within it to the Chinese or to China as the suzerain power, made it clear that there was a recognition that Tibet possessed the power to negotiate and enter into treaties with a foreign power directly. In fact, Article IX of the convention could be interpreted as having granted Britain, 'a special position as a kind of Protector of Tibet'.[14]

For London, what was missing was Younghusband's failure to get the amban to sign off on the convention, or to get his 'signature to a separate treaty of adhesion'. He was supposed to undertake the latter as part of the directions he had received from London.

Convention of 1906

Two years later, the Anglo-Chinese Convention of 1906 was signed. The British were unable to get the Chinese to simply acknowledge the Convention of 1904 with its amendment of the indemnity clause, as the Chinese insisted on a clear recognition of China's sovereignty over Tibet. The British had to make certain concessions that, in effect, recognized the status of China in Tibet as the suzerain without mentioning that term in the text of the convention.

Fundamentally, the Convention of 1906 was an instrument to meet London's objectives of diluting the Convention of 1904, particularly its Article IX, by bringing in China within its ambit and thus removing the imperative from the term 'to any Foreign Power'. It also specified that the prohibitions of Article IX (d) did not apply to China and in return for this concession it was agreed that Britain could lay telegraph lines between India and the trade marts located within Tibet. The fixation for London being Russia, apart from the concessions Whitehall was making to accommodate the Chinese, Article II of the convention states in categorical terms, 'The Government of Great Britain engages not to annex Tibetan territory or interfere in the administration of Tibet.'

Not satisfied with merely stating this position, Article II further goes on to grant China a right to prevent any other foreign power by the undertaking that it would not 'permit any other foreign state to interfere with the territory or internal administration of Tibet'.

It was obvious that Britain was not interested in maintaining the provisions of the Convention of 1904 that granted it an effective say in how Lhasa dealt with external powers and also, to an extent, the authority to act as a suzerain. Instead, Britain exhibited an interest to restore the hollowed-out authority of Manchu China over Lhasa. The only area of emphasis was the retention of all provisions pertaining to trade.

A noticeable element was that there was no direct reference to China being the suzerain in Tibet. This appeared to be an area that was kept up their sleeve by British negotiators as in the Anglo-Russian Convention of 1907[15] that was the next development on Tibet, with both sides stating in the chapeau to the 'Arrangement concerning Thibet' that the two governments 'recognizing suzerain rights of China in Thibet, and considering the fact that Great Britain, by reason of her geographical position, has a special interest in the maintenance of the *status quo* in the external relations of Thibet ...'

In its Article I, it was agreed that both would respect 'the territorial integrity of Thibet' and to not interfere in its internal administration. In its Article II, both parties agreed that 'in conformity with the admitted principle of suzerainty of China over Thibet, Britain and Russia engage not to enter into negotiations with Thibet except through the intermediary of the Chinese Government'.

While retaining the British emphasis on trade, the article grants British commercial agents the right to deal with Tibetan authorities in keeping with the agreement reflected in Article V of the Convention of 1904. There is also a detailed reference to the indemnity clause and the amended figure of reparations to be paid by Tibet to Britain and the reduced period of occupation of the Chumbi Valley from seventy-five years to three years as referred to in the declaration made by the viceroy of India at the time of ratifying the Convention of 1904 that was appended to it.

What is apparent from the content of the Conventions of 1904, 1906 and 1907 (arrangement relating to Tibet) is that the British home authorities were concerned about the relations with Russia where Tibet was being looked upon as a buffer between the Russian and British empires. There was a power vacuum in Tibet caused by a weak China, where incidentally both Russia and Britain held a position of strength, and could serve a similar purpose in Tibet as well.

Perfidious Britain was taking care of its own interests, irrespective of the immorality of its actions. It effectively forced a Tibet that had shrugged off Chinese control to remain under the thumb of a weak and irresolute power that was soon to be blown away by the republican revolution. Britain was also ever ready to look upon India's strategic and security interests as secondary to its own interests. In the case of the Curzon proposals, the politics of the moment that reflected the differences between him and the secretary of state for India got precedence over the merit of Curzon's suggestions that were based on his understanding of not only the needs of India but, more importantly, those of Britain and its empire.

Contentious Chumbi Valley

Perhaps nothing puts this into focus than the reaction of the British representative in Moscow, Charles Hardinge, who even objected to the diluted indemnity clause and the limited period for which the British proposed to hold the Chumbi Valley. In Hardinge's reckoning, 'It seems to me that the occupation of the Chumbi Valley, though for three years, is a dangerous measure ... to finally resolve itself into annexation ... I do not see that the occupation presents any material advantage to us.' His main contention was that by this measure Britain was providing an opportunity to the Russians to renege on 'their engagements to us in Persia and Afghanistan'.

Here was a person sitting in Moscow with limited, if any, knowledge of the geographical and historical meaning of the Chumbi Valley to India. He was evaluating the Anglo-Tibetan developments almost entirely from the perspective of Russia's understanding with Britain elsewhere in Central Asia. As the British representative, he was of course within his rights to analyse a possible fallout on Anglo-Russian ties and convey his analysis to the home government. The crux of the problem was that the political views in London over Tibet's significance to India were being shaped by officials who looked on Curzon's views with a jaundiced eye. They were intent on opposing his suggestions as his advice contradicted the widely held view that Tibet was of little significance to Britain's interests.

Foreign Secretary Lansdowne, a former viceroy to India, was an equal partner in this political game and ended up focusing on the Russian angle. He agreed with the contentions on Tibet and the Chumbi Valley put across by Hardinge, stating, 'I have been perturbed about it. Younghusband seems to have taken the bit between his teeth, and we are placed in a very embarrassing situation.'[16]

In contrast, and what puts the whole British approach in perspective, Curzon justified the occupation of the Chumbi Valley, as it 'lay on the southern side of the Himalayan watershed and its inhabitants were hostile to Tibetans from other regions. Britain's political influence in Tibet had both to be exclusive and supreme. If such an objective could be secured without a protectorate, the idea could be readily dispensed with; if not, Britain would be driven to it ...'[17]

This view carried no import in a London that was being guided largely by its European interests, where the issue of Tibet carried little weight or relevance. Whitehall believed that Curzon had the propensity to attach greater emphasis to India's geographical interests and in the process lose sight of the broader picture of Britain and its imperial interests.

A close reading of the implications of the Conventions of 1890 with the appended Regulations of 1904, 1906 and 1907 drives home the fact that Britain's approach was governed by the twin factors of underwriting China as the suzerain power in Tibet and containing the advance of the Russian empire in Asia and thus preventing a threat to Britain's Asian empire. By reaching an agreement with Russia that both of them would pursue their dealings with Lhasa through the Chinese, London reached the conclusion that Tibet was now ideally placed to act as a buffer between the Russian and British empires.

The power vacuum being filled by a weak China served the interest of both countries. The irony was that they were assuming that China would remain a weak nation where Britain and Russia could continue to influence the government's behaviour on Tibet. They were soon to be disabused of this notion.

After the Conventions of 1906 and 1907 had been ratified and operationalized, Britain made it clear that the states of Nepal, Sikkim and Bhutan now lay outside the political and administrative reach of both the Tibetan Dalai Lama and the Chinese Emperor.

Notes

1. Lord Curzon's Despatch of 8 January 1903: Its impact on his Tibetan policy as noted by Dr P.L. Mehra from his doctoral dissertation (at John Hopkins) entitled 'The Younghusband Expedition, an Interpretation'.
2. Curzon's communication made the point that 'accepting the Chinese proposals, but of attaching to them the condition that the Conference shall take place … in Lhasa, and that it shall be attended by a Tibetan representative who shall participate in the proceedings. In this way alone … we shall escape the ignominious position of having an Agreement … formally concluded with the Chinese and subsequently repudiated by the Tibetans.' Quoted from *Tibet: Pawn or Pivot of the Great Game*, Premen Addy, 2018.
3. Lord G.N. Curzon's despatch of January 1903 to the secretary of state of India in London.
4. Alexandre Andreyev in *Tibet and Her Neighbours: A History*, ed. Alex McKay, Thames & Hudson, London, 2004, pp. 167–173.
5. *Ibid.*, p. 15.
6. *Ibid.* p. 169.
7. Note on Tibet by Sir W. Lee-Warner, *Home Correspondence India*, Volume 196, No2151, 17 September 1902. Also cited by Alastair Lamb in *British India and Tibet*, p. 212.
8. *India and Tibet*, Francis E. Younghusband reprinted by AES, New Delhi and Chennai 1993, 2005.
9. Article I of the Lhasa Convention states that: 'The Government of Tibet engages to respect the Anglo-Chinese Convention of 1890 and to recognize the frontier between Sikkim and Thibet, as defined

in Article I of the said Convention, and to erect boundary pillars accordingly.' The Chinese endorsed this by the Anglo-Chinese Convention of 1906 in its Article I that states that: 'The Convention concluded on September 7, 1904, by Great Britain and Tibet, the texts of which … are attached to the present Convention … both of the High Contracting Parties engage to take at all times such steps as may be necessary to secure the due fulfilment of the terms specified therein.'

10. Ampthill Papers (E233/37) proposed by him as acting viceroy, while Curzon was on Home Leave, in Britain to the secretary of state for India, Brodrick. Letter dated 14 September 1904.
11. Letter from Brodrick to Ampthill (E233/37), 1 July 1904. Taken from *British India and Tibet: 1766–1910*, Alastair Lamb, Routledge and Kegan Paul, London and New York, 1960, p 247.
12. UK Foreign Office Papers 17, 1749. Lansdowne to S. Rice, 4 May 1904.
13. *India and Tibet*, Francis E. Younghusband reprinted by AES, New Delhi and Chennai 1993, 2005, p. 305.
14. *A Short History of Tibet*, H.E. Richardson, E.P. Duton & Co., 1962.
15. The full title was 'Convention between Great Britain and Russia relating to Persia, Afghanistan and Tibet. Signed at St. Petersburg, August 31st, 1907'.
16. 'Lansdowne Papers' as quoted by Premen Addy in his book *Tibet: Pawn and Pivot of the Great Game* published by Academic Publishers, Kolkata, 2018.
17. *Ibid.*, p. 79.

11

CHINESE MISADVENTURES IN TIBET (1906–11)

One important consequence of the 1904 invasion of Lhasa by Younghusband's British expedition was the reinforcement of China's feeling of vulnerability at Britain's hands after the two Opium Wars. Peking realized that if Britain came to control Tibet with a permanent presence in Lhasa, it could result in a threat to China's outlying provinces of Sichuan and Yunnan. The threat was made more real due to a weakened Manchu court which only retained nominal control over these provinces.

A military tactician and warlord of Sichuan, the Han Chinese Chao Er Feng (Zhao Erfeng), made his own assessment of the situation and decided that to safeguard China, Tibet's eastern territories that bordered Sichuan should come under his control. One of the messages that the British wanted to convey through the Anglo-Chinese Convention of 1906 was that they intended to take a backseat on Tibet and grant China a free hand to deal with

Lhasa. This was an opportunity for Chao and Peking to tighten China's hold over Tibet.

Leaving nothing to chance, the Chinese adopted two interlinked measures to gain absolute control over Tibet. The first was an aggressive move on eastern Tibet by Chao Er Feng. This was in clear violation of the Sino-Tibetan Treaty of 821–822, whose provisions both Tibet and China had accepted would prevail in perpetuity. The second was the Chinese commissioner appointed to Lhasa overriding the Tibetan government and putting monasteries under pressure. To Peking, at this stage, it did not matter that this would be perceived as a threat by the Dalai Lama, who had emerged from his retreat undertaken during the Younghusband expedition in 1903–4.

Violation of Past Treaties

These actions were a clear message that China's adherence to treaties and the commitments enveloped in them was only to the extent that it suited them. The invasion of eastern Tibet and the use of force to gain control over Lhasa was in direct violation of China's time-honoured historical commitments arising out of the Sino-Tibetan Treaty of 821–822 where both China and Tibet had accepted a permanent frontier of peace and tranquillity (as detailed in Chapter VIII).

The wording of the Sino-Tibetan Treaty of 821–822 was clear in placing the Chinese and the Tibetans on a footing of equality, where the Chinese Emperor, having been at the receiving end, was signing a treaty in perpetuity to ensure peace between the two countries, setting a permanent boundary between the two kingdoms. As has been previously mentioned, to underscore this agreement, pillars were erected to mark the frontiers between the two countries.

There is a Mongolian account that clarifies that the treaty was inscribed on three pillars: one placed at Lhasa, the second at

Chang'an, the capital of Tang China, and the third at the border of the two countries that the Mongolian text mentions as rMe ru. L. Augustine Waddell identifies this place as Ch'ing-shui where the compact was sworn between the two emperors. Waddell concludes that rMe ru was the pass that was a 'few miles to the east of the city of Ch'ing-shui-hien'.[1]

S.W. Bushnell's translation of the Chinese text of the treaty, that was published in the *Journal of the Royal Asiatic Society* in 1880, located the city by the name that it was known then as 'the modern city of Ch'ingshuihsien in the prefecture of Kungch'angfu in Shensi'.

Waddell confirmed Bushnell's identification of the frontier city as Ch'ingshuihsien, and went on to fix the location as lying 'in the line of the other boundaries enumerated on either side of it, from the north to the south, clarifying that this line forms a natural frontier … following as it did the water-parting of the Lung Mountain range and the corresponding range to the south of the River Wei'.

The sanctity of the Sino-Tibetan Treaty of 821–822 had never been questioned by the Chinese nor had it been revoked. More importantly, it underscored the fact that these were two independent nation-states that, by an agreement through this treaty, accepted that violations of their borders or acts to defend their independence and territorial integrity by any one party could result in retaliation and that 'nothing that the other party may do by way of retaliation shall be considered a breach of the treaty on their part'.

This provision makes it clear that Lhasa, feeling itself in jeopardy as China violated its commitment, could as part of its defence call on any source to come to its aid. It did this in 1950, seeking United Nations' intervention as well as India's aid. It was a political failure on India's part not to have formally put Tibet's request before the

United Nations, including declaring it an independent country that should be made a member of the United Nations.

The patron-priest relationship that developed in later centuries between imperial China and Tibet assured the latter that the former would come to its rescue whenever Tibet and its Buddhism faced an external threat. These moves were, however, to be made by imperial China whenever there was a request from Lhasa that was also backed by the Chinese amban. Developments that followed the Conventions of 1904 and 1906, where the British showed no inclination to deal with Tibet except in the area of trade, came at a time when local conditions in China granted the strong warlord, Chao Er Feng, an opportunity to carry out his ambitions.

The latter half of the Manchu period was one where local strongmen could adopt measures that did not necessarily have the sanction of the court. This is what happened with the Sichuanese warlord Chao Er Feng's invasion of eastern Tibet and the brutality shown by him in putting down any opposition, including dissent from the lamas and monks. Protests made by Lhasa at the Manchu court did not put a stop to the invasion as, by this time, Peking had lost control over the outlying provinces of Sichuan and Yunnan.

In Lhasa, the Chinese were set on exploiting the space that the British had granted them to assert their hold on Tibet proper. The British historical view of events was patently contradictory. They had undertaken the Younghusband expedition to Lhasa as they were aware that the Manchu court, whatever its earlier hold on Tibet at the time of the Qianlong Emperor was, did not exercise any control over Lhasa after his demise. The Tibetans had made it clear that they did not accept the contention that the Chinese had any right to represent them or their interests. Their actions had left no room for doubt that the Emperor was not in a condition to force his will on Lhasa. Despite knowing this, under pressure from

Whitehall, the British in India had receded into the background, letting China impose its will on Tibet.

The Chinese, having read British intentions and using the Tibetan fear of the British as a hold over them, adopted measures to contain and, where possible, frustrate British interests in Tibet. To remove Britain's presence from the Chumbi Valley that the Chinese had rightly assumed granted them a strategic position in their dealings with Sikkim and Bhutan, they agreed to pay the Tibetan indemnity in full, aimed at an early departure of the British from the valley.

The Chinese had no difficulty accepting the British strategy that Tibet be placed as a buffer between the British and Chinese empires. However, they also took into account that the Younghusband invasion of Tibet had led to China itself becoming vulnerable to the expansionist ambitions of both Russia and Britain. Hence, China arrived at the conclusion that it needed control over Tibet to safeguard its own borders.

All these events of deep importance to Tibet were taking place at a time when Britain, under a Liberal government was even more reluctant to be seen as exerting 'any political influence over Tibet'. It was anxious to let the Chinese take charge of Tibet to keep Russia out.

Chinese Oppression of Tibet

Commissioner Chang Yin-tang, cast in the same mould as Chao Er Feng, took charge in Lhasa backed up by a Chinese military force of 2000 men.[2] He took over the administration of the country and used force to put down dissent, both by laypersons and by religious orders. Opposition soon surfaced as the Tibetans realized that they had to meet force with force against a China that had refused to show respect to the Dalai Lama and the Buddhist religion.

The Chinese had twice deposed the thirteenth Dalai Lama. First was when he left Lhasa in 1904 to avoid dealing with Younghusband. Amban You Tai, to facilitate the negotiations for the finalization of the Convention of Lhasa, had deposed the Dalai Lama. This was a tactical move as it served the mutual interests of both the Chinese amban and Younghusband. This measure facilitated negotiations towards the drafting and signing of the treaty in Lhasa that recognized Britain's strategic and commercial interests in Tibet.

The Dalai Lama had finally ended up in Peking where he had been subjected to treatment that Richardson described as 'censorious and slighting', resulting in his looking at China in unfavourable terms. He was restored to power in 1908 by a royal Manchu decree, with the Manchu court expecting him to be subservient to the Chinese and abide by Peking's diktat. Understandably, he resented this treatment and was further upset when, on his return to Lhasa in the latter half of 1909, he found the Chinese commissioner Chang Yin-tang in full control, having side-lined the Tibetan authorities.

Charles Bell summarized the entire situation in a few but telling words. Referring to the withdrawal of British forces from Lhasa, he mentioned that in his opinion the British government 'did the right thing'. 'The Tibetans were still suspicious of our motives. The Chinese still held the confidence of the country to the extent of being able to increase Tibetan suspicions of our designs.' This was the case between the signing of the Conventions of 1904 and 1906. 'Later on, China invaded Tibet, seized a great part of the administration, desecrated monasteries and oppressed the people.'

The aggressive behaviour adopted by the Chinese created a situation that had never occurred in this fashion in Tibet proper. It was the first time that a Chinese armed force had entered Tibet uninvited, and it led to an immense upheaval in Tibet at large.

The Tibetans now came to look upon Britain as possibly a more trustworthy partner and its support as a protector of Tibetan rights would be a welcome development.

The Dalai Lama, faced with the overwhelming interference and the use of brute force, realized that the only way out was to remove himself along with all his ministers and his seals from Lhasa. This time, he decided to seek the assistance of the British and fled to India. In a letter that he wrote to Charles Bell, he clarified the position:

> The Chinese have been greatly oppressing the Tibetan people at Lhasa … I was obliged, together with my six Ministers, to make good my escape. My intention now is to go to India for the purpose of consulting the British Government …
>
> I have left the Regent and Acting Ministers at Lhasa, but I and the Ministers who accompany me have brought our seals with us … I now look to you for protection, and I trust that the relations between the British Government and Tibet will be that of a father to his children.

This letter was a clear invitation seeking British intervention and protection for Tibet. The Chinese intrusion in Tibet had forced the Tibetans to seek an end to Chinese presence in Lhasa and Tibet proper.

Himalayan States in Jeopardy

Chang's actions were not just confined to Tibet. He had a greater ambition of wresting control over other Himalayan states, from Ladakh onwards. He also attempted to reassert Chinese suzerainty over Sikkim and Bhutan and threatened the north-eastern parts of tribal India. This was a foretaste of what India would face 'if China obtained a firm hold over Tibet'.

To make his intentions clear, Chang started efforts to promote a policy steeped in Chinese symbolism, urging the 'blending of the five colours, i.e. China, Tibet, Nepal, Sikkim and Bhutan, and had likened Nepal, Bhutan and Sikkim to the molar teeth lying side by side in a man's mouth'.[3] Chang separately reached out to Bhutan and Nepal as well.

To the representative of Nepal in Lhasa, he suggested, 'Tibet and Nepal being united as brothers, under the auspices of China, should work in harmony for the common good.'[4] This conveyed the suggestion that like Tibet, Nepal should also look upon China as its suzerain.

With Bhutan, attempts were made by the Chinese amban to get them involved in helping out against the British in Sikkim. The amban wrote to the chiefs in Bhutan, the Deb Raja and the Penlops of Tongsa and Paro, that as the Bhutanese were 'subjects of the Emperor of China, who is the Lord of Heaven, all of you have no option but to obey the orders of your ruler'.

According to Political Officer Bell, the Chinese leadership was keen on neutralizing Britain's influence on Bhutan with the intention of bringing it under their control to fulfil China's expressed desire to make Bhutan 'the gate on the south which prevents entry'.[5] The message was clear—if Britain did not prevent Chinese advances to Bhutan's leadership, it would have the Chinese in Bhutan creating a direct threat to India's north-east.

To forestall Chinese moves on Bhutan, Bell suggested that a new treaty be negotiated with Bhutan that would place the conduct of its foreign relations under the British government, while Bhutan would retain full control over its internal affairs. An Anglo-Bhutan treaty specifying these two provisions was signed on 8 January 1910.

As Bell put it, after the signing of the treaty, 'thus with the consent of all and the blessings of its all-powerful priesthood, Bhutan was joined to the British Empire'.[6]

Unlike the foggy notions that the Government of Britain held in its conduct of Tibetan policies, to the British Indian officials dealing with the Himalayan states, the Chinese occupation of Tibet was recognized as a threat to India's security. This official assessment was unequivocal and it was a part of British records that identified a Tibet under the full control of China as a major security threat to independent India. Obviously, this serious strategic concern was not on Prime Minister Jawaharlal Nehru's mind, as he focused on his Asia Vision, central to which was Sino-Indian cooperation aimed at building a resurgent Asia awakening from the coils of colonialism.

Returning to what was happening in Tibet, the Chinese were not only busy establishing their control but, to gain their way, they were openly violating the many provisions of the conventions between them and the British. This was true for both political commitments and trade issues. Every barrier in the way of adequate implementation of trade regulations was being adopted by the Chinese officials while their overpowering presence was creating a great deal of unease among the Tibetans at almost all levels.

The British in India understood the need to bring an end to the brutality that Chang was visiting upon the Tibetans but they remained on the side-lines. Britain was holding back on taking any action as their interference could be seen as a violation of the understandings that the British and the Russians had committed to, of letting China exercise a free hand in Tibet while they maintained strict neutrality over the kingdom. In other words, the British were turning a Nelson's eye to developments in Tibet till conditions reached a position where a negative fallout surfaced and the Chinese threatened to occupy north-eastern India.

This apart, the Chinese decided to challenge the British arrangements with the Himalayan states that were a part of the Cis-Himalayan states, including Sikkim, that they had acknowledged under the Convention of 1890 as a British protectorate. It would appear that the Chinese, despite the political turmoil that the republican revolution had brought, had taken the view that they needed to maintain their hold over Tibet as a tactical necessity, where both Sikkim and Bhutan were seen as essential strategic outliers.

Britain Strengthens China's Position in Tibet

To make matters worse, the Government of Britain, against Curzon's advice and overruling his opposition, continued to display a willingness to accommodate the Chinese. It not only permitted China to strengthen its control over Tibet but even to reverse earlier policies. Visits by Indian pilgrims to Manasarovar were forbidden as travel by British subjects to any part of Tibet beyond Gyantse were deemed illegal. This came about as a result of an Anglo-Chinese agreement on 'Tibet Trade Regulations, 1908' signed at Calcutta on 20 April 1908.[7] In effect, it was an extension of the Regulations of 1893 with amendments concerning the establishment and operationalization of new trade marts at Gartok and Gyantse.

Article III of the Tibet Trade Regulations of 1908, entered into by Britain with China,[8] made it clear that Tibetans would be placed under the supervision and control of the Chinese. It went to the extent of saying that any disputes that could not be settled 'by agreement between the Trade Agents and the Local authorities shall be referred … to the Government of India and the Tibetan

High Authorities at Lhasa'. For this purpose, a stepped system was agreed to, where the Lhasa authorities were to be approached through a reference by the Government of India to the Chinese imperial resident at Lhasa. A failure to resolve the issue at this level would then be kicked upstairs to be taken up and resolved at the level of the governments of Britain and China in 'accordance with the terms of article I of the Peking Convention of 1906'.

Article IX made clear that 'British officers and subjects' were barred from proceeding beyond Gyantse, confining themselves to the routes between Yatung to Gartok and Gyantse and vice-versa. The 'natives of the Indian frontier, who have already by usage traded and resided in Tibet, elsewhere than at the trade marts shall be at liberty to continue their trade, in accordance with existing practice'. All other visits by Indians, including for pilgrimage, were not provided for.

What Britain had done was to leave a weak Tibet in the hands of an obdurate Manchu China that was already on its way out of power. By 1908, the British had relinquished their position of influence in Lhasa, limiting their Tibetan concerns to the realm of trade. When the Dalai Lama sought British intervention after reaching Darjeeling, his requests merely resulted in a mild protest citing a 'subversion of existing political conditions' that had been undertaken by Peking without a reference being made to Britain.

The note did, however, point out that the understanding derived from the conventions was that an 'effective Tibetan Government should be kept in being with which they could maintain their treaty relationship'[9]. This protest was brushed aside by Peking, stating that the British authorities need not be worried—all treaty obligations would be carried out. There was no reference to the issue of an effective Tibetan government being kept in place.

When the then Government of India conveyed its concerns to the home office over Chinese behaviour and the apparent violations of the Anglo-Chinese understandings on Tibet, the secretary of state for India, Lord Morley's view, endorsed by the Government of Britain, was that the Chinese were 'simply making their suzerainty effective, which would probably result in a strong internal government in Tibet'. His suggestion was that unless there was a specific breach of the treaty obligations there was no need for Britain to act.

By now, it was obvious that the difference in perspective between London and Calcutta had worked to the advantage of China. What was more baffling was that despite being aware that both Chao Er Feng and Commissioner Chang were acting in their own interests and were outside Peking's control, Britain decided to conveniently discount that fact, as also the news that Commissioner Chang's strong-arming tactics in Lhasa were being openly challenged by the Tibetans.

Britain continued to ignore developments in Lhasa. While the Dalai Lama had once again been deposed by the Chinese, he had not lost the support and faith of his subjects. During his and his ministers' absence from Lhasa, the Chinese tried to get the Panchen Lama to head a Tibetan administration, an attempt that was foiled by him. The Tibetan National Assembly, the Tsongdu, remained hostile to Chinese actions and kept in touch with the Dalai Lama in Darjeeling with its messages denouncing Chinese actions being passed on to Calcutta.

Peking soon realized that without the presence of the Dalai Lama in Lhasa, it would not be able to control Tibet. Attempts to persuade him to return were defeated over the terms that he wished to impose. He had also made it clear that whatever the relations that existed in the past between him as the Dalai Lama and the Chinese

Emperor were now part of the historical past. With the ending of monarchy in China, the old relationship of priest and patron had ended. With the unwarranted invasion of Tibet and the violation of its borders by the Chinese, whatever remained of the old relations had also ended.

The thirteenth Dalai Lama was looking to reassert Tibet's independence and a return to the position that the country held in the period of the fifth Dalai Lama. To this end, he modified his approach by granting sanctity to the Anglo-Tibetan Convention of 1904, implying that he was willing to accept the protection of the British.

Events in China were moving in a manner that spelt the end not only of the Qing dynasty but also of the monarchical system. In 1911, the republican revolution broke out and the impact was soon reflected in Tibet where Chinese troops mutinied and were set upon by the Tibetans. In many parts of Tibet, Chinese troops were annihilated and Chinese officials everywhere were under threat. The British tried to persuade the Dalai Lama to intervene and save the lives of the Chinese including the amban. By June 1912, the Chinese had lost all control over Tibet except some parts of eastern Tibet.

Following the republican revolution, the British attitude changed to the extent that they were now committing themselves to a policy of full internal autonomy for Tibet under Chinese suzerainty, but without Chinese interference in its internal administration. The policy now was more in tune with the original intent that had been promoted by Curzon, that Anglo-Tibetan relations be guided by the Tibetans following, in letter and spirit, the agreements both political and commercial underwritten by the conventions and regulations relating to trade between British India and Tibet.

Britain was now recognizing that it was Tibet that would implement the provisions of the various treaties outside the control of China, as it was established beyond reasonable doubt that China could not impose its will on Tibet except by resorting to an armed occupation of that country.

Notes

1. 'The Early History of Tibet', S.W. Bushnell in the *Journal of the Royal Asiatic Society of Great Britain and Ireland*, new series, Vol.12, No4, October 1880, pp. 435-541.
2. This was the first time an invasive force had entered Tibet without a request from Lhasa. Earlier expeditions by China in 1720, 1728, 1750 and 1792 had entered Tibet at the request and consent of Lhasa.
3. *Ibid.*, p. 106.
4. *Ibid.*, pp. 100–101.
5. *Ibid.*, p. 106.
6. *Ibid.*, p. 103.
7. This is where for the first time on the insistence of L.W. Dane (he was British India's foreign secretary) the Tibetan representative was treated, despite Chinese objections, as of equal status to the Chinese negotiator. The Agreement was signed in April 1908 after very tortuous negotiations, by E. C. Wilton for Britain, Chang Yin-tang of China and Wang Chuk Gyalpo for Tibet.
8. Agreement between Great Britain, China and Tibet amending the trade regulations in Tibet of 5 December 1893. Signed at Calcutta, 20 April 1908, known as Tibet Trade Regulations, 1908.
9. *A Short History of Tibet*, H.E. Richardson, E.P. Duton & Co., 1962, p. 98.

12

IMPACT OF REPUBLICAN CHINA

Even though the Kuomintang-led republican revolution had drawn the curtain on Manchu rule in China, it did not end the Chinese desire to seek control over Tibet. A fair part of eastern Tibet was still occupied by China. The new government in Beijing reiterated its intention to keep its armed forces in eastern Tibet, with the added inclination to send a force to subdue Lhasa.

To create the grounds in support of the policy of intervention, the president of the newly founded Republic of China, Yuan Shikai, proclaimed in April 1912, 'Mongolia, Sinkiang and Tibet were to be treated on the same basis as provinces of China and were to be considered as integral parts of the Republic', of China.[1] This proclamation came despite the fact that the thirteenth Dalai Lama had made it clear that he intended to free Tibet, making it independent of Chinese hegemony.

The British had finally realized that their policy after the Convention of 1906 had failed to preserve Tibet's right to exercise control over its internal affairs. To the Chinese, the use of the term 'suzerainty' was meaningless; it had never been defined and there was no equivalent in their language for it. Britain now made it clear that it would not accept the Chinese claim that Tibet was an integral part of China. In practice, the British expected that Lhasa would remain in control of Tibet's domestic affairs, but under a kind of protection of China that would deal with Tibet's external affairs. An armed invasion of Tibet was certainly not what the British had expected.

Instability in the Himalayas

In historical terms, the priest-patron relationship between Tibet and China (detailed in earlier chapters), had resulted in a special relationship between imperial China during the rule of the Yuan dynasty that was further reinforced during the Manchu dynasty. Historian Dawa Norbu, author of the book *China's Tibet Policy*,[2] defined this relationship as one of 'indirect rule', that was heavily influenced by their (the Chinese, Mongol and Tibetan) belief in Buddhism. Hence, the most accurate way to define the historical relationship between China and Tibet was a special one bounded by Buddhism. This special relationship was damaged and, in fact, destroyed by the actions of Chao Er Feng in eastern Tibet and Commissioner Chang in Lhasa.

There was a feeling that Chao's intervention was largely based on the assumption that China faced a threat from a British-controlled South Asia. Britain, by forcing its way into Lhasa in 1904, had created a situation where China felt that if it did not control Tibet, its frontiers could be breached. Commissioner Chang, in keeping with this view, was asserting China's sovereignty over Tibet to ensure that the British in South Asia were kept at bay

At this stage, the two factors that influenced British policy were Viceroy Minto (appointed after Curzon's resignation in 1905) drawing the attention of the secretary of state to the atrocities visited upon the Tibetans by the Chinese, and the possibility that Nepal, fearful of an aggressive Chinese presence in Lhasa posing a threat to it, might decide to invade Tibet. While Britain was analysing these developments and had yet to settle on a policy, a more serious issue was appearing on the horizon.

China, observing Britain's lack of response to its actions in Tibet, decided that it was free to take the next step. It now put forward the contention that it held suzerainty not only over Tibet that had been recognized by both Russia and Britain, but, by extension, to Nepal, Sikkim and Bhutan as well. China's actions in Tibet created the impression that it may be looking to assert its suzerainty over the three Himalayan states as well. The British representative in Peking warned both London and Calcutta that China was likely to carry out this intention and pointed out the implications such actions would have on the security of India. This forced the hand of the British and a note was finally presented to the Wai Wu (the foreign office in Peking) that Britain would not 'allow any changes China might make in Tibet to impinge on the territorial or political integrity of Nepal, Sikkim and Bhutan'.[3]

The Chinese response was a typical case of obfuscation. In the face of pressure, the British charge d' affairs, Max Muller, was informed that Peking had no intention of interfering in Sikkim and Bhutan, but, cleverly, no declaration was made on Nepal. The reason was soon apparent—China was claiming suzerainty over Nepal. China's overlord in Lhasa, Commissioner Chang Yin-Tang, had made public in 1909 that he considered Tibet, Nepal, Sikkim and Bhutan as part of China. Britain at that time had ignored Chang's statement, making no attempt to counter it or straighten out the Chinese claim.

Britain's actions, if anything, were full of contradictions. Its decision to claim and exercise paramountcy over Nepal, Sikkim and Bhutan was linked to the essentialness of these states to the security of India. This should have led to an immediate action to put things right with Peking and ask it to discipline its official in Lhasa to reverse his claims. This did not happen.

Another interesting proposal, and from India's security point of view a very relevant one, was Whitehall ignoring the advice of colonial officials and, more importantly, of experts of the British-Indian military intelligence, to include the Chumbi Valley as a part of Sikkim due to its primacy to India's security. Surprisingly, an independent India also followed in Britain's footsteps and turned down expert advice to take over the Chumbi Valley as China came to aggress and occupy Tibet in 1950–51.

Finally, the developments in Lhasa forced London to make it clear to Peking that Britain would no longer give countenance to any attempt by China to push its way into Tibet through the use of force. A strong note spelling out the conditions was formally presented to the Wai Pu. It stated that:

- His Majesty's Government formally recognised the suzerain rights of China in Tibet;
- Never recognised, and not prepared to recognise right of China to intervene actively in the administration of Tibet, which should remain as contemplated by the Treaties in the hands of Tibetan Administration.
- While the right of China to station a representative with a suitable escort at Lhasa, with authority to advise the Tibetans as to their foreign relations is not disputed.
- The British Government was not prepared 'to acquiesce in the maintenance of an unlimited number of Chinese troops either at Lhasa or in Tibet generally.'[4]

Sir John Jordan, the British envoy to the imperial court at Beijing, had spelt out the British position in 1909 when he stated that Britain 'would not tolerate any attempt to reduce Tibet, who had independent treaty relations with Great Britain to the condition of a province of China, warning the Chinese Government, that grave complications might ensue if the Chinese expedition crossed the frontier into Tibet'.[5] This was the strongest warning issued by Britain, clearly setting the parameters within which it was willing to deal with a Sino-Tibetan relationship.

Sticky Myth of Chinese Suzerainty

With the collapse of the Qing dynasty in early 1912, the thirteenth Dalai Lama asserted Tibet's independence by forcing all Chinese troops and officials out of Lhasa and central Tibet. Britain, however, refused to accept the Dalai Lama's assertion of independence. It informed him formally that the Government of India saw the situation within the context of an autonomous Tibet under Chinese suzerainty, with the added conditionality that all treaty obligations were to be carried out and cordial relations were to be maintained between Tibet and India. The relations between the British and the thirteenth Dalai Lama and his senior ministers had reached a level of comfort where both parties had come to respect each other, with the Tibetans relying on the British to protect Tibet against Chinese depredations.

In equal measure, the British position had also hardened over attempts that the republican government in Peking was making to change the status of Tibet. It saw China's attempts as a deliberate bid at violating the provisions of the Convention of 1907, by which the Russians and the British had jointly acknowledged Chinese suzerainty over Tibet, but not its sovereignty.

While these developments were taking place, the question about the diplomatic legitimacy of the new Chinese republic also cropped up. The situation in China was fluid, as the republican government in its attempt to retain the nature of the relations that had existed between the Chinese emperors and the Dalai Lamas, restored the latter's titles. In Tibet, however, the view was that with the ending of dynastic rule in China, their old relationship no longer existed.

Within these complex new developments, it was not only China's relationship with Tibet that was at stake. The Russians, taking advantage of a weakened China, extended recognition and support to the new Mongolian regime that headed an independent Mongolia. This brought into play a new dynamic that the British in India had to take into account while drafting their policy on Tibet.

For the British to extend recognition to republican China, it was necessary that Sino-Tibetan relations remained within the ambit of internal autonomy for Tibet and Chinese suzerainty over it stayed within the limits that the British had set. The peremptory proclamation of Yuan ShiKai that Tibet should be treated as a province of China had complicated matters. According to Dawa Norbu, who had carried extensive research of the relations between Tibet and China covering all the historical periods, this was the first time that such a claim had been made by Peking.[6]

In the meanwhile, the Russian Buddhist lama, Agvan Lobsang Dorzhiev had returned to the scene and a treaty between Mongolia and Tibet had been worked out and signed. The fact that Mongolia was now under Russian influence created its own set of problems that the British had to take into account to counter any expansion of Russian influence over Tibet. It was here that Lord Charles Hardinge, viceroy of India from 1910 to 1916, was able to help Britain adopt a policy that moved issues along the direction that India inherited in 1947. In his telegram to the secretary state for

India in London, dated 7 November 1912, he detailed how British India felt the issues could be dealt with:

> Reference to your telegram of 23rd October. Tibet. The question has undergone considerable development since my telegram of 23rd March, and it appears evident that conditions of recognition of new Chinese Government will not suffice to effect settlement of Tibet question … The threat most likely to prove effective is that if China enters Tibet our agreements with China regarding that country will no longer hold good, and we will give active assistance to Tibet in opposing Chinese advance, and in establishing and maintaining Tibetan independence.

Hardinge also suggested that in keeping with the spirit of the Anglo-Russian Convention, Britain would invite Russia to assist us on joint action.

The viceroy's opinion firmed up the British response to China. In Peking, the British representative formally protested President Yuan ShiKai's proclamation of Tibet being a province of China and his decision to send troops to eastern Tibet. Yuan ShiKai reversed his position on Tibet, formally conveying to the British Minister in Peking that there was no intention of incorporating Tibet in the Chinese Empire.[7] This was of symbolic importance, and it should have led both the British colonial authorities and subsequently independent India to extend full diplomatic recognition to Tibet as a free country.

Yuan ShiKai, however, asserted that he would send troops not to invade but to maintain the sanctity of China's borders with Tibet. This was typical Chinese sophistry at work because he did not clarify what he considered as the border between the two countries. The correct action by the British at this stage should have been to point out that China and Tibet must adhere to the borders that had been defined under the Sino-Tibetan Treaty of 821–822, but they failed to do so. Differences between where the Tibetans insisted their border with China lay and what China claimed as its traditional territory encroached by Tibet, created conditions for the British to step in and help resolve the issue.

The British, however, maintained the myth of Chinese suzerainty over Tibet, confusing the situation to the point that the rest of the world, and particularly independent India, also kept applying the same terminology to describe the Sino-Tibetan relationship. This was in contradiction to the fact that from the period 1912 to 1949, Tibet had both in fact and in action been an independent country. In keeping with this dichotomy that continued to afflict Britain's Tibet policy, its envoy at the conclusion of his discussions with the Chinese president, handed a memorandum that reaffirmed that the Government of Britain 'was prepared to recognise Chinese suzerainty over Tibet but not to admit the right of China to intervene in the internal administration of the country or to maintain an unlimited number of troops there'. The Chinese remained obdurate but the actions taken by the Dalai Lama to reclaim eastern Tibet and push the Chinese out acted as its own corrective.

China at 'the Gates of India'

The complexity of the situation in Tibet, where multiple stakeholders were involved, led the British to conclude that a formal arrangement was needed to settle the borders between Tibet and China, India and Tibet, and Tibet and the Cis-Himalayan states that would keep other powers like imperial Russia out of the equation. The British also felt it necessary to place the relationship between China and Tibet on a firmer footing to ensure that Tibet would be in control of its internal affairs within an autonomy that would not prevent it from conducting its external affairs as and when required. The Chinese position of suzerainty was recognized but its exercise was limited to external affairs in purely nominal terms.

Sir John Jordan's memorandum, submitted to President Yuan ShiKai in 1912, had clarified and placed the British understanding of the relations between Tibet and China in perspective. It stated that Great Britain 'would not tolerate any attempt to reduce Tibet, who had independent treaty relations with Great Britain to the condition of a province of China and warned the Chinese Government that grave complications might ensue if the Chinese expedition crossed the frontier into Tibet'[8]. Jordan's memorandum by implication suggested that Britain would not tolerate any attempt by China to dilute the rights granted to Great Britain by Article I of the Convention of 1906.

The stage was now set. The thirteenth Dalai Lama had for all practical purposes shrugged off Chinese presence and thrown out the amban, reverting relations to the pre–Kang Hsi and Qianlong Manchu period. He had further conveyed that in the new circumstances, the kinship that had existed between the two nations from the time of Kublai Khan and the Sakya Lama had come to an end. The Dalai Lama's forces had evicted the Chinese west of the Mekong–Yangtse watershed in eastern Tibet. His forces were battling the Chinese to remove them from Amdo and from most of the Kham region. Attempts to bridge the gap between Lhasa and Peking over consensus on borders had failed. The British realized that they had to take matters into their own hands and keep any other party out. The British government in India insisted that the initiative to deal with the Sino-Tibetan situation best remain with it, cutting out the British foreign office with its bias towards European affairs and its history of confused handling of the Tibet–India relations.

Another factor had come into play by this time. Chao Er Feng, while conducting his operations in eastern Tibet, had threatened the north-eastern part of India. By 1910, both eastern and central Tibet had fallen into the hands of the Chinese, creating conditions that turned the India–Tibet border into a live issue. The British press now came to focus on the threat that the Chinese hold over Tibet could pose to British India. London's *Morning Post,* in its editorial of 28 February 1910, according to Lamb, summed up the situation well enough from the British point of view. What the editorial stated is prescient and applies to what India was faced with when the PRC came to occupy Tibet in 1950; it is worth acquainting ourselves with it.

> A great Empire, the future military strength of which no man can foresee, has suddenly appeared on the North-East Frontier of India ... The men who advocated the retention of Lhasa have proved not so far wrong ... The evacuation of the Chumbi has certainly proved a blunder. The strategic line has been lost ... China, ... has come to the gates of India ... It is to be hoped that the Indian Government will ... use the presence of the Dalai Lama [in India] as a lever for securing from the Chinese Government ... in frontier rectification.[9]

The reference to the strategic aspects of Tibet as a whole for India and the particular importance of the Chumbi Valley was underlined in this editorial. Another factor that the British in India had to now take into account was the threat that the Chinese occupation of the Kham area of eastern Tibet posed to the north-eastern parts of India and northern Burma. This was particularly true of the area described as lying to the south of the crest of the Assam Himalayas in India and the areas of Burma south of the Himalayan watershed.

To set the record straight, the Chinese occupied Tibet in 1910 and instituted an active intervention designed to take over the north-eastern parts of India, particularly focusing on the Assam provinces' northern borders with Tibet. As China moved into eastern Tibet, it showed that it had every intention to ignore the existence of the traditional frontier between Assam and Tibet and to wrest control over Assam's tribal areas. To bolster its claims to the area, China brought out a map of 1890, delineating the Qing empire and claiming Assam as its tributary.

Charles Bell, as advisor on Tibet to the Government of India, had pointed out in 1909 that Assam's tribal areas that lay south of the Himalayan watershed were vulnerable to Chinese threats. He suggested that there was an urgent need to put in place a proper administrative structure to prevent any Chinese ingress into that area. His suggestions included the need for identification of areas that were suitable for cultivation to encourage agricultural development, and the establishment of appropriate structures that would attract the tribes to cooperate with the administration.

The main factor, of course, was that the area should be clearly seen to be under the British Indian administration to prevent any attempts by the Chinese to gain entry into the area. Bell's suggestions only received attention a year later, in 1910, when he was able to confirm to the Indian government that his fears of Chinese intervention in the tribal areas had come true.

Chinese troops had advanced into the tribal area of the Hkamti tribe in the north-eastern corner of India. A couple of months after the Chinese move into the Hkamti tribal area they arrived in Rima, in Tibet, that lay opposite the Mishmi tribal area and 'ordered a neighbouring Mishmi chief to cut a track from Tibet to India'.[10]

As Alastair Lamb put it,[11] Chinese patrols had 'penetrated the Assam Himalayas, contacting tribes and planting boundary markers in a region which had hitherto been entirely insulated from international interests'.[12] These developments drove home the fact that China was inclined to push into the tribal areas. This would violate the traditional frontier guarded by the natural barrier that the 50-mile depth of the Himalayan rage provided. Their intention was to establish themselves overlooking the plains of Assam. This remains a Chinese ambition directed at India's Arunachal Pradesh that they claim to be part of Tibet.

These actions by China finally roused the British Indian government and attempts were made to secure the area. Given the nature of the threat, it was logical for the British to draw a line setting out the Indo-Tibet border that came to be known as the famous McMahon Line.

Any reading of the situation made it clear that a Chinese occupation of Tibet would threaten the security of India. It was in India's interests that Tibet be kept free from any external power, ensuring that the latter continued to act as a buffer between India and all powers to its north and east.

Outer Mongolia and Russia

With a weakened Manchu China being replaced by a chaotic republican regime that did not have full control over China's outer regions, Outer Mongolia seized the opportunity to declare its independence from Peking with Russia assuming the role of its benefactor and protector. The Chinese had no choice but to give in to Russian demands in order to save face and be recognized as the nominal suzerain in Mongolia, dispossessed of any power to interfere in Mongolian affairs. Rumours quickly reached India that the Tibetans and Mongolians had arrived at a treaty among themselves, understood to have been negotiated and signed on behalf of Tibet by the infamous Dorzhiev who claimed to possess credentials issued by the thirteenth Dalai Lama to do so

This treaty granted ease of access for the movement of Mongols and Tibetans to each other's territories. The British realized that unless they stepped in to resolve the issues that were complicating China's relations with Tibet, they may be confronted with Russian intervention in Tibet. Russia's presence in Mongolia and Manchuria granted it the Buddhist credentials that it could leverage in its relations with Lhasa, compromising Britain's and India's interests in Tibet.

Furthermore, Dorzhiev's interactions with the Russian military had resulted in a group of Russian Buryats providing military training to the Tibetans along with a flow of Russian arms into Tibet. These developments were raising alarm bells in the dovecotes of the British administration, particularly in India. The thirteenth Dalai Lama on his return to Tibet had given every indication that he was willing to have Britain as Tibet's protector. He also expected material supplies from Britain to assist him in his efforts to free the whole of eastern Tibet from Chinese incursions. The dilemma Britain now faced was that if it did not act to safeguard its relations with Tibet, Lhasa may turn to Russia.

Britain had to act to fill the political vacuum, recognizing that the Tibetans would fight any attempt to foist Chinese suzerainty on them. The Indian colonial administration now proposed that Britain assume paramountcy over Tibet while ensuring that the Dalai Lama and his government exercised complete control over Tibet's internal affairs. These proposals ran into opposition as the British foreign office endorsed the advice of the British representative in China that nothing should be done to exploit the weakened position of China under the republican government that was still in the process of trying to consolidate its position. The assessment was that this was a short-term problem and Britain should keep long-term considerations in mind.

British policy, however, had to take ground realities into account as well. It had now come to favour a stable and fully autonomous Tibet outside the control of China except in a nominal sense. This change in attitude suited the Government of India in order to resolve the issues confronting the triangular relations (of Britain, Tibet and China) so that stability was restored to the region and India's security and strategic interests were taken care of. To achieve this, they wanted the parties involved to keep certain factors in mind:

- There had to be a clearly defined border between China and Tibet. Such a border should keep China away from those areas of eastern Tibet that could pose a threat to both India's north-east and British Burma's northern areas.
- Britain would recognize Tibet as a fully autonomous state that could enter into treaty relations on its own, thus reversing its earlier policy where the Convention of 1904 was seen as an aberration that needed to be corrected by gaining China's endorsement through the Anglo-Chinese Convention of 1906.
- Trade would be dealt with as a part of a British India and Tibet agreement and there would be no outside interference in the conduct of trade relations.

It was also clear at this stage that to bring about a settlement of all these factors, a new treaty had to be entered into where all three parties, Britain, China and Tibet, were officially recognized as being of equal status. This, both in action and effect, was a recognition that Tibet was an independent country.

Notes

1. *A Short History of Tibet*, H.E. Richardson, E.P. Duton & Co., 1962, p. 103.
2. *China's Tibet Policy,* Dawa Norbu, Routledge, New Delhi, 2001.
3. *Tibet: Pawn and Pivot of the Great Game*, Premen Addy, Academic Publishers, Kolkata, 2018.
4. *The Northern Frontier*, Parshotam Mehra, Vol. I, Oxford University Press, Delhi, 1979.
5. *China's Tibet Policy,* Dawa Norbu, Routledge, New Delhi, 2001.
6. *China's Tibet Policy,* Dawa Norbu, Routledge, New Delhi, 2001.
7. *A Short History of Tibet*, H.E. Richardson, E.P. Duton & Co., 1962, p. 104.
8. *China's Tibet Policy,* Dawa Norbu, Routledge, New Delhi, 2001.
9. *British India and Tibet: 1766–1910*, Alastair Lamb, Routledge and Kegan Paul, London and New York, 1960, p. 276-277.
10. *Tibet: Past and Present,* Charles Bell, Motilal Banarsidass, New Delhi, 2000.
11. *British India and Tibet: 1766–1910*, Alastair Lamb, Routledge and Kegan Paul, London and New York, 1960, p. 276. Also referred to by Wendy Pence in her study, *The British Empire and Tibet, 1900–1922* published by Routledge as part of its Routledge-Curzon Studies in the Modern History of India series, 2005.

13

SIMLA CONVENTION OF 1914

Britain assumed the role of mediator to resolve the issues between China and Tibet. To achieve an agreement, it was felt that negotiations should take place outside China and Tibet, and India was offered as neutral territory to host the conference between the three parties. Shimla, or Simla as it was then known, was British India's summer capital and was chosen as the location of the conference.

The British attached lower priority to the achievement of an agreement relating to the Tibet–China boundary, than to the defining of the status of Tibet and the nature of the relations between it and the new China. This question assumed importance as what had defined the relations between the two countries was the priest-patron arrangement. This had now disappeared along with the idea that China exercised control over Tibet.

The British, however, were reluctant to treat Tibet as their protectorate. This forced the situation towards the construction of a relationship that on the surface retained China as the suzerain but in a very loose arrangement, China had a special diplomatic relationship with Tibet without having any right to impose itself on Tibet in whatever manner.

The main British concern was the removal of any possibility of China threatening India's security. In 1909, Britain had signed a treaty with Bhutan where the latter agreed to the former controlling its foreign relations, directed specifically by the aim to keep Chinese influence out of Bhutan. The next step was to adopt a 'forward policy' to make effective the Himalayan barrier as a buffer between Tibet and north-eastern India. This also applied to the safeguarding of British Burma's northern frontiers. These steps were implemented over the years 1911–13.[1]

Contentious Convention

The agenda of the convention was to redefine relations in a manner where the Chinese recognized Tibet as fully autonomous at a conference where all three parties were represented on a basis of equality. To put pressure on China, the British refused to permit passage to Chinese officials to enter Tibet through India. This, as Bell put it, 'proved a weapon of considerable force, as the Tibetans consistently prevented the entry of Chinese through their eastern borders'.[2] The Chinese were forced to agree not only to the conference taking place in India but also that all three delegations were of equal standing and had plenipotentiary powers to enter into a binding agreement.

The Simla Convention finally arrived at a compromise that was initialled by all three parties—Ivan Chen for China, Lonchen Shatra for Tibet and Henry McMahon for Britain. For most of the negotiations, McMahon played the role of mediator attempting to bridge the differences between the positions held by the Tibetan and the Chinese representatives. The British came up with the compromise solution that would divide Tibet into two parts. In

Outer Tibet that lay 'west of the historic Yangtse frontier', an area over which Lhasa had exercised unrestricted jurisdiction 'for many centuries', China would remain the nominal suzerain.

The rest of the area of Tibet that lay to the east of the frontier of Outer Tibet would be known as Inner Tibet, that is best described in the words of H.E. Richardson as 'extending in the north to the Altyn Tagh range and in the east to the old provincial borders of Kansu and Szechwan', where 'the population was mainly Tibetan by race and religious affinity'.[3] In Inner Tibet, the Chinese could appoint Chinese officials for administering the area with the proviso that the area would be 'included in the ban against the conversion of Tibet into a Chinese province'.

For India, the division of Tibet had its own implications. Lhasa being in full control over managing both its internal affairs and its dealings with India, would remove any real threat to India's security. In this case, Tibet would continue to be a buffer between China and India and Tibet's other neighbour, Russia.

The loose arrangement that was to cover Inner Tibet, however, could cause problems as a Chinese authority exercising control over that region could resume the threat that the Chao Er Feng occupation of eastern Tibet had posed to north-eastern India. The fact that the McMahon Line had been accepted by Lhasa and ratified by it, may have been considered satisfactory as a permanent preventive against the Chinese playing mischief in these areas of India. But as is often the case, history had something else in store.

For India, a matter of concern was not only that the British attempt to define a permanent solution to the Tibet–China issue had failed. The British also failed to get the Chinese to formally agree to the part of the Simla Convention that referred to the borders with India, in particular, the McMahon line that covered the Tibet–India border and stretched across the northern border of

Burma that at that time was part of British India. This failure came to, and continues to, haunt India.

This was a monumental failure on the part of McMahon and London as they refused to accept the advice of British officials on the ground who had greater understanding of Chinese behaviour and who suggested that China be pressured to agree to a side agreement endorsing the McMahon Line and the traditional borders of Tibet with India.

Not to insist on such a side agreement was a tactical blunder that could have gained traction if the British were finally ready to see Tibet as an independent and sovereign nation. However, all British interactions showed that they were still not ready to grant such a status to what they had come to see as Outer Tibet. They were hopeful till 1918 that a final tripartite settlement could be arrived at but the efforts that Eric Teichman, the British vice counsel at Tajchienlu had put in, did not fructify. By then it was clear that the Simla process had failed to settle the border and the status issues where the relations between Lhasa and Peking were concerned.

Before ending this part, we have to take note of the fact that the British continued their efforts with the Chinese to get them to accept the designation of the border with Tibet in accordance with the map of Inner Tibet that had been appended to the Simla Convention—in this regard they kept Lhasa out of the loop in the sense that it was not informed that the British were continuing to extend the lure of recognizing China's suzerainty over Tibet as long as it signed and ratified the Simla Convention. The republican Chinese continued to delay and procrastinate. This remained the case till the events of the Second World War intervened and the battle lines were drawn, with Britain, the United States and China as allies operating against the Japanese invasion of China and other parts of Asia.

The thirteenth Dalai Lama had taken all measures to see the end of Chinese interference in Tibet and, for all practical purposes, had declared Tibet an independent state. As a show of his independence and his control over Tibet's external relations, he communicated directly with the king of England. When the First World War broke out, the Dalai Lama wrote a letter to the British king that Tibet would be willing to make available a thousand troops to side with Britain and informed him that the lamas and abbots throughout Tibet were offering prayers for Britain's victory in the war.

At the end of the war, he sent a letter congratulating Britain 'on the glorious results of the Great War'.[4] This correspondence was an obvious attempt by the Dalai Lama to establish that he was the head of a sovereign state, following a protocol that presented him in the eyes of the world as such. It also showed to what degree the British presence was now welcomed by Lhasa and the kind of friendly relations that, at least in the eyes of the Tibetans, had replaced Chinese influence.

After 1912, the presence of the Chinese had all but disappeared in Tibet. Even the posting of a Chinese resident that would have followed if the Chinese had accepted the terms of the Simla Convention of 1914 along with its enclosures did not take place as the Chinese had not signed it, questioning the borders of what was designated as Inner Tibet. Perhaps the last shot in this regard was fired by the British Memorandum of August 1943. The memorandum in its intention was quite clear.

Eden Memorandum to Define Trilateral Relations

The memorandum addressed by the British foreign secretary Anthony Eden to Dr T.V. Soong, the Chinese foreign minister, dated 5 August 1943, was in response to Dr Soong querying Britain's 'attitude' towards Tibet. Eden responded, stating that 'since the Chinese Revolution of 1911, when Chinese forces were withdrawn from Tibet, Tibet has enjoyed de facto independence. She has ever since regarded herself as in practice completely autonomous and has opposed Chinese attempts to reassert control.'[5]

The Eden Memorandum went on to state that:[6]

1. The 'rock on which the Convention [Tripartite Convention between India-Tibet-China of 1914] and subsequent attempts to reach an understanding were wrecked was the question of the boundary between China and Tibet, since the Chinese Government claimed sovereignty over areas which the Tibetans claimed belonged to their autonomous jurisdiction.'
2. That in 1921 Lord Curzon as Foreign Secretary of Britain's Government informed the then Chinese Minister Dr Wellington Koo, 'that the British Government did not feel justified in withholding their recognition of the status of Tibet as an autonomous State under the suzerainty of China, and intended dealing on this basis with Tibet in the future.'
3. That in principle they were prepared to 'recognise Chinese suzerainty over Tibet but only on the understanding that Tibet is regarded as autonomous.'
4. That while India and Britain did not have any territorial ambition in Tibet they were 'interested in the maintenance of friendly relations with, and in the preservation of peaceful conditions in an area that was coterminous with the North-East frontiers of India.'

The key elements of British policy, also the policies of British India, were: the stress on complete Tibetan autonomy and a loose suzerainty over Tibet to be exercised by China but only if the latter accepted in its entirety the Simla Convention of 1914. Significantly, the British were now only offering suzerainty as a lollipop to a China that in any case was weakened considerably by a civil war that had temporarily been set aside, by the nationalist government and the communist insurgents agreeing to jointly fight the Japanese invasion that had made deep territorial inroads into China.

While pointing out that Tibet was to all intents and purposes independent, by recalling that ever since the Chinese revolution of 1911 led to the withdrawal of Chinese forces from Tibet it 'has enjoyed a de facto independence', the British continued to maintain a willingness to grant China the status of suzerain if it signed and ratified the Simla Convention. This they did without consulting Lhasa, even though they were aware that Lhasa, after China's failure to sign the Simla Convention, had withdrawn this concession to Chinese sentiment that had been forced on them by the British.

The British projected a policy where partition was seen as a solution to resolving differences since a compromise was difficult to reach. Dealing with the differing claims put forward by China and Tibet, Britain adopted a position where China's invasion would be rewarded by it gaining administrative control over eastern Tibet. This was being done in the face of the fact that the Chinese, by their invasion of eastern Tibet, had violated the time-honoured Sino-Tibetan Treaty of 821–822 that had fixed the boundaries between the two countries 'in perpetuity'.

Research carried out by Britain's experts had identified the border at 'Ch'ing-shui'. Ignoring this historical aspect borne out by the evidence that the Tibetan representative had amply demonstrated as fact, the British as mediators proposed as part of the Simla Convention the division of Tibet into two parts, permitting the Chinese an overriding position in eastern Tibet, now largely redefined as Inner Tibet. The rest of Tibet, defined as Outer Tibet, was to be the domain over which the Dalai Lama would preside unhindered. The Chinese disputed the boundary of Inner Tibet proposed by the British and as a compromise accepted by Tibet.

It was a fact that Tibet had for all intents and purposes functioned as an independent state since 1912, which was categorically endorsed by its signing and ratifying of the Simla Convention as an equal partner to the negotiations that had preceded it. It was thereafter in a treaty relationship with Britain. This status was enjoyed by it till the People's Republic of China, in total disregard of the historical relations that had existed between Buddhist Tibet and imperial China, invaded Tibet and enforced its colonial rule over it.

Notes

1. Enclosure to McMahan report on the tripartite negotiations. Quoted by Clive Christie in his article titled 'Great Britain, China and Status of Tibet, 1914–21' published in the *Journal of Modern Asian Studies*, Vol. 10, 1976.
2. *A Short History of Tibet*, H.E. Richardson, E.P. Duton & Co., 1962.
3. *A Short History of Tibet*, H.E. Richardson, E.P. Duton & Co., 1962, p. 111.
4. Stated by John Shuckburgh, political secretary at the India Office.
5. From legal materials on Tibet held by the Tibet Justice Center titled 'Memorandum of British Foreign Secretary to Chinese Foreign Ministry', (Eden Memorandum), dated 5 August 1943. Also, *China's Tibet Policy,* Dawa Norbu, Routledge, New Delhi, 2001, p. 175.
6. *Ibid.*

PART III

INDIA, TIBET AND SIKKIM

14

NEHRU AND HIS FLAWED TIBET POLICY

Anyone finding oneself at the Nathu La would have little difficulty understanding the strategic importance of Sikkim to India. The reality was that in geographical terms, Sikkim occupied the strategic heights, particularly of the Chola mountain range, that overlooked the Chumbi Valley. By being at these heights, the Indian armed forces were granted an advantage that was of prime importance to the country's security.

Gangtok was the service point in Sikkim that fed the 17th Mountain Division, both in the eastern and the northern sectors of Sikkim. The other part, south of Nathu La, had the two important passes of Jelep La and Dok La, where Dok La lay at the trijunction between the Chumbi Valley, Bhutan and Sikkim and was under the jurisdiction of the 27th Mountain Division headquartered at Kalimpong. These two mountain divisions had shown the capability to defeat any attempts by Chinese forces to dislodge them from the heights they occupied during the skirmishes of 1967.

Gangtok in 1967 was a small town of 18,000 residents, with a clear rural dimension to it. In structure, there was little to distinguish it from any small Indian hill station. The market area, with its two cinema halls, small eating joints and hotel bars, was the centre of social activity. Below the market area, overlooking the football stadium, lay the Norkhil Hotel.

Towering above Gangtok was the majesty of the Kanchenjunga and its range of mountains. To my mind, this was a mountain that in its natural beauty scored over most if not all the other Himalayan peaks. Gangtok had in the past been one of the beneficiaries of Indo-Tibetan trade across Nathu La. Given the nature of Indo-Chinese relations in the post-1962 period, all such cross-border trade had come to a standstill. It was reopened along this route after a gap of forty-four years on 6 July 2006.

The demographic plurality of Sikkim was reflected in the composition of the population of Gangtok, where the domination of the Bhutia minority in governance was obvious, as were the rumblings against this domination. The leading political theme that was kept somewhat unsuccessfully under the surface did not take long to emerge during the very first discussions that I was exposed to soon after my wife, Aruna, and I had settled down. The main issue was the lack of representative politics and the controls being exercised by the palace coterie. The role that the ruler was playing to suppress the views of the majority was at the centre of this discontent. The political office's continued shoring up of the ruler against popular will also attracted a good deal of criticism.

As I had mentioned earlier, my first real initiation into the strategic dimension of Sikkim was the briefing on the 1967 skirmishes by Major General Sagat Singh. That briefing had roused my interest in looking into Tibet and the reason why the British wanted it as a buffer between India and Central Asia and China. It was a position that independent India had inherited in 1947 along with all the extra-territorial rights that the British had acquired as a result of the several conventions and trade agreements that they had signed with Tibet and imperial China, and the memoranda that had been served by it subsequently on republican China. The political office at that time had gathered all the papers dealing with Tibet, Sikkim and Bhutan from the days of the first political officer, John Claude White.

These archival papers opened up for me the various approaches to the negotiations that took place in Simla from 1913 to 1914 when the convention was initialled by all three parties. It gave me a glimpse into the ratification that took place between McMahon and the Tibetan Lonchen Shatra about the border between Tibet and India and the various attempts to get the Chinese to ratify the arrangements. These archives also helped me realize that India's security had been threatened not just after the Chinese occupation of Tibet in 1950, but earlier when the Chinese had gained control over Tibet soon after the signing of the Anglo-Chinese Convention of 1906.

The British had turned a blind eye to the brutality that the Chinese had let loose on Tibet till the time the Chinese interference had come to pose a direct threat to the security of India, not only along the borders of the Cis-Himalayan states but also India's north-eastern tribal areas. It was this knowledge that set me on the path of investigating where Sikkim stood in the thick of things concerning India, Tibet and Maoist China.

Tussle over Tibet

After 1919, for all practical purposes, the British treated Tibet as an independent nation. The Eden Memorandum of 1943 made the British position quite clear, particularly as it served as an official reply that refused to accept the contention of the nationalist government of China—that Tibet was a Chinese colony and thus seeking that Britain keep away from interfering as a third party in affairs that were primarily to be settled by internal dialogue between the Tibetans and their Chinese masters.

Chiang Kai-shek was attempting to get the British to accept that China was not the suzerain but the sovereign of Tibet. The Eden Memorandum unambiguously stated that Tibet was 'de facto independent'. Additionally, Anthony Eden and Leopold Amery, the secretaries of state for India and Burma (1940–45), had authored in 1943 for Britain's war Cabinet a proposal to counter Chinese moves. They mentioned that either Britain could withdraw its recognition of Chinese suzerainty over Tibet or let the matter rest for now. While mentioning that China did not even have a nominal role to play in Tibet, they felt that as a counter to the expanding Japanese presence, it was convenient to maintain the fiction of Chinese suzerainty over Tibet.

However, what neither the Eden Memorandum nor the Eden–Amery note took cognisance of was the deceitful position adopted by both Yuan Shikai and Chiang Kai-shek in contradiction to Sun Yat-sen, the first leader of the Kuomintang and the provisional first president of the Republic of China. According to Sun Yat-sen, all territories outside Han China should have the right to self-determination in respect to the relationship they would like to have with republican China. Given the nature of the developments in Tibet at that time, any act to implement what Sun had formulated would have seen Tibet opt for independence.

Charles Bell, while on his mission to Lhasa, had pointed out the pitfalls of British policy of sitting on the fence on the Tibet–China issue and in the process denying the promised military support pledged to Lhasa that would be used to strengthen the Tibetan armed forces, enabling them to defend themselves against any aggression launched by China. He had also pointed out that the Dalai Lama might seek the support of the Japanese, as had been done by the Mongols, a move that would create a problem for India's northern borders with Tibet as they would 'fall under Japanese, as well as under Chinese influence'. He added that given these developments, India would 'no longer have what is perhaps the best land frontier in the world, the lofty plateau of Northern Tibet … this inhospitable table-land is the real barrier of India to the north'.[1]

Bell was making the point that should have served as a warning that it was against India's strategic and security interests for Tibet to be overtaken by any power that would change its status as a buffer state between India and the countries beyond Tibet's northern, eastern or western borders. This warning was not hidden from Delhi and should have been part of the official discourse on independent India's foreign policy.

Unfortunately, India's first prime minister, Jawaharlal Nehru, was looking on China and the part he expected it to play in his Asia Vision. His appreciation for China was reflected in the joint India–China declaration that was issued at Brussels in February 1927 at the International Congress against Colonial Oppression and Imperialism. Drafted by Nehru, it bore 'the marks of an outlook which was to remain unchanged for over thirty years. Friendship with China was the core of his pan-Asian feeling.'[2]

Nehru looked upon India's ties with China in the colonial context, suggesting that the 'close cultural ties between the peoples of India and China for over three thousand years', had been forced apart by the actions of Britain. The resolution called upon the two sides to take on Britain and mentioned that India and China 'must now resume the ancient personal, cultural and political relations between the two peoples. British Imperialism which in the past has kept us apart and done us so much injury, is now the very force that is uniting us in a common endeavour to overthrow it.'

Call to 'Common Endeavour'

This call to a 'common endeavour' encouraged the nationalist Chinese foreign minister T.V. Soong to suggest to Anthony Eden that Britain should refrain from interfering in Tibet that was China's colony and in return the Chinese would refrain from interfering in Britain's colony, India. The Chinese were trying to use the example of colonialism to attain their objective of taking over Tibet and making it an integral part of China. Second, they were indicating that India would have a secondary position in Asia where China would be the main player. This was something that appeared not to have roused any hackles on the part of the Indian nationalist leadership either, as they were probably unaware of the discussions that took place between the British and Chinese foreign ministers. It was also possible that Nehru, heading the interim government in 1946, had not consulted Olaf Caroe, who was then foreign secretary and had a clear idea of the Tibet–China situation and the importance to India of a Tibet outside direct Chinese control.

The first glimpse of how an independent India would look on Tibet and the claims on it that were being put forward by China occurred at the informal Asian Relations Conference hosted by the Indian Council of World Affairs at New Delhi in April 1947. It had been called at the behest of the Nehru-led interim government of India. As S. Gopal describes it in his biography of Nehru, 'It was to be a nonofficial conference of representative of all shades of opinion in the countries of Asia (plus Egypt).'[3]

When President Chiang Kai-shek of China objected to the presence of Tibet as a separate delegation from the Chinese, he was persuaded that it was an informal conference and Tibet was being invited as a neighbour. It was referred to as such in Nehru's inaugural statement, in which he mentioned that 'from our neighbours Afghanistan, Tibet, Nepal, Bhutan, Burma and Ceylon to whom we look especially for cooperation and close and friendly intercourse'.[4]

Referring to China, Nehru went out of his way to extend recognition to it by stating, 'We welcome you delegates and representatives from China, that great country to which Asia owes so much and from which so much is expected.' Nehru was making it clear that he expected India and China to work together to restore Asia to its rightful place within the post-war global order.

What Nehru was ignoring was that the Chinese delegation, which had representatives of both the nationalist government and the Chinese Communist Party (CCP), had unitedly maintained that Tibet was a part of China. This was a message that presented danger to free India's security and should have led to the adoption of a Tibet policy recognizing the importance of Tibet as an independent country to India's security.

By giving in to the Chinese, India was ignoring the ground reality that Tibet, since 1912, had been de facto an independent country and de jure fully autonomous. It had kept the Chinese out, and the British had held, ever since 1919, that unless the Chinese accepted the terms of the Simla Convention of 1914 on the borders with Tibet, Britain would not recognize China as having even nominal status as Tibet's suzerain.

The message that Nehru seemed to have sent out, giving in to Chinese pressure, was that he was willing to compromise on India's strategic interests at the altar of his larger Asia vision. His attitude on Tibet probably contributed to the misunderstanding that Chiang Kai-shek harboured that independent India would accept Tibet as an integral part of China.

Notes

1. *Tibet: Past and Present,* Charles Bell, Motilal Banarsidass, New Delhi, 2000.
2. *Jawaharlal Nehru: A Biography,* Volume I, S. Gopal, Oxford University Press, 1975, p. 102.
3. *Ibid.*
4. *Ibid.*

15

TIBET'S IMPORTANCE TO PEACE ON INDIA'S FRONTIERS

Olaf Caroe was foreign secretary to the British government of India during the Second World War. In his assessment, in the long term, China was 'a potential great power ... sorely tried, in economic chaos and facing internal revolution, yet inclined to arrogance and always purposeful in her policies'.[1] Caroe in a sense, like Nehru, anticipated that China would be authoritarian, adding to it his judgement that it would also display 'some of Japan's ambitions'. This was said in 1944, reflecting the fact that both he and the Viceroy's Study Group (set up by Olaf Caroe to study the strategic imperatives that confronted India as it moved towards independence) understood the strategic importance of Afghanistan and Tibet as buffer states to undivided India.

The Tibet issue, in particular, had come to carry added weight in the discussion on India's strategic interests. These assessments were available to the successor government, after independence, and should have been considered for the formulation of the policy that independent India adopted on Tibet. Unfortunately, the emotional attachment to anti-colonialism seemed to have overcome strategic realities of the situation that India would be confronted with if the rights it inherited in Tibet were not openly acknowledged as assets that granted it a bargaining leverage.

W. Kirk in his study, 'The Inner Asian Frontier of India', was being prescient when he contended, 'The assumption of responsibility for a former imperial frontier has always been one of the most difficult tasks that a successor state can be required to perform.' He pointed out, 'The successor state has in many instances been born in opposition to the imperial power and in the early stages of its independence turns away from things imperial.'

This analysis could be applied without any reservation to the manner in which Nehru considered Tibet within the tools of foreign policy that he formulated for a newly independent India. As he said at the inauguration of the Asian Relations Conference in New Delhi on 23 March 1947, 'We propose to stand on our own feet and to cooperate with all others who are prepared to cooperate with us. We do not intend to be the play-things of others.'[2]

'The Strong Always Rule the Weak'

At the time of this conference, Nehru was leading an interim government, but the foreign policy plank had already been thought out, and the issue of frontiers should have been decided upon based on a careful reading of the security imperatives that were dictated by geostrategic factors. This was the reality of the frontiers that Nehru had to take into account and it was essential that neither his policy of non-alignment and the Asia Vision nor his anti-colonial emotionalism, should have overlooked the importance that lay in managing India's frontiers with those countries.

Regrettably, Nehru permitted sentiment to overshadow reality, where he refused to take into account the nature and character of Chinese thought, best illustrated by a quote of a Chinese intellectual cited by Joseph R. Levenson, 'In the world there is only power—there is no other force. That the strong always rule the weak is in truth the first universal rule of nature.'[3] This is a philosophy that Mao Tse Tung projected by coining the slogan, 'Political power grows out of the barrel of a gun.'

While Nehru was intellectually smart, and almost prescient in his judgement of the directions that a people and its leaders would take, he tended often to let emotion override his intellect. Nehru had read the prevailing situation in China accurately when he visited it in 1939. While establishing a warm and close friendship with Chiang Kai-shek and his wife, he concluded that the Communist Party and its seasoned warriors would come to dominate China. He even foresaw that Chinese nationalism would drive its relationship with Soviet Russia where it was unlikely that Mao would permit the Soviets to dominate Chinese policy.

In September 1946, Nehru had made it clear that non-alignment was the tool that would enable India 'to keep away from power politics of groups, aligned against one another, which have led to world wars in the past and which may again lead to disasters on an even vaster scale'. The other aspect that he stressed was that India was 'particularly interested in the emancipation of colonial and dependent countries and peoples'. While non-alignment was an enlightened foreign policy tool, it was crucial to distinguish between what satisfied India's interests, particularly its security, and what did not, including establishing arrangements that met India's strategic needs. Tibet under Chinese domination had to be avoided and all the leading countries of the West should have been canvassed to contain communist China's ambitions over Tibet.

Till 1952–53 the belief in China was that 'the newly independent Asian states were all puppets of the West'. This was reflected in a Chinese official publication describing Nehru as, 'a rebel against movement for national independence, a blackguard who undermines the progress of the people's liberation movement, a loyal slave of imperialism'. Elsewhere, he was also referred to as a running dog of imperialism. These and similar negative descriptions of Nehru and India did not change Nehru's commitment to his Asia Vision where he expected China to take a leading position along with India.[4]

Understandably, the manner in which Nehru regarded India's relationship with Tibet after independence could not be kept segregated from the way Nehru looked upon the Cold War–driven world and his Asia Vision. On 15 August 1947, independent India inherited the rights and obligations of the Simla Convention of 1914, signed by both the British and the Tibetan plenipotentiaries. Despite Nehru's anti-colonial leanings, he did not renounce these inherited rights. One of the main elements was the transfer of extraterritorial rights that British India had held in Tibet. Among these was the seamless transfer of the British legation in Lhasa to become the Indian legation with the Indian tricolour replacing the Union Jack.

These were rights that obviously could be modified in the context of the new imperatives that would guide independent India's relations with its neighbouring countries as well as the overarching elements that would come to determine the directions that India's foreign policy would adopt as it set out on its journey as part of the global community of free nations. Within this, India would need to defend its interests, particularly the frontiers, that it had inherited. India was a newly constituted entity that, for the first time in its history, could be defined as a nation with settled frontiers, as the Republic of India.

This nation from its very inception was faced with a hostile Pakistan that not only created problems along India's west and north-west, in the geographical construct of East Pakistan, it projected a threat to the narrow Siliguri Corridor that connected the rest of India to its north-east. The security threat to the Siliguri Corridor from East Pakistan had to be factored into defence arrangements by the Government of India. Not surprisingly, the manner in which Pakistan carried its intent to force the state of Jammu and Kashmir to accede to it resulted in a concentration of India's defence mechanisms on Pakistan. During the period defined by the developments of 1947–48, there was little attention being paid, except in purely diplomatic terms, to dealings with Tibet.

'A Palm with Five Fingers'

In the meanwhile, relations between Tibet and China were coming to a head. Lhasa, in a formal demarche, sought the immediate vacation of territories in eastern Tibet that were still under Chinese occupation. The demarche was hand-delivered to the foreign ministry of the nationalist government in Peking and clearly spoke to the fact that Tibet was addressing China as an equal. The Chinese told the Tibetan delegation that such matters lay in the domain of China's national assembly and the Tibetan delegation should participate in its discussion to convey their concerns. The Tibetans, in a display of true naiveté, fell into this trap. The Chinese of course did not address the concern that lay behind the Tibetan demarche. They tried instead to portray that the Tibetans had attended the national assembly as Tibet was part of China. These developments were not hidden from India, which did not grant to them the serious attention they deserved.

As the Maoist forces were taking over China, Lhasa, worried over the communist takeover and the threat that it posed to Tibet, expelled the Chinese mission along with some Chinese traders who they felt were committing acts against the interests of Tibet. Acknowledging India as the successor to the British, Lhasa looked to India to come to its aid against an aggressive Chinese regime, seeking the supply of military equipment and training of its defence forces.

By early 1950, communist China was calling for the 'liberation' of states on its periphery, like Tibet, which they were claiming were an integral part of China. This should have come as a warning to the Indian government as the possibility of the occupation of Tibet had now resurfaced and the threat to the security and integrity of India that the Chinese had posed during their occupation of Tibet, post the signing of the Anglo-Chinese Convention of 1906, was again rearing its ugly head.

India should at this stage have taken into account that if China occupied Tibet, there would no longer be a buffer state between India and China. Delhi should have also taken into account the moves that the Chinese had made in the period 1910–11 on the tribal areas of Assam, now designated as the North-East Frontier Agency (NEFA), that lay well to the south of the Himalayan watershed covered by the 1914 McMahon Line that the Chinese had not endorsed. Clearly, a Chinese occupation of Tibet would be against India's territorial interests.

Mao had called Tibet a palm with five fingers—Ladakh, Nepal, Sikkim, Bhutan and the Assam tribal areas (NEFA). Claiming that if Tibet, the 'palm', was an integral part of China, its five fingers—areas that were vassals of Tibet—were thus automatically parts of China. This made it quite clear that when China occupied Tibet, it would once again make a play for the states of Nepal, Bhutan and

Sikkim, along with NEFA. This meant that the now-Indian states of Ladakh and NEFA were under threat. Delhi had to work out a plan to meet and counter Chinese threats that were a reaffirmation of a policy that had been earlier followed during the Chinese occupation of Tibet from 1907–11. Unfortunately, this did not happen.

Olaf Caroe's Warning Note

'Boundaries … as such they are of solid value so long as they are made strong enough and secure enough to prevent their violation and infringements.'[5]

'The crux of the Sino-Indian strategic rivalry is this; if the Chinese power elite consider Tibet to be strategically important to China, the Indian counterparts think it is equally vital to Indian national security.'[6]

As the independence of Tibet came under serious threat, Prime Minister Nehru and the Indian government should have given detailed thought to the policy that the outgoing British had adopted on Tibet in the context of its importance to India's security. The Indian foreign office headed by Sir Olaf Caroe had examined the issue of Tibet as a buffer state essential to the security of India's northern borders.

Caroe's thinking on the subject was detailed in a note entitled 'The Policy towards Tibet' addressed to the secretary of the external department, India Office, dated 19 September 1945. In it, Caroe covered the Tibet issue from the strategic and security angles, and outlined its importance to India in maintaining the 'general policy of support for Tibetan autonomy'. He drew attention to the measures undertaken to consolidate administrative controls within the areas delineated by the McMahon Line.

The main thrust of the note was the importance of Tibet as a buffer state, a strategic element in keeping China away from India's borders. He drew London's attention to the threat to India's security by China when it came to occupy Tibet during 1906–11, including its claims to Nepal and Bhutan as China's vassals. These claims had continued to be made by the Chinese even after the collapse of the Manchu empire.

Caroe drew attention to 'Chinese ambitions in tribal areas of Assam' being revealed 'by their maps that claim "China"—not as Tibet—territory stretching almost as far as the Brahmaputra in the plain of Assam'. Caroe reiterated that Tibet, for all practical purposes, had acted as an independent state since 1912, 'and has conducted such relations as it had with foreign countries without the mediation of the Chinese Government'. In the case of Tibet, the application of the term 'suzerainty' needed to be 'interpreted with regard to the factual position … On this criterion, Chinese suzerainty over Tibet since 1912 has been nominal since it has involved the exercise by the Chinese Government *of no control* over either the internal affairs or the external relations of Tibet [emphasis added].'

Caroe's note clearly enunciated the factors that needed to be taken into account:[7]

1. The maintenance of the Tibetan buffer is a matter of utmost importance for India both from the point of view of defense and in the interests of India's internal administration.
2. Tibet should enjoy internal autonomy and the right to conduct direct foreign relations, recognising Chinese suzerainty by more or less ceremonial formalities.
3. Support for Tibetan autonomy should be by the strongest and most outspoken diplomatic pressure to be increased

at the present time ... by publicity for the realities of Tibet's position over the last 33 years, and by the supply of munitions and equipment if sought by the Tibetan Government.

4. There may be advantage in bringing the position of Tibet before the United nations, but it is realized that the Chinese may be able to render such a course ineffective ...

Caroe's note on Tibet included the recommendations of the war department after it had 'reviewed the interests' of the Indian government in Tibet 'from the point of view of defense'. His note made it clear that whatever may have been the understanding of 'the physical difficulties of Tibet's mountains and high altitude plateau have given India a valuable buffer against aggression. This however cannot be regarded as immutable.' The administration was being warned that technology had reduced the effectiveness of the Himalayas as a physical buffer, making it all the 'more important to maintain as far as possible a political buffer'. The war office note was a strong endorsement of the need to keep an autonomous Tibet as a physical and political buffer which made it clear that everything possible should be done to prevent a 'natural defensive barrier to pass under the control of any potentially hostile power'.

The war office pointed out that 'from the military point of view that the autonomy of Tibet should be maintained and potential aggressors kept at a distance for as long as possible'. The final suggestion, also endorsed by Caroe and the British Indian government, was, 'Tibetan autonomy can best be maintained by strong diplomatic support coupled with the provision of such arms and ammunition as the Tibetans may ask us to supply.'

Intimations of Colonization

All this material was available and should have provided the incoming Indian government with a well worked out brief on the implications of any other power breaching Tibet's borders. In this context, India should have seen the Chinese behaviour on Tibet's presence at the Asian Relations Conference as a warning sign. That was when India should have pointed out that it considered Tibet to be an independent state of strategic importance and that it would extend the same diplomatic recognition to Tibet as it would to the Republic of China.

This, of course, was not the route Nehru took and the first shots of ambiguity in thinking over Tibet had been fired as Nehru gave in to Chinese demands. Nehru should have kept in mind the Simla Convention of 1914 where the Chinese had accepted the negotiations on a triangular basis among equals. Unfortunately, Nehru allowed his emotional attachment to his Asia Vision and anti-colonialism to override the high priority that he needed to grant to the Indo-Tibetan relationship to counter the possibility of a Chinese occupation.

Persisting in the belief that a democratic India and a communist China could deal with each other in a spirit of cooperation and understanding, where India could influence the policy that PRC would adopt on Tibet, was patently delusional. In fact, S. Gopal in his biography on Nehru bluntly states, 'Nehru's assessment of China's attitude to India was also naïve.'

Nehru failed to take into account Caroe's observation on Chinese ambitions where he said that China 'makes no secret of its ambitions to reassert its sway over its former territories, it recalls that it claimed suzerainty over Nepal and Burma'. In what was a prediction, that has since been borne out as fact, Caroe mentioned that once China 're-established control over Tibet and the Yunnan Province', it would look southwards towards the 'Indian Ocean by way of Burma'. There was then the warning that 'the shrinkage of distance and the opening of land and air routes between Bengal and Yunnan may well turn the attention of the Chinese imperialists to new and dangerous paths'.[8]

Initially, due to what was a tactical mistake by Lhasa, India was faced by a demand for the return of Tibetan territory that the former claimed had been occupied by British India. Subsequently, there was a formal announcement by Lhasa accepting that the relationship they had with the British was now transferred to the successor Government of India. Lhasa had evidently reversed its position as it came to realize that communist China posed a threat to its independence, while hoping that an Indian involvement would help in containing China's ambitions.

The main issue of concern for India should have been the security threat that a Chinese occupation of Tibet posed. The threat that China posed to India when it assumed full administrative control over Tibet in the 1907–11 period should have been carefully examined along with the map it had produced to claim as its own Indian territories in the North-east.

There was no lack of information available to Delhi on the manner in which the Chinese had behaved towards India and its territorial and Cis-Himalayan interests during that period, making it more than clear that a Chinese occupation of Tibet would project a threat to India's territorial integrity. India should have taken steps to negotiate Tibet's adherence to the Simla Convention of 1914, extended diplomatic recognition to Tibet as an independent country and supported its move to become a member of the United Nations.

There was little doubt that Maoist China was acting as an imperial power bent on colonizing Tibet. This should have roused Nehru's anti-colonial sentiments. Instead, he permitted his romantic engagement with China and its civilization to overtake the adoption of a pragmatic policy on Tibet.

Notes

1. *The Future of the Great Game*, Peter John Brobst, University of Argon Press, 2005, p. 60.
2. Nehru at the inaugural address on 23 March 1947 to the Asian Relations Conference called by the Indian Council of World Affairs in New Delhi.
3. 'The Problem of Intellectual Continuity', *Confucian China and its Modern Fate*, Volume One, Joseph R. Levenson, Routledge, 2016.
4. Most of this was reflected in Communist China's newspapers at that time. It is also covered in *Jawaharlal Nehru: A Biography*, Volume II, S. Gopal, Oxford University Press, 1975. He quotes Nehru's letter to President Soekarno of Indonesia on page 64. This also appears in reports from the Indian Mission in China.
5. T.H. Holdich as the superintendent of Frontier Surveys in British India.
6. Observation by Dawa Norbu quoted by Tsering Topgyal in his study 'Chartering the Tibet Issue in the Sino-Indian Border Dispute'.
7. The summing up is at the end of Sir Olaf Caroe's note, 'The Policy towards Tibet', dated 19 September 1945.
8. A note from Sir Olaf Caroe, foreign secretary to the Government of India, on the policy towards Tibet, addressed to the secretary, external department, India Office, London, dated 19 September 1945.

16

INDEPENDENT INDIA AND SIKKIM

Nehru had taken upon himself the responsibility of dealing with the Himalayan states of Bhutan, Nepal and Sikkim in 1947, placing all three outside the ambit of India's home ministry and its adjunct, the ministry of states. Here, a clear anomaly could be noted. Unlike Nepal and Bhutan, Sikkim had for all practical purposes been a part of the federated states of India and, in 1922, had become a member of the Chamber of Princes.

By keeping it out of the ambit of the ministry of states, Nehru had taken the position that Sikkim would be treated as a state outside India. In the initial period after independence, India had worked out standstill agreements with all three Himalayan states maintaining that existing treaty relations that they had with British India would remain in place till new treaties were signed between them and independent India.

What India had to take into account was that it was Sikkim that was geographically located on the crossroads across the Himalayan watershed that provided easy access to the trade marts in Tibet and the Lhasa offices. Apart from the Gangtok–Nathu La link to the Chumbi Valley that connected India to Yatung and Phari, there was also the route from Gangtok via northern Sikkim that linked it to Khamba Jong and Gyantse. The other route of significance was the one that linked Darjeeling, via Kalimpong and Jelep La, to the Chumbi Valley and the trade marts of Yatung and Gyantse.

Himalayan Dilemma

After independence, it did not take long for the geostrategic importance of Sikkim and its communication links to India to sink in. At this stage, Delhi was confronted by the demands of the Sikkim State Congress, seeking Sikkim's merger with India, paralleling the arrangements that India was signing with the Indian princely states.

This was also the time when treaties were being negotiated and signed with Nepal and Bhutan, while negotiations with Sikkim were put on the backburner. The Indian government had before it the extensive analysis that had been made by British Indian officials, including the very sobering assessment by Charles Bell in 1909 that the Chinese harboured a design to colonize not only eastern Tibet but also the more fertile Bhutan and the tribal belt of Assam. Both the Caroe notes and the note by Bell referred to the Chinese commissioner Chang, when he took charge at Lhasa in 1907, claiming that China, Tibet, Nepal, Sikkim and Bhutan formed a unity as a blending of 'five colours'.

To substantiate the Chinese design, Chang had alluded to Nepal, Bhutan and Sikkim 'as the molar teeth lying side by side in a man's mouth'.[1] It was this threat that had finally led the British to negotiate a fresh treaty with Bhutan in 1910, 'to place her foreign relations under the British Government' as well as to extend the administrative domain over the Assam tribal belt.

Chinese motives had been spelt out, making it imperative that the Indian government take this threat seriously and, in turn, ensure that Nepal, Sikkim and Bhutan lay in India's area of influence.

The first treaty to be negotiated and signed was between India and Bhutan on 8 August 1949, which was ratified by both sides towards the end of September, becoming effective on 22 September 1949. Its title reflected the nature of the relations between two friendly nations—'Treaty of Perpetual Peace and Friendship'. In principle, it followed the main provisions of the Treaty of 1910, with India being substituted for Britain in the text:[2]

1. Non-interference in the internal affairs of Bhutan,
2. Bhutan to 'be guided by the advice of the British Government in regards to its external affairs,'
3. Payment of an annual allowance to the Government of Bhutan.

This treaty was replaced by a new treaty in 2007 that reflected the changed circumstances once Bhutan became, with Indian collaboration, a member of the United Nations.

The Indo-Nepal Treaty was signed on 31 July 1950. It formalized the special relations between the two countries, covering freedom of movement, extending reciprocal rights of national treatment, residence and participation in economic activities. In another special feature, the two countries undertook to 'inform each other of any serious friction or misunderstanding with any neighbouring state likely to cause any breach in the friendly relations subsisting between the two Governments'. This provision took into account the Chinese moves on Tibet.[3]

In the case of Sikkim, two factors had to be taken into account. The first was the insistence by Maharaja Kumar Palden Thondup Namgyal that Sikkim was not legally an Indian princely state. There was a prevailing contradiction in the manner in which the British treated Sikkim. By treaty, it was a protectorate; by action, it was a federated Indian state. The British political officer in Gangtok functioned, for all practical purposes, as the resident, typical of an Indian princely state during British rule.

British India had devised a set of norms determining the manner in which they dealt with the Indian princely states. On top were the independent states managed by the prince; second were those where the prince was incompetent, a minor and so on, and appointed a minister to manage the state; and third were 'the residentials', where a British political functionary in person, or by officers of his selection, managed the territory of the prince. Sikkim fell in the third category and was patently seen by the British as an Indian princely state.

Under the Government of India Act of 1935, Sikkim was treated as any other Indian state and the political officers were enabled to continue to conduct Sikkim's political and administrative affairs. However, in contradiction to this, the state continued to be placed under the political department of the secretary of state for India that in a sense differentiated it from the other princely states.

To make this contradiction even more apparent, Sikkim, as a member of the Chamber of Princes, had participated in the discussions that the Chamber's representatives had with the Indian government before the enactment of the Government of India Act of 1935. This implied that Sikkim had accepted that it was on par with any other Indian state. As a result, in tandem with its protocolar status, Sikkim was allocated a fifteen-gun salute.

It was obvious that the British had created a degree of confusion on the real status of Sikkim. The representations that were made by its ruler in this regard to the Government of India led Jawaharlal Nehru to move a special resolution in the Constituent Assembly, stating that 'this Assembly resolves that the committee to confer with the negotiating committee set up by the Chamber of Princes and with the representatives of the Indian States for certain specified purposes shall in addition have power to confer with such persons as the committee thinks fit for the purpose of examining the special problem of Bhutan and Sikkim and to report to the Assembly the result of such examination'.[4]

The implication of this resolution was that Bhutan and Sikkim, whatever may have been the position they were granted during the British period, were now to be looked upon by independent India as Himalayan states that it had a special relationship with.

In a sense, Nehru was granting credence to the position articulated by A.J. Hopkinson, who was the political officer in Gangtok at the time of the visit of the Cabinet Mission to India. He had pointed out that the 'Paramountcy Memorandum failed to take into account the special position that Sikkim occupied because of its being surrounded on three sides by foreign territory and as such fell in a special category.'[5]

Political Ferment in Sikkim

In addition, there was the emergence of political parties in Sikkim that were influenced by the political developments in India. As acknowledged by Sunanda K. Datta-Ray,[6] political activity had emerged in Sikkim in 1945 and coalesced into the emergence of a combined political party—the Sikkim State Congress (SSC)—on 7 December 1947. The three independent parties that came together were the Praja Sudharak Samaj led by Tashi Tshering, Praja Samalen led by Gobardhan Pradhan and the Praja Mandal led by Kazi Lhendup Dorji Khangsarpa.

Tashi Tshering was elected the leader of the new party. On 8 December 1947, he led a delegation to meet Maharaja Tashi Namgyal and presented to him a three-point memorandum that had the following demands:

- Abolition of landlordism
- Formation of an interim government with the objective of putting in place democratic governance
- Accession of Sikkim to the Union of India

To counter these moves by the SSC, Maharaja Kumar Palden Thondup manipulated the formation of what was in effect the 'Kings Party'—the Sikkim National Party (SNP), mainly comprising the Bhutia elite with some Lepcha and token Nepali representatives. Following Palden Thondup's lead, the SNP opposed the SSC's proposals, particularly on the question of merging with India, mentioning that Sikkim's relations were based on a political arrangement between two independent countries.

The SNP put across the argument that Sikkim in historical, cultural and religious terms was closer to Bhutan and Tibet than it was to India. This was a position that had been scripted by the Maharaja Kumar and should have alerted the Indian government to his ambitions on the status of his kingdom that would, in time, create pressures that would impact Sikkim's political stability. Palden Thondup was, of course, disregarding the fact that it was Sikkim's relationship with British India (now assumed by independent India) that had led to the restoration of its territories that Nepal and Bhutan had seized from it.

Interestingly, before the standstill agreement had been signed, the ministry of states in keeping with the manner in which it was approaching all Indian princely states, presented the Maharaja of Sikkim with the Instrument of Accession, seeking his signature. Sikkim protested this move and Delhi acceded to Sikkim's request, offering instead a standstill agreement. This was happening while there were enough indications that the political situation in Sikkim was fragile.

Palden Thondup, in a shrewd move to try and neutralize the opposition that the SSC represented, decided to nominate three of its members to serve as secretaries to the Government of Sikkim. He then used the influence of pelf and position to gain their confidence and had them convey to the SSC leadership, at a meeting in June 1948, that after reviewing the requisite state papers, these three members had arrived at the consensus that Sikkim should remain independent. They were, however, unable to produce the concerned papers to back up their position and it was obvious that they had identified themselves with the administration and were no longer representing the interests of the SSC.

Thereafter, Tashi Tshering, as president of the SSC, accompanied by general secretary Chandra Das Rai, visited Delhi and called on Prime Minister Nehru, presenting him with the three-point agenda. Nehru requested them not to press for the accession of Sikkim to India, as negotiations towards the signing of a treaty were underway. On the issues of democracy and abolition of landlordism, he gave an assurance that this paralleled India's thinking and he would support its implementation in Sikkim. By the end of that meeting, he had bought time.

Eventually, however, the political party would be let down by India on all three points after the signing of the 1950 treaty with Sikkim. Nehru's approach to the three Himalayan kingdoms and Tibet was largely in a political context, driven by his commitment to anti-colonialism. In the case of Sikkim, this attitude led to the Indian government supporting Palden Thondup's authoritarian approach to internal affairs. Anti-colonialism had defeated the aspirations of the people of Sikkim to a democratic form of governance.

The political situation in Gangtok soon worsened as the SSC resorted to satyagraha and invoked Mahatma Gandhi to force a decision on the abolition of landlordism and the formation of a democratic government. Its leaders were arrested and were released only after the intervention of Political Officer Harishwar Dayal. To bring about an amicable settlement, the political officer suggested fresh negotiations between the SSC leadership and the Maharaja Kumar–dominated Sikkim durbar. With Palden Thondup stubbornly adhering to his position, the talks failed. The SSC now began a second satyagraha, forcing the ruler and his family to seek shelter at the political officer's residence, and the Indian army had to intervene to restore law and order.

Maharaja Tashi Namgyal finally accepted Harishwar Dayal's advice and agreed to install a five-member 'interim government'. It would include two members nominated by the durbar and three by the SSC. Tashi Tshering, along with Dimik Singh Lepcha and Chandra Das Rai, as well as the two durbar nominees, Dorji Dadul and Reshmi Prasad Alley, formed the interim government on 9 May 1949. Tashi Tshering was elected prime minister.

Immediately, problems arose, with the Cabinet demanding full powers to administer the country, while Maharaja Kumar ensured that all administrative powers and controls were exercised by him as head of the executive authority. The real problem was that the ruler Maharaja Tashi Namgyal had for all practical purposes recused himself from administering the country and it was his son, Palden Thondup as Maharaja Kumar, who was wielding authority.

Tashi Namgyal had been praised by the British for his handling of complex domestic issues and he had been able to carry his people along with him. Palden Thondup, in contrast, was immature and unable to assess the value of compromise as a means to finding solutions to the SSC's political demands which represented the complex demography of the state. His attitude was one that held no sympathy for the wishes of a majority of the population, creating conditions of chaos in the process. However, he was cunning enough to suggest that he was taking actions to prevent any challenge to India's presence in Sikkim by an irresponsible political party.

As the differences appeared irreconcilable, the ruler, Tashi Namgyal, realized that an impasse had been reached. He followed what had been the practice from the days of Claude White, and sought the intervention of the political officer and requested him to take over the state's administration. The Indian government dispatched minister B.V. Keskar to examine the situation, who informed Delhi that there was no alternative to the political officer taking over. It was also decided that an Indian civil servant with the necessary administrative experience be appointed as dewan to manage the state. J.S. Lall took charge of the administration from Harishwar Dayal on 11 August 1949.

The first experiment at democratic rule in Sikkim had failed in less than a month, with India having to take on the responsibility of bringing political peace to Sikkim. Significantly, the Indian army had to be summoned to ensure the safety of the ruler and his family and to restore law and order that the durbar managed by Palden Thondup had failed to maintain.

It is noteworthy that the Indian intervention had not been in support of the people, who in their majority had backed the SSC. It had been to safeguard the interests of the ruler whose son was already well on the road to force his will on the people and serve his own ambitions of seeking a reduction of Indian presence in Sikkim. He felt this would create conditions that would force India to extend to him the same position that India had accorded to the ruler of Bhutan.

Harishwar Dayal, according to the records that I saw at the political office, did have in mind that the dewan, after restoring order, would help create a constitutional system where the state would be administered by a council of ministers, with the ruler's role reduced to the status of a constitutional monarch.

Dayal had obviously failed to gauge the ambitions that Palden Thondup harboured. At least till 1971, Delhi would assume that India's strategic interests would be better served with domestic power in Gangtok being held by the ruler. As India looked on and did nothing to support the promise that Nehru had made to the SSC, Palden Thondup came up with an ill-judged political formula. He forced through an arrangement where representation to the legislature would be of equal numbers representing the Nepali majority and the Bhutia–Lepcha minority, equating the minority 20 per cent of the population with the majority 75 per cent.

The unfortunate fact was that the Indian government colluded with the ruler under the delusion that a known devil was easier to deal with than the unknown element of popular will. This remained the case until large-scale political instability in Sikkim prompted the then prime minister of India, Indira Gandhi, to overrule any opposition to Sikkim's merger with India. The international opposition to this move, not unsurprisingly, came from the People's Republic of China and Pakistan.

Indo-Sikkim Treaty, 1950

When the treaty with Bhutan was signed in early August 1949, the situation in China was still unclear. The nationalist forces were facing defeat but the civil war was still on. Eventually, on 1 October 1949, the People's Republic of China came into being. A month earlier, in September 1949, the Chinese Communist Party (CCP) had proclaimed its policy of incorporating Tibet, Taiwan, Hainan Island and the Pescadores Islands as part of the forthcoming PRC. The Chinese however were aware that Tibet would resist such an incorporation. To force Tibet to the negotiating table, Mao ordered the People's Liberation Army (PLA) to forcibly occupy Chamdo in eastern Tibet. This carried a direct threat to India's security and needed to be countered.

The treaty India signed with Nepal on 31 July 1950 did show the impact of the developments in the neighbourhood. The wording of Article 2 of the treaty, where the two sides undertook to 'inform each other of any serious friction or misunderstanding with any neighbouring State likely to cause any breach in the friendly relations subsisting between the two Governments', was an indication of this. It was obvious that the 'friction or misunderstanding' was a reference to Tibet and the Chinese intent to colonize that country. However, it was also obvious that Nehru was not willing to take a hard stand against China.

Yaacov Y.I. Vertzberger in his seminal work, *Misperceptions in Foreign Policymaking: The Sino-Indian Conflict, 1959–1962*, arrives at the following conclusion that is of significance:

> Nehru saw the problem not only as a border dispute in a wider political context pertaining both to overall Sino-Indian relations and to the entire Asian sub-system, but also as inseparable from global events. This conclusion likewise emerges from the analysis of Nehru's psychological environment, in which the geo-strategic factor is only third in importance.[7]

The main issue at this stage was that the Indian leadership was in a pacifist mode with Nehru even questioning the need for India to have an army, believing that no one threatened India and India threatened no one. The most foolish part of this belief was the lack of interest in placing even a minimum number of observation posts at key positions on India's borders with Tibet. The Indian government had not given any real thought to showing the flag to demonstrate the prevalence of India's administration along key parts of its borders. This lacuna resulted in India being unaware of the movement of PLA forces out of Sinkiang through the Indian territory of Aksai Chin on their way to occupy western Tibet. A violation of Indian territory had thus taken place in October 1950 but because India had completely disregarded the geostrategic factor, it was unaware of this development.

Once China had occupied Tibet, it presented India with a reality that could no longer be ignored. Accordingly, Palden Thondup's ambition to be placed on a par with Bhutan no longer carried any weight. The treaty negotiated with Sikkim expanded India's role in the state, declaring it a protectorate whose external affairs, defence and communications were placed entirely within India's domain. Subject to these categorical provisions, the state was to 'enjoy autonomy in regard to its internal affairs'.[8]

The strategic considerations central to India's concerns were spelt out in Article III(1), that held the Indian government 'responsible for the defence and territorial integrity of Sikkim. It shall have the right to take such measures as it considers necessary for the defence of Sikkim or the security of India, whether preparatory or otherwise, and whether within or outside Sikkim. In particular, the Government of India shall have the right to station troops anywhere within Sikkim.'[9]

This article did make the point that the Indian government would 'as far as possible' take the measures spelt out in Article III(1) 'in consultation with the Government of Sikkim'.[10] The words 'as far as possible' made it clear that the consultation was not compulsory or binding, and that India had no compulsion to gain the prior acceptance of the Government of Sikkim to undertake steps to implement its responsibilities.

The India–Sikkim Treaty was signed on 5 December 1950. Unlike the treaties signed with the other east Himalayan states, this treaty clarified the unequal status of Sikkim by the fact that the subjects of Sikkim were to travel on Indian travel documents and were to be treated as 'Indian protected persons' by Indian diplomatic representations abroad, on par with the treatment meted out to citizens of India.

The treaty mentioned that India had the right to appoint a 'Representative' to 'reside in Sikkim and the Government of Sikkim shall provide him and his staff with all reasonable facilities', etc. Nowhere did it state that this was a diplomatic appointment. This was done deliberately, in order to make it clear that Sikkim was not being treated as an independent state; albeit to meet the requests of the ruler, India had agreed not to treat it as an Indian princely state. To drive home the point that Sikkim had limited political identity, the treaty mentioned that in the case of any dispute that could not be settled through mutual consultation, it should be 'referred to the Chief Justice of India whose decision thereon shall be final'.

The Indo-Sikkim Treaty was a document that plainly, but only in a limited sense, addressed the concerns that had arisen in India as a result of the Chinese occupation of Tibet. It was also obvious that the Chinese presence in Tibet had turned the border between India and Tibet into a live one. The Indian presence in the Himalayan states was now a strategic necessity. Sikkim's geographical position granted it particular importance in this scenario. India needed to develop a closer strategic relationship with Bhutan, too, on military grounds as both Sikkim and Bhutan were placed in the physical position of overlooking the Chumbi Valley. India now had to assess threats to the Siliguri Corridor on two fronts. To its south was East Pakistan, while to its north lay Tibet's Chumbi Valley, now occupied by China and strategically placed to threaten the Siliguri Corridor.

Both Nepal and Bhutan bordered the Siliguri Corridor, and India also needed to keep in mind the defence interests of both these Himalayan states. It was in this context that a pacifist Nehru adopted a hardline position in Parliament, stating that any threat posed to the integrity of the Cis-Himalayan states would involve India coming to their defence. This once again sets out the dichotomies of India's China policies. Nehru was consistent in projecting the view that he attached 'great importance to India and China being friends. I think the future of Asia and to some extent of the world depends on this.' He was expressing this opinion in the Lok Sabha in December 1950. At a time when the Chinese had ignored all attempts by the Indians to safeguard Tibet's autonomy and taken Tibet over in the best practices of a colonial power, he was still extending the hand of friendship in line with his Asia Vision.

At the same time, he was aware that the Chinese presence in Tibet had changed equations and a threat perception was now needed to be made a part of India's relations with China. He, however, qualified his approach where the defence of India was concerned, by adopting the notion that 'the Himalayas were such an effective defense line that even an airborne fleet could not cross them'. Carrying this myth further, he stated that 'in a military confrontation no outside power would prove a useful ally, as the type of aid that one gets from abroad is machines and in these mountain areas those machines do not reach'.[11]

Nehru made this riposte to Patel's warning that China's occupation of Tibet posed a direct threat to India. His belief and faith in the Himalayas as a formidable barrier safeguarding India's security was at best naive and at the worst intellectually dishonest. Nehru should have at the very least, keeping in mind that the country was already facing a major threat from Pakistan, taken seriously the advice that India should take over the Chumbi Valley as Maoist China expanded its physical presence in Tibet.

Notes

1. *Tibet: Past and Present,* Charles Bell, Motilal Banarsidass, New Delhi, 2000, p. 106.
2. India–Bhutan Treaty of 1949.
3. India–Bhutan Treaty of 1950.
4. Dissertation submitted by Rajiv Rai 'The State in the Colonial Periphery: A Study on Sikkim's Relations with Great Britain', p. 86.
5. *Ibid*, Chapter III.
6. *Smash and Grab: Annexation of Sikkim*, Sunanda K. Datta-Ray; first published by Vikas Publications in 1984 with a revised edition being published by Westland India in 2013.
7. *Misperceptions in Foreign Policymaking: The Sino-Indian Conflict, 1959–1962,* Yaacov Y.I. Vertzberger, Routledge, London, 2019.
8. This is provided for in Article II of the Indo-Sikkim treaty signed on 5 December 1950
9. *Ibid*. Article III (1).
10. *Ibid*. Article III (2).
11. *Misperceptions in Foreign Policymaking: The Sino-Indian Conflict, 1959-1962*, Yaacov Y.I. Vertzberger, Westview Press/Boulder, Colorado, 1984, p. 107.

17

THE CHUMBI VALLEY

In purely geographical terms, the Chumbi Valley lies to the south of the Himalayan watershed that rests to the south of the town of Phari. Phari is often described as the 'head' of the Chumbi Valley. This valley was a recognized part of the kingdom of Sikkim and the Namgyal family that came to rule the state had its origins in it. Because of the ancestral linkages and the milder climate of the valley, the rulers of Sikkim, till the Treaty of Tumlong, resided in Chumbi and tended to administer the entire kingdom from there.

For the British, the links between Sikkim, Chumbi Valley and Lhasa were seen, not in strategic terms related to the security of India, but purely for the geographical benefit that they provided to promote trade between Britain and Tibet. Their strategic importance to India only came to the forefront as Britain gave in to Lord Curzon's demands that Tibet assume the role of a buffer state safeguarding India's security. It was also no coincidence that there had been several occasions when British officials dealing with the Himalayan kingdoms, Tibet and the security of India had proposed that the Chumbi Valley be occupied or taken over. This had been turned down by London over its commitments to Beijing and Moscow.

Historical Discord

The Anglo-Tibetan Convention of 1904, also known as the Lhasa Convention, in its unamended format had included the retention of the valley for a period of seventy-five years, to ensure that the Tibetans adhered to the payment of an annual indemnity of Rs 1 lakh to Britain as well as the enforcement for the implementation of commercial commitments. London intervened to force a revision of this provision as it appeared in its eyes to create a problem with the Russians as both parties had made the commitment that neither was interested in annexing or claiming Tibetan territory.

Accordingly, the indemnity was reduced to Rs 25 lakhs and the retention of the valley to a period of three years. Another mistake was the insistence by London that the Chinese sign a formal agreement to endorse the Lhasa Convention. This was a step that granted the Chinese a status in Tibet that they had never really exercised. The very reason behind the Younghusband expedition was the inability of the Chinese to enforce their will over Tibet and to implement the commitments that they had undertaken on its behalf.

What followed after 1906 was a retreat from Tibetan affairs by Britain, engineered by secretary of state Brodrick and acting viceroy Amptill, in their efforts to cut Curzon down to size. The Chinese took advantage of the British retreat to wield a heavy hand in administering Tibet, at the same time adopting policies that threatened the borders of India and British India's interests in the eastern Himalayan kingdoms. It was clear from that point onwards that any power inimical to India's interests that came to exercise control over Tibet would create a threat to India's security.

This threat would be even more acute if the Chumbi Valley was occupied by China, as apart from its physical advantage it also enabled that country to attempt to influence Sikkim and Bhutan against India. This situation had been neutralized as the thirteenth Dalai Lama took charge and literally threw the Chinese out of Tibet, declaring Tibet an independent country and strengthening Indo-Tibetan ties. This situation lasted till Mao and the CCP took over the reins of power in China and forced their way into Tibet, thus removing Tibet as a strategic buffer between India and China.

Communist China's moves on Tibet should have caused little surprise as Chiang Kai-shek had also maintained the myth that Tibet was a part of China. He did however admit that Tibet was in a special relationship that permitted it a degree of internal autonomy. No such concession to Tibetan autonomy was on Mao's mind.

The Chinese Perspective

Ambassador K.P.S. Menon had held discussions with Dr George Yeh, the Chinese vice-minister for foreign affairs at the Kuomintang capital of Nanking. His report, conveyed to Delhi on 21 October 1947, was a significant pointer to what India could expect even if Chiang and the Kuomintang retained full control of China.[1] The important points it mentioned were:

- The Indian government be approached 'with a view to the abrogation or modification of the agreements which were entered into between China and Great Britain in the days of the Unequal Treaties'.
- The Trade Regulations of 1908 'were not in force and have been a dead letter since 1914 as they were suspended by

the Trade Regulations of that year between Great Britain and Tibet'. In the same breath, Dr Yeh mentioned that the 'Simla Convention was not recognized by the Chinese Government'. The Chinese were claiming that all the trade arrangements that had been entered into between Britain and Tibet, and which India had inherited, were no longer valid. It was a position that was disputed by both Britain and India.

- To the position taken by Ambassador Menon that 'we regarded Tibet as an autonomous territory under Chinese suzerainty', Dr Yeh mentioned that 'the Chinese Government too had taken notice of the special position of Tibet'. He then mentioned that the Chinese national Assembly 'treated Tibet as a special territory'; and President Chiang Kai-shek himself had offered to concede 'a very high degree of autonomy' to Tibet.

These discussions had taken place within the context of a proposed new treaty between China and India covering trade relations with the latter that 'included Tibet'. Menon did make the point that the treatment of Tibet was a matter for discussion, maintaining quite categorically that 'nothing in the Treaty should be construed to affect the existing trade relations between India and Tibet'.

Another reference by George Yeh was the claim that Nehru, during the Asian Relations Conference, had mentioned that the Indian government would be glad to enter into conversation with the Chinese government regarding the status of Tibet 'without the intervention of any third party'. This he had conveyed to President Chiang, and it was Yeh's understanding that by 'third party' Nehru meant the British and not the Tibetans. Menon correctly pointed out that it was 'unlikely that' the Indian government 'would enter into any formal conversations with the Chinese Government to settle the status of Tibet over the head of Tibet itself'. 'To do so would be to repudiate the autonomy of Tibet which the "GOI" had recognized for the last 33 years.' This was a very clear enunciation of the policy of the Government of India on Tibet, one that Menon's successor Panikkar would fail to maintain.

China's nationalist position on Tibet, where it was willing to consider India's point of view on Tibet as an autonomous entity, was reversed by the communist government. The new government reasserted the claim that Tibet was a part of China and had been so from the time of the Yuan dynasty. Initially, they showed some deference to the Indian position and maintained that Tibet would be treated as autonomous under China. Soon, however, this assurance was overturned, with Beijing turning Tibet into its colony, where total control of its administration was placed in Han Chinese hands.

It also did not take much time for Beijing to show its hand by asserting its claim to suzerainty over the Himalayan kingdoms of Bhutan, Nepal and Sikkim, or in projecting the view and questioning India's relationship with them. It was obvious that the same argument could, with equal felicity, be turned to claim that the British had prevented China from exercising its historical rights vis-à-vis the Himalayan kingdoms and territories including, in this respect, Ladakh and NEFA.

Delhi should have evaluated the problems Mao's position on Tibet would create for India and its security, weighing in the process all the measures, political and diplomatic, that India could adopt to meet the situation. It was in India's interest for Tibet to retain its de facto position as an independent nation. The first step at this stage should have been to consult with the American and British establishments and commence diplomatic relations with Lhasa as an independent nation, backed up by both material and military supplies. This would have sent an appropriate message to Beijing. At the same time, a coordinated attempt should have been made at the UN to grant Tibet membership of that body. In all probability, the Soviets and the nationalist Chinese occupying the permanent seats at the Security Council would have refused membership to Tibet. Even so, the message would have gone out that the world stood behind Tibet and its independence, and this would have kept Mao and his Tibetan ambitions in check, with Tibet receiving the support that could have enabled it to defend its territory.

There is now enough evidence available from declassified documents that the Americans were willing to help India if it would agree to take action on securing for Tibet at least the status of a fully autonomous nation. Nehru, among other reasons, allowed his distrust of the Americans and a misapplication of his belief in non-alignment to blind his judgement. Fortunately, this did not apply to the issue of Sikkim, whose geographical location was now being seen in Delhi as one of importance to India's security and for ensuring India's influence on Nepal and Bhutan.

Even so, the relations with Sikkim did not in their logic cover the issue of the Chumbi Valley and the need to look at its strategic value to India and its security. The political office in Gangtok and the legation in Lhasa had looked at the entire issue of what would transpire if the Chinese moved on Tibet, and had suggested in 1949 that Delhi should seriously consider moving into the Chumbi Valley and taking it over. Here, India could have made good tactical use of the physical evidence that at 'old Chumbi', some distance up the Amo Chu, were located the palace and adjoining complex that had housed the rulers of Sikkim and the Royal Advisory Council to administer Sikkim.

Charles Bell, who had governed the valley during the period it was held by the British after the Convention of 1904, described it as some 700 square miles in area with a small population. He called it 'a wedge of territory that cuts between Bhutan and Sikkim to within twenty-five miles of the plains of Bengal'.[2] Bell's description highlighted the valley and its strategic importance to India by quietly focusing on what its occupation by the Chinese would mean to not only Bhutan and Sikkim but, more importantly, to India.

Bell's observations also pointed out, once again, that in geographical terms, the valley lay south of the Himalayan watershed; it had for long been a part of Sikkim; the majority of the people who inhabited it were non-Tibetan having their origins in Bhutan; it was of strategic value to India; and its main waterbody, the Amu Chu, flowed on to Bhutan and entered the plains of India as the Torsa Nadi finally falling into the Brahmaputra.

Harishwar Dayal's Proposal

China has shown since the early 1960s that it would like to push India out of the commanding and strategic heights that the latter had reached under the Indo-Sikkim Treaty of 1950. Satellite images grant a deep insight into what we are faced with in the sector that overhangs the Siliguri Corridor. The expansionist actions that have been undertaken by China's PLA not only in Ladakh but also at Naku La, a pass in northern Sikkim, since April 2020, is a clear message, assuming that the political class needed such a reminder, that China intends to ramp up its border claims and push India out of areas that it contends are important to meet its strategic concerns.

The implementation of China's carefully crafted expansionist policies since 1949 included the complete takeover of Tibet and the displacement of its Tibetan population by a large-scale settlement of the Han Chinese. In an ironic twist of fate, while colonizing

Tibet, they carried out a systematic destruction of Buddhism and the Tibetan way of life. It had been the Chinese who had warned Lhasa that it should keep its distance from the British as Britain was an expansionist Christian power that threatened Buddhism and the Tibetan way of life.

In a detailed note that Harishwar Dayal[3] addressed to Delhi from Lhasa on 20 October 1949, he pointed out that with the rapid advance of the communist Chinese into Tibet, the Indian government must consider as a 'matter of great urgency, their policy in Tibet on matters (i) military, and (ii) political'. He pointed out that the Chinese 'have already announced their intention of "liberating" Tibet at an early date' concluding that 'Tibet is in imminent danger.'

Dayal did not pull any punches, pointing out that 'the occupation or domination of Tibet by a potentially hostile and possibly aggressive Communist power would be a threat to the security of India'. He drew the attention of the government to the fact that the occupation of Tibet 'would encourage the Chinese Communists to press their country's long-standing claim to a large portion of the Assam Tribal Areas and also revive the pretensions to suzerainty over Ladakh, Sikkim, Bhutan and Nepal'.

Dayal pressed the point that the diplomatic recognition that the Indian government intended to extend to the People's Republic of China should be conditional. 'I have already suggested that, when the time comes to recognize the Communist Government, it should be stated in general terms that such recognition is without prejudice to the existing rights and commitments of the Government of India, but the present view of the Government of India appears to be that recognition should be unconditional.'

Dayal's approach was clear-headed, in direct contrast to the woolly headedness on display in Delhi and the romance with

Maoist China that Panikkar was coming to display while suggesting that China's invasion of Tibet should be seen as an 'internal affair' and India should not interfere in it. Foreign Secretary Menon had rightly questioned this point of view, but there was no corrective advanced by Nehru to contain Panikkar's inclination to place greater credence to the doings of the Beijing leadership while simultaneously attaching little importance to the impact these happenings would have on India's interests. What was ironical and had apparently been forgotten was that in a despatch that Panikkar had addressed to Delhi on 20 November 1948, he had advanced the opinion that Tibet should be recognized as an independent nation.

Dayal in his despatch reiterated that India should take possession of the Chumbi Valley,[4] emphasizing the trade Agencies that had been 'provided for in the Convention of 1904 with Tibet (confirmed by China by the Anglo-Chinese Convention of 1906) and have existed for over 40 years'. He went on to state, 'It would in my view be justified to meet any military threat to these posts with force.' While military operations in Tibet would have their difficulties, 'there seems a reasonable chance that a foothold could be retained—at any rate in the Chumbi valley—even against a direct communist attack', warning that a 'lack of such a foothold would greatly complicate the task of guarding India's north-east frontier'.

Dayal's contention was backed up by geography. With a hold on the Chumbi Valley, the Chinese threat to the Siliguri Corridor, to western Bhutan and to eastern and north-eastern Sikkim would be avoided. In fact, by including the Phari area of Tibet that lies at the head of the valley, India would have the added advantage of overlooking the Gyantse and the Shigatse areas of Tibet. These have come to serve as the crossroads for much of Chinese road infrastructure in Tibet, including the link to Sinkiang.

Unfortunately, Delhi failed to grasp the strategic and security interests that lay behind Dayal's proposal as it did not fit in with the view of China that Nehru harboured. Dayal was seen as questioning Nehru's belief that the Himalayan range provided an impregnable defence of India. The suggestions also went against the prime minister's firmly held belief that China had no intention to attack India or challenge the borders established between Tibet and India. Panikkar had contended that Beijing would continue to adhere to existing treaties, with the option to negotiate fresh treaties in the future. This shored up the belief that all matters between India and China relating to Tibet could be resolved diplomatically.

Prime Minister Nehru's note of 9 July 1949 mentioned what he had in mind 'on policy toward Tibet', putting forward the argument that 'we should be very careful in taking any measures which might be considered a challenge to Chinese Communist Government or which might mean an invasion of Tibetan sovereignty'. Further, 'I do not think any question arises, at present at least, of our occupying any part of Tibetan territory. This in itself would be a provocation and it would have bad international reactions.'[5] This was an interesting position to adopt in the face of communist China's clearly expressed intention to take Tibet by force, despite the interventions of India, suggesting that Tibet's autonomy be preserved and that it was in China's interests to arrive at a peaceful settlement with Lhasa.

Further, any international repercussions on India taking over the Chumbi Valley could be answered by pointing out that India was only rectifying what the British had done to excise the Chumbi Valley from Sikkim to meet their selfish commercial and business ends. As S. Gopal in his biography of Nehru points out, 'Nehru's assessment of China's attitude to India was also naïve.' Further evidence of this was provided in the same note by Nehru, suggesting that 'whatever may be ultimate of Tibet in relation to China, I think there is practically no chance of any military danger to India arising from any possible change in Tibet'.[6]

Then going against all evidence that the technologies that had been on display during the Second World War had shown that mountains were no longer a formidable natural barrier, Nehru maintained that 'geographically, this is very difficult and practically it would be a foolish adventure'. In keeping with this assessment, he made it clear that there was no need 'at present for our Defence Ministry, or any part of it, to consider possible military repercussions on the Indian-Tibetan frontier'.

It is perhaps understandable that in the first half of 1949, the dangers of the Chinese occupation of Tibet were being underplayed. But by November 1950, this could no longer be the case. On 4 November 1950, Sumal Sinha heading the Indian legation in Lhasa, had informed both Gangtok and Delhi that the Chinese forces at Chamdo were 'regrouping for a final assault on Lhasa'. He also informed the Indian government that the Tibetans now feared an all-out assault to 'pulverize Tibetan resistance and to intercept the Dalai Lama's flight to India'.

Harishwar Dayal, in a telegram dated 21 November 1950, reminded South Block that Tibet 'in the recent past have asserted a claim to Ladakh, Darjeeling, Sikkim, Bhutan and part of the Assam Tribal areas; large sections of the India-Tibet border in the western Himalaya are undefined and there have been border disputes between the Tibetans and Kashmir and Tehri Garhwal.' Subsequently, Tibet had confirmed that it would adhere to the commitments made under the Simla Convention. What Dayal was warning about was not that Tibet would by itself revive these claims, but that once Chinese forces occupied Lhasa, these claims may be put forward by the Chinese suggesting 'we must therefore be prepared for the aggressive assertion of a variety of claims, either directly by the Chinese or through Chinese sponsored Governments in Tibet and elsewhere'.

Within the logic of the developments that were taking place with the Chinese march into Lhasa now a distinct possibility, political officer Harishwar Dayal once again proposed that India should consider taking over the Chumbi Valley. To make his argument more palatable, he hinted at the geostrategic advantage that valley offered to the defence of India. He also once again reiterated that the valley had been part of the territory of Sikkim. In making this point, he was obviously hinting at India reversing a historical wrong that had been done to Sikkim earlier by the Tibetan administration and subsequently by the British colonial authorities. Unfortunately, his suggestions failed to gain Nehru's concurrence.

Dayal worded his proposal in terms that would fit the Nehruvian commitment—that he would defend the Himalayas with all the force at his command. Referring to the original suggestion on the subject that had come from the Indian legation in Lhasa, made as far back as June 1949, he explained that this proposal had been made 'as a purely defensive measure and with no aggressive intention'. He then drew attention to the fact that if 'an attack on Sikkim and Bhutan call for defensive military operations by the Government of India. In such a situation occupation of the Chumbi Valley might be a vital factor in defence.'

To grant greater heft to the proposal, Dayal put forward the strategic value of the valley, describing it as 'a thin wedge between Sikkim and Bhutan and through it lie important routes to both these territories. Control of this region means control of both Jelep La and Nathu La routes between Sikkim and Tibet as well as the easiest routes to Western Bhutan from the Tibetan side and our side. It is a trough with high mountains to both east and west and thus offers good defensive possibilities. *I would therefore suggest the possibility of occupying the Chumbi Valley be included in any defensive military plans* [emphasis added].' He, like a good civil servant having read the mind of the prime minister, wrapped it within the condition that 'this step would not be taken unless we become involved in military operations in defence of our borders.'

What Dayal should have included as additional background were two vital elements. First, was to draw attention to the aggressive intent that the Chinese had shown towards Sikkim, Nepal and Bhutan when they had taken command of Lhasa in the period 1907–11 and the moves that China had made on the tribal areas of Assam when Chao Er Feng had occupied eastern Tibet from 1905 onwards. This was the situation till the thirteenth Dalai Lama was able to reassert his hold over Tibet in 1912 and drive the Chinese out of most of eastern Tibet.

The second was the so-called five-finger strategy put forward by Mao Tse Tung as far back as 1939, where he claimed that Tibet was the palm and Ladakh, Nepal, Sikkim, Bhutan and what is now Arunachal Pradesh but was then known as NEFA were the five fingers. Both the threat and the intent were obvious. He should have also drawn attention to the fact that the Chinese republic had, after it took over power, published maps where the Assam tribal areas had been shown as part of China and not Tibet. This was a matter of record that should not have been ignored by the Indian government.

Deepening Fault Lines

Despite the fact that communist China did not hesitate to express its criticism of Nehru on Tibet, when dismissing India's protest of 21 October 1950, Beijing stated, 'As for India's protest, China cannot but consider it as having been affected by foreign influence hostile to China in Tibet ...'[7] The problem was that Nehru was unable to understand that the Chinese were bent on taking over Tibet, in the fullest sense of the term. And, while for practical reasons the Chinese were willing to adopt a stepped approach that would ultimately lead to Tibet's full integration with China (including the local administration), this was purely tactical and certainly not because the Chinese were driven by any concern over maintaining friendly relations with India.

In 1950, in an assessment, the distrust that the Chinese had for India was made clear. Their view of Nehru was that he was an expansionist. In a briefing on 24 November by China's ministry of foreign affairs, to a select set of ambassadors, in what amounted to a policy statement, it accused India of desiring to 'interfere with our internal affairs, prevent our liberation of Tibet, and maintain Indian and capitalist privileges in Tibet'. They alleged that India was joining hands with the British to prevent the Tibetan delegation that was supposed to negotiate the terms of the Chinese takeover ('liberation') of Tibet.

The irony behind this was that Nehru believed that by extending an early and unconditional diplomatic recognition to the People's Republic of China and by accepting it as the suzerain power in Tibet, India would be in a better position to negotiate a deal with it to secure Tibet's autonomy. Instead, his efforts were rejected by China as interference in their internal affairs, pointing out that 'Tibet is an inalienable part of China and the People's Liberation Army must enter and liberate Tibet and safeguard the frontier of China.' The question here was—'liberation' from whom? Tibet was an independent nation and had removed any Chinese links after 1912. Hence the correct word was not 'liberation' but 'colonization' of Tibet.

While India was suggesting a peaceful installation of the suzerainty of China in Tibet, the Chinese were negating that position by asserting their sovereignty over Tibet and questioning India's intentions. China was bent on reasserting the claims that Commissioner Chang and warlord Chao had made from 1907 to 1911. Unfortunately, the lessons of that period were ignored to India's cost and peril.

What was to follow once again showed up Nehru's naiveté in handling the relations with China over Tibet. China did not hesitate to say that it viewed India's treaty-related rights in Tibet, rights that had been endorsed by China in 1906, as being exercised by an alien power, where at Article 1 of the Sino-Tibet seventeen-point agreement it expected the 'Tibetan people shall unite and drive out imperialist aggressive forces from Tibet'. The only so-called 'imperialist forces' present in Tibet were the ones from India within the compass of the Convention of 1906 and the subsequent trade agreement of 1908. This should have served as an eye-opener and India should have rejected the seventeen-point agreement that had in any case been forced on Tibet, literally at gunpoint. At that time, the young Dalai Lama had left Lhasa residing at the Chumbi Valley trying to make up his mind on how to tackle the Chinese menace. If India had acted, it could have provided an opportunity for an international move to condemn the Chinese intrusion on Tibet.

Maoist China was casting India's rights as capitalist and imperialist intentions that were to be dishonoured and destroyed. However, despite the open hostility on display, India entered into an 'Agreement between the Republic of India and the People's Republic of China on Trade and Intercourse between Tibet Region of China and India'. It was signed between the two parties on 29 April 1954. Here there were two specific points to consider. First, India had given up its extraterritorial rights without securing a specific agreement over its borders with Tibet where Chinese maps were already claiming large parts of Indian territory. Second, for all practical purposes, India had endorsed the PRC's claims that Tibet was an integral part of China by accepting that the agreement was 'between Tibet Region of China and India'.

Any right-minded Indian government should have at the negotiations leveraged its legal presence in Tibet and insisted that India would agree to bring these rights within the corrective of a bilateral agreement for China. In turn, China would have to recognize India's existing borders with Tibet. What made it worse was the inclusion in the chapeau of the five principles, or Panchsheel, where the very first principle, 'mutual respect for each other's territorial integrity and sovereignty', made little sense as the territories were not defined, leaving the whole issue at the mercy of display of goodwill by both parties to arrive at an agreement at some time into the future.

The irony of the situation was that a briefing note prepared by Zhang Jingwu[8] on the Sino-Indian negotiations that finally led to the signing of the 1954 treaty, in very clear terms held 'the assumption' that 'India intends to capitalize on this opportunity to have some benefit in Tibet', as mentioned in 'your correspondence'. He then made the point that 'based on the information that we have at hand about Tibet, particularly our insufficient understanding of imperialist privileges in Tibet, we still need Indian cooperation in some international issues'. Here is the rub that comes in, where Jingwu made his assessment that 'India is capitalizing on our temporary difficulties in Tibet … As well as our need for India's cooperation in various areas, to gain benefits by offering a general solution to the Tibet issue'.[9]

He then pointed out that the Indian documents emphasize that 'India and China have no territorial disputes'. He here refers to

Nehru's statement to this effect in the Rajya Sabha. He then said, 'This is where the plot of India lies. Today, India occupies Dawang (Tawang) Region, according to the 1914 Simla Accord. However, it claimed the absence of territorial disputes just to force us into implicitly acknowledging and legitimizing their occupation. We must stay alert in this regard.'[10]

He then offered his opinion:[11]

1. We must declare abolishment of the old accord, i.e. the Simla Convention.
2. Must ask India to withdraw from Chinese Tawang and lower Luyou which it currently occupies.
3. China and India may discuss the dividing lines between both countries. It is impossible to fundamentally settle the issues regarding the accord and the border. It is in our interests to delay the settlement of these issues.

He went on to make the point that declarations must be made that ensured that China did not leave behind any impression that it had 'implicitly acknowledged the status quo'.[12] China was set to taking the Indian government for a ride and it succeeded in its efforts.

A redeeming feature in all of this was that despite taking the line that the Himalayas offered an impassable barrier to any threat that China's occupation of Tibet may portend, Nehru was wise enough to look on the relations with Sikkim from the strategic point of view. He did not permit his avuncular feelings towards Maharaja Kumar Palden Thondup Namgyal to stand in the way of signing a treaty that not only declared Sikkim an Indian protectorate but, more importantly, weighed in the defence factor, that after 1962 added greater emphasis to the relations with Gangtok.

There is, however, no indication that Nehru came to regret the fact that India did not consider the strategic factors that the Chumbi Valley would have served to keep China at bay. Today, one can see that the Chinese have taken full advantage of the geostrategic factors that the valley has come to serve, helping their designs to keep up the pressure on India. The Doklam standoff in the summer of 2017 made it clear that the threat posed to the 'chicken's neck' is now even more acute, with the infrastructure that China has established in the valley enabling it to speedily move against India whenever it suits them.

Notes

1. Report dated 21 October 1947 cited at *India-China Relations, 1947–2000*, Avtar Singh Bhasin, Geetika Publishers, New Delhi, 2018, pp. 49-51.
2. *Tibet: Past and Present,* Charles Bell, Motilal Banarsidass, New Delhi, 2000.
3. Top-secret Memorandum dated 20 October 1949 by the political officer to the secretary to the Government of India, ministry of external affairs, in *India-China Relations, 1947–2000*, Vol. I, Avtar Singh Bhasin, Geetika Publishers, New Delhi, 2018, pp. 155–161.
4. This suggestion had originally been made in its 'Express Letter No. 3' dated 15 June 1949 by the Indian legation in Lhasa.
5. Note by the prime minister on the policy towards Tibet in *India-China Relations, 1947–2000*, Vol. I, Avtar Singh Bhasin, Geetika Publishers, New Delhi, 2018, p. 121.
6. *Ibid.*
7. Reply of the Central People's Government of the People's Republic of China on 30 October 1950 reported in *India-China Relations, 1947–2000*, Vol. I, Avtar Singh Bhasin, Geetika Publishers, New Delhi, 2018, pp. 374–75.
8. He was a lieutenant general in the PLA and from 1952–65 the CPC committee secretary of the Tibet Autonomous Region. Cited from

the cable dated 21 October 1953 by Zhang Jingwu forwarding his note titled 'On Issues of Relations between China and India in Tibet'; taken from Wilson Center Digital Archive of declassified Chinese documents, available at http://digitalarchive.wilsoncenter.org/document/114754.

9. *Ibid.*
10. *Ibid.*
11. *Ibid.*
12. *Ibid.*

18

THE MERGER WITH INDIA

On the demise of Tashi Namgyal in 1963, his second son, Palden Thondup Namgyal, took over as the twelfth ruler of the Namgyal dynasty of Sikkim. Thondup was originally slated to be ordained as a Buddhist monk, and was trained as such till he was eleven, having been recognized as a reincarnated Rinpoche. In 1941, he was enthroned as the Maharaja Kumar, replacing his elder brother, Paljor, who died in a plane crash while serving as an officer in the Royal Indian Air Force.

Palden Thondup was an able administrator, unfortunately with an authoritarian bent of mind, in contrast to the more accommodating personality of his father. Tashi Namgyal had turned into a recluse after his wife, Kunzang Dechen, returned from Tibet bearing an illegitimate daughter. She was banned from entering the palace while Sir Tashi was alive. Palden Thondup was very close to his mother and promptly reopened the social and political doors to her after he took over as Maharaja. She added her weight to her son's ill-advised policy that granted the Bhutia element an overriding political advantage over the majority of the populace.

Being of Tibetan origin with links to Tibetan aristocracy, she was responsible for influencing her son to maintain his Tibetan links and fed his ambition of being treated by India at the same level as the Bhutanese monarch. All these characteristics were to come in the way of his understanding that India's relations with Sikkim were being influenced by China's occupation of Tibet. His other weakness was his inability to bring a greater balance to the politics of the state; he did not take into account the political aspirations of the Nepali majority.

Palden Thondup had a stammer, that was more pronounced when he was under stress and lying. He was also rather superstitious and, at times, felt guilty of having betrayed his calling as a Buddhist lama. Another factor that from time to time played on Thondup's mind was the belief in the myth that only a Namgyal with a physical deformity could rule over Sikkim. His brother, Paljor, who had been popular and whose personality appealed to the people of Sikkim, had died before he could assume the throne because he was physically whole. Subconsciously, this played on his mind and he tended to find relief in the bottle.

Palden Thondup married twice. His first wife, Samyo Kushoe Sandeki, was from the Tibetan aristocracy and died in 1957. Sandeki was a popular figure in Sikkim and was widely respected by the people. Palden met a young American socialite, Hope Cooke, in Darjeeling and married her in 1963. His coronation as the Maharaja took place on an astrologically determined auspicious date, 4 April 1965, although he had taken over as ruler on 2 December 1963 after his father's death. The coronation was a grand ceremony, covered by American and European media that were attracted by another American marrying royalty, following the wedding of Hollywood actress, Grace Kelly, with the ruling Prince of Monaco.

Palace Intrigue

Hope Cooke was ambitious and allowed her naiveté to overcome the reality of her position as an 'outsider'. She was caught early in the web of palace intrigues and shallow politicking. When my wife and I made our first call on the Chogyal and Gyalmo (queen consort), our initial impression of Hope Cooke was of a young person who had adopted the outward poise of Tibetan aristocracy, reducing the soft tones in which Tibetan ladies expressed themselves to a mostly incomprehensible whisper. She obviously did not realize that she was not taken as seriously as she thought she was by senior courtiers. What is more, she was at the receiving end of Palden Thondup's favourite sister, Princess Pema Tsedeun, also known as Kukula. Kukula was urbane and politically savvier than her brother. There was an immediate clash of personalities between her and Hope Cooke, with each in her own way trying to exert her influence on the ruler.

Our first meeting with the Chogyal—whose request to be addressed as such and not Maharaja had been acceded to by the Indian government—and the Gyalmo took place in an intimate private sitting room at the palace. It was just the four of us around cups of tea and cakes from Calcutta's Swiss bakery and cafe, Flurys, along with an array of Sikkimese snacks. The Chogyal was his charming self, ready to discuss everything including politics. It was clear to me that he was trying to gauge whether I would be useful to him in the games he indulged in, of sharpening differences between officials of the political office and the political officer.

The same attempt was also in play where the relations between the political officer and the divisional commander of the 17th Mountain Division, were concerned. Prior to the visit, I had discussed the call with my boss, N.B. Menon, who let me have his insight into the mind of the Chogyal and his ways. I had little difficulty in reading his motives and the ideas that lay behind them. He was intent on creating confusion that he could take advantage of, in order to achieve his political ambition.

I managed to convey, indirectly, that I would not be part of any political game-playing, suggesting that given the norms of protocolary behaviour as first secretary (I was yet to be promoted to that status), I would of course be in touch with his principal secretary, Jigdal Densappa, and the concerned officials at the Sikkim secretariat. Palden Thondup took the hint and soon thereafter arranged for Karma Topden, the son of his political confidante, Martem Topden, a senior politician and legislator from the Sikkim National Party, to be the one to interact with me on political issues. This was, of course, along with Jigdal Densappa, who was Karma's mentor.

Karma Topden had been trained in intelligence and was part of the so-called Study Group that was the backup in both political and socio-economic spheres to serve the ruler's ambitions and interests. It was also the think-tank that advised the Chogyal on all matters related to India. Hope Cooke was involved in broader policy formulations that emerged out of the deliberations of the Study Group that had Jigdal as its administrative head. It was this group, along with a set of legal advisors, that fed the Chogyal's ambitions to the point where he tended to fail to realistically evaluate the possible.

One of the outcomes of the deliberations of this group, where Hope Cooke had taken the lead, was to resurrect the controversy surrounding the grant of Darjeeling to the East India Company, adding the twist of asking for its return from India. What lay behind this attempt was the supposition that by placing the Indian government under this kind of pressure, it could force Delhi to negotiate a fresh treaty with Sikkim where in return for a settlement on Darjeeling, Sikkim would ask to be treated as an independent state in a special relationship with India.

Expanding Ambition

To grant credence to this ambition, Hope Cooke published an article in 1967, putting forward the claim that all land within the territory of Sikkim belonged to the ruler in eternity and as such could only be held in trust till he sought its return. She demanded the return of Darjeeling and its surrounds to the kingdom of Sikkim,[1] suggesting that this was what her husband was seeking by revoking the trust deed that had granted Darjeeling to the East India Company. This article contributed to the atmosphere of distrust between the Chogyal and the Indian government, and it was felt that Hope Cooke was a 'trojan horse' planted by the Central Intelligence Agency (CIA) in Sikkim. It was also a wake-up call to the mandarins in South Block, both at the prime minister's office and the ministry of external affairs.

The Chogyal was informed in no uncertain terms that this attempt at muddying issues was unacceptable and that his wife was stepping into dangerous waters. Hope Cooke, of course, was also playing to the gallery. By bringing Darjeeling into the Sikkim–India equation, she felt that both the Bhutia and the Gurkha elements of the Nepali population would ensure that they endorsed her husband and his will to get a revision of the Treaty of 1950. In this endeavour she was unsuccessful, as the bulk of the Nepali and many among the Bhutia hierarchy were suspicious of her. This was also part of the palace politics and intrigues let loose by Kukula against her sister-in-law, the Gyalmo.

Even among the top Sikkimese bureaucracy, there were quite a few who resented Hope Cooke's attempts to interfere and put barriers in the way of their dealings with the palace on matters of administration and policy. This resentment was to reach a climax when a pliant Indian Civil Service officer, I.S. Chopra, was selected by Foreign Secretary T.N. Kaul to take over the post of the principal administrative officer in Gangtok. Chopra, falling under the blandishments of Palden Thondup, accepted the title of 'Sidelong', a Tibetan title equivalent to the designation of 'prime minister'. He in turn bent before the Chogyal and Hope Cooke's wishes to the point where he pressurized the chief secretary to divert plan funds provided by India in favour of projects that benefitted the Bhutia interests adding to the feelings of alienation of the Nepali majority.

I.S. Chopra was unfit for the job entrusted to him. He was protocol-conscious and attempted to undercut N.B. Menon, who may have been junior to him in the foreign service but was the senior interlocutor between Delhi and the Chogyal. P.N. Haksar as the principal secretary to Prime Minister Indira Gandhi had no confidence in Chopra, describing him as someone who had 'no loyalties to anything and least of all to his own country. But he was a friend of the Foreign Secretary (T.N. Kaul) and has always been a smooth operator. Having become the Dewan of Sikkim, he could not care less what happened to Indo-Sikkimese relations.' [2]

By 1967, it had become clear that the Chogyal was in the mood to challenge the position of the Indian government on Sikkim. He was willing to work all channels, domestic and external, to modify the 1950 treaty so as to severely curtail India's role in Sikkim. As a first step, he worked towards upgrading Sikkim to enjoy the same level of freedom that had been granted to Bhutan under its treaty with India. The Study Group, which also included a Nepali representation of loyalists like M.M. Rasailly and K.B. Thapa, had worked out a multipronged strategy that could be followed to create both domestic and external pressure to force Delhi to revisit Sikkim's status. A part of this strategy was the utilization of Hope Cooke's and Palden Thondup's contacts in the United States and the United Kingdom to create a publicity campaign that would help influence public opinion to side with Sikkim and its ruler's ambition.

Among the many failings of Palden Thondup was his handling of the domestic political pressures, such as the discrepancy of representation between his majority Nepali subjects and the Bhutia–Lepcha subjects. This remained a political undercurrent, always threatening to become more demanding. So far, people's movements against the Sikkim durbar had been contained by interventions of the political officer and Indian security forces. Failing to realize that this was a factor that had kept him unscarred on his throne, Palden Thondup, under the machinations of his wife, favourite sister and the officials of the Study Group led by Jigdal Densappa, failed to read the mood in Delhi. In Delhi, Sikkim's strategic importance to India was a matter of overriding concern and it was sinking in that the Chogyal's ambitions would work against India's interests.

Palden Thondup had over time come to believe that India needed his goodwill to keep the Sikkim–India relations on an even keel. Aided by his key advisors, he concluded that he could exploit India's vulnerability on strategic issues to get his way on all other matters while agreeing to a degree of Indian presence in Sikkim, primarily for defence. In fact, here too he felt, again based on advice that he was getting from his Indian and foreign legal advisors and some of Hope Cooke's American contacts, that once Sikkim, like Bhutan, had gained membership of the United Nations, he could reduce India's defence involvement to a nominal level, underwritten by an exchange of letters outside any amended treaty agreement. Unfortunately, he had also assumed that he could bring the Chinese into this equation, forcing India to bend to his will.

What was apparent, as I gained a deeper insight into the developments, was that before the signing of the 1950 treaty and after, both sides had made mistakes that could lead to an impasse in their relations in the future. Prime Minister Nehru had reposed considerable trust in the youthful Palden Thondup, who in a sense he had mentored. This had led Thondup to assume that he would be left to deal with the politics of Sikkim on his own terms. The fact that India had come to his rescue in the face of popular movements by his subjects had led him to believe that India was against Sikkim being placed in the hands of a democratic polity. At this stage, he welcomed the protectorate status as a tactical factor to help him gain control. Due to India's soft-handling of Sikkim's politics, Palden Thondup hoped that as matters settled, he would be able to manipulate his subjects so he could both reign and rule for the foreseeable future.

Multiple Players and Layers

After Nehru passed away in 1964, Palden Thondup was confident that Indira Gandhi, whom he had got to know during his time with her father, would continue to take a friendly interest in him and look on his ambitions with sympathy. In the early years as prime minister, she granted him a degree of access that bordered on friendship. He, however, misunderstood her resolve and level-headed approach when it came to matters of strategic concern that had security implications woven into them, to the point where she came to question the policy that her father had adopted vis-à-vis the Himalayan states and their relations with India.[3] Sikkim was not excluded.

Another aspect that emboldened Palden Thondup's thinking evolved from the relationship that his sister, Kukula, had established with the CIA and the American Consulate in Calcutta. She had also developed links through her marriage with the Tibetan aristocracy, with the Tibetan émigré leadership that included the Dalai Lama's brother, Gyalo Thondup, in Kalimpong. The Americans had utilized the occasion of the young Dalai Lama's self-exile in the Chumbi Valley to escape the PLA's advance on Lhasa, where he had taken residence at Yatung on 16 December 1950, to persuade him to fall in line with their strategy against communist China. They had moved away from the support that they had advanced to the Kuomintang's claims on Tibet to a policy oriented towards containing communism. As per this new policy, they were advising the Dalai Lama to quit Tibet, disavow the Sino-Tibet seventeen-point agreement, and in exile become the spiritual face of Buddhism that opposed communist China. The young Dalai Lama insisted that Washington spell out its proposal to him officially and in writing. This Washington was unwilling to do, unless it was able to get Delhi's support, which was being denied to it by Jawaharlal Nehru.

The American policy towards the Dalai Lama was influenced by their understanding of Delhi's concerns. Enough hints had been dropped by the American ambassador, Loy W. Henderson (1948–51), that any stand that India adopted to oppose the Chinese position on Tibet would gain American support. Nehru, however, permitted his prejudices against America and anti-colonialism to cloud his judgement.

China's moves on Lhasa at the end of 1950 coincided with similar moves in North Korea against the UN forces led by America. The Americans were hoping that the Chinese aggression on Tibet would have a salutary impact on Nehru and the attitude that he had so far displayed of 'obeisance towards China, and a critical wariness towards Washington'.[4] What the declassified American papers of the period clearly indicate is that the Americans were willing to extend material support, including military equipment, to Tibet to meet its defence needs. However, they could do this only if the Indian government was a willing partner and looked at an independent Tibet as a strategic asset.

In his assessment, Dean Acheson,[5] the American secretary of state, expressed the hope that the open display of 'duplicity' by the Chinese in their dealings with the Indian government on Korea 'should leave no doubt regarding absence of moral principles Peiping regime and its and its cynicism in conducting international relations'. Dean Acheson was hoping that this would cause the Indian government to reassess its views on the character of the Peiping regime, and bring Nehru closer to Washington's reading of communist China. This was not to be.

At a private dinner conversation that Ambassador Loy Henderson had with Nehru on 3 November 1950, he conveyed Dean Acheson's message that 'the US would be willing to help in any way possible' referring to the developments in Tibet. Nehru rebuffed the offer, saying that the 'US could be most helpful by doing nothing and saying little just now'.[6]

Kukula was by nature and inclination comfortable using intrigue to get her way. She was manipulative and this part of her character had been further honed at the courts of Lhasa. She was fiercely loyal to her brother and had no hesitation in extending all help to serve Palden Thondup's ambitions. She developed a relationship with the CIA officials based in Calcutta and modelled herself as an important informant on Tibet and India–Sikkim relations. Her CIA links had behind them the desire to get Washington to influence Delhi to revise the 1950 treaty in accordance with what Palden Thondup wanted. In this, she did not meet with much success as the CIA in Calcutta was concentrating on Tibet. Subsequently, she allegedly established links with officials of the PRC in Hong Kong. It was Kukula who drew her brother's attention to the Chinese suggestion that the Himalayan kingdoms along with some of the other erstwhile Indian princely states bordering Tibet could form a Himalayan Confederation to act as a buffer between India and Chinese Tibet.

This Chinese plan had also won the attention of King Mahendra of Nepal. Being the largest and the most populous Himalayan state, Nepal saw itself dominating the Confederation. That it would have an anti-Indian flavour was the other attraction for him. Bhutan made it clear that any such proposition, unless it included Tibet at its head, would not be agreeable to it. Bhutan also said it was comfortable in its relations with India. This effort failed.

The Chogyal of Sikkim, however, decided to try his hand at a revised version of a Himalayan Confederation that would keep Nepal and Bhutan out but would encompass erstwhile Indian princely states, including Ladakh. He addressed letters to all the rulers, inviting them to join the Confederation. One of the invitees, the Raja of Stoke, informed the Indian government of Palden Thondup's proposition, passing on a copy of the letter he had received. The Confederation did not ultimately take off, failing to gather requisite support, and the exercise led to Delhi losing trust in Thondup.

Unfortunately, the Chogyal learnt nothing from the failure of this attempt and continued to rely on his relations with Secretary T.N. Kaul in Delhi and the assumption that Prime Minister Indira Gandhi had a soft spot for him. He went on with his attempts to have the 1950 treaty rewritten in his favour, where India's position would be reduced to an advisory one. In this, he did not suggest that the defence relationship be done away with but that it should be largely reduced while India helped him build a larger Sikkimese military force. His intention was probably also to marginalize the political majority that was increasingly questioning his authority.

Palden Thondup was aware that the idea that he should be reduced to the level of a constitutional monarch was gaining traction among some political leaders. If it came to pass, it would effectively be the end of the authoritarian Namgyal rule that he had helped put in place. He and his advisors, among whom were legal professionals both in India and abroad, were misreading the signals they were getting from Delhi. This, in a sense, could be largely laid at the doors of T.N. Kaul.

An impatient Thondup now decided to create a public situation that he hoped would pressurize Delhi to agree to his demand to revise the 1950 treaty to his liking. He organized a 'popular' demonstration against India's domination of Sikkim. The anti-India demonstration was carried out by schoolchildren carrying slogans asking India to quit Sikkim, to coincide with India's Independence Day celebrations on 15 August 1968.

The demonstrating students gathered on the road just below my house and the whole show was directed by Jigdal Densappa, M.M. Rasailly and K.B. Thapa, editor of the palace-supported tabloid *Sikkim*. The nature of the protest, the involvement of his principal advisors and the fact that it was carried out on India's Independence Day with the aim to mar an official function hosted by the political officer that had the Chogyal and the Gyalmo as guests of honour, was seen for what it was. The Chogyal was throwing down the gauntlet and challenging the authority of Delhi.

T.N. Kaul, on behalf of the prime minister, admonished Palden Thondup, but due to the cordial nature of their relationship, the lesson was lost. Deputy Prime Minister Morarji Desai came to Sikkim a month later and held discussions with the Chogyal, but this did not have the salutary effect that had been hoped for. K.B. Thapa was one of the Chogyal's Nepali supporters who received financial assistance from the state to run his publication, *Sikkim*. In it, Thapa continued to attack India, allegedly as a voice of the people seeking freedom from India and for Sikkim to find its rightful place as an independent state.

A Liability

This propaganda that was seen to be organized by the Chogyal and his principal advisors soon created the conditions where Prime Minister Indira Gandhi concluded that the Chogyal was becoming a liability. In a visit to Gangtok in 1968, following a two-day visit to Thimphu, she made it clear to Palden Thondup that he was treading on dangerous ground and he should realize that India set great store by its peaceful relations with Sikkim. She also pointed out to him that the Chinese had shown in 1967 that they harboured the intention to claim Sikkimese territories and were willing to use force to achieve that. It had taken stern military action on the part of the Indian army to safeguard Sikkim's territorial integrity. Here was a reminder that the strategic factor remained a major imperative and India would not agree to any compromise that would weaken its position in that regard.

The Chogyal did not seem to take any of this seriously, obviously under the impression that he could play on India's commitment to democracy and fear of China to gain his ends. What he had lost sight of in all of this was the fact that if it was not for Indian intervention, he would have been severely reduced in status at the hands of the popular will of his own people. His continuing actions to undermine India's position in Sikkim led Mrs Gandhi to realize that the Chogyal was an impediment and there should no longer be any attempt to shield him from the will of the people of Sikkim. She did not close the door to him, though, hoping that he would come to his senses and mend his ways.

I left Gangtok at the end of April 1970. I could sense that despite the efforts of Foreign Secretary Kaul to shield him and his doings from the leadership in Delhi, Palden Thondup and his antics were creating a situation where the prime minister's office was increasingly critical of his behaviour. I had been posted to the

Permanent Mission of India to the United Nations in Geneva. Palden Thondup would visit Geneva regularly where he held consultations with an eminent legal advisor on international law and also with a representative of the International Committee of Jurists. I had been told by Foreign Secretary Kaul that I would have to keep in touch with the Chogyal on his visits to Geneva and look after him. During this period, between mid 1970 to early 1973, Palden Thondup visited Geneva three or four times and was quite open in his discussions with me.

As the East Pakistan issue came to a head towards the end of 1971, Palden Thondup continued his efforts to force a revision of the 1950 treaty. This time, he tried to take advantage of the fact that Chinese support for Pakistan could create pressure on India and force it to bend to his will. There were indications that he had tasked Kukula with contacting Chinese officials in Honk Kong and that he too had met with them during his trips abroad. By early 1972, Prime Minister Indira Gandhi had taken the advice to keep Palden Thondup at an arm's length and had come to the conclusion that India should place its trust in the people of Sikkim. In a note dated 14 March 1972, principal secretary to the prime minister, P.N. Haksar, made two points:[7]

1. 'Sanction behind any political framework has to be the people if the framework is to prove durable.' In this context he suggested that 'we can establish contact with the people of Sikkim, develop relationship and earn their goodwill and use that as a real lever against the vagaries of the Chogyal.' In effect, what Haksar was suggesting was the reversal of the policy that had been followed by the Indian government till 1972, of preventing the people from gaining the upper hand against the Chogyal, who had used authoritarian measures to maintain his rule over them.

2. Till such a time that the Prime Minister has 'made up her mind, she should not see the Chogyal ...' This had been accepted by Indira Gandhi and he was refused access to her.

Palden Thondup brought this up with me when he came to Geneva in early 1972. I had decided that I should be blunt with him this time. I suggested that he should critically examine certain facts. He had managed to persuade Nehru to treat Sikkim as a special case when even Olaf Caroe had made it clear that the British had treated Sikkim as an Indian princely state. He had been saved several times by Indian intervention when the popular will in Sikkim was openly in favour of joining India and subsequently, the Indian government had ensured the preservation of the status quo. It was quite clear that Delhi was in no mood to accommodate him and his wishes any longer. Once the people realized that they were being given a free hand, he was likely to feel the backlash of the populace for which he should be prepared.

The impression I had was that Prime Minister Gandhi now wanted to deal with the people of Sikkim directly. In my discussions with the Chogyal, it was clear that he had realized that he was now on a slippery slope but was still hopeful that his friend T.N. Kaul would pull his chestnuts out of the fire. Before the developments in Tibet came to a head, Kaul was even convinced that India would not follow the British policy of having Sikkim as a 'protectorate'. After the Chinese came to occupy Tibet, he changed his view and understood the strategic necessity of India declaring Sikkim a protectorate. He also endorsed the view that India would be responsible for 'good government'.

Will of the People

Triloki Nath Kaul, a former Indian Foreign Secretary, concluded that as the Chinese hold over Tibet strengthened in 1951, 'India had to strengthen her defence, communication and security in and through Sikkim'.[8] Here there was no ambiguity of the strategic importance of Sikkim to India. Kaul recognized that his friend Palden Thondup was 'fickle by nature' and that this weakness in his character was manipulated by his American wife and her 'friends', where he 'started giving pin-pricks to India, on matters, big and small. He antagonised 75% of the population which was of Nepalese origin and stifled democratic elements among *Bhutias and Lepchas* also.'[9]

Kaul did make a last-ditch effort to save the situation in September 1972. He sent Thondup a draft for the revised treaty that spelt out an agreement where a 'democratic autonomous Sikkim' would be fully in control of all its affairs while granting India control over the areas of 'defence, communications and security'. By signing this, Sikkim would succeed in removing the 'the ugly appellation of "Protectorate" from the treaty'. A draft of the new treaty, that Thondup had agreed to, was then sent to him for signature. At this stage, he went back on his agreement. He was badly advised by his friends, led by his wife and the Study Forum, as well as his legal team that had both Indian and external experts on it.

As Kaul left Delhi, with him departed the last bit of trust that anyone in Delhi had for Palden Thondup. What brought things to head was his controversial visit to Kathmandu to attend the coronation of King Birendra of Nepal in 1975. He met with the Chinese vice-premier and held detailed discussions with him. Thereafter, at a press conference, he stated that he would fight to preserve the independent identity of Sikkim and called into question the associate status that had been extended to Sikkim under the Indian Constitution in 1974. He had gone against the mass will and the wishes of the popularly elected Government of Sikkim. His antics at Kathmandu contributed to the demand for Sikkim's full merger with India.

Prime Minister Indira Gandhi had recognized that Palden Thondup had become an obstacle impeding India's interests and could no longer be trusted. She had concluded that the people of Sikkim were clearly on the side of India as they consistently maintained that Sikkim should be merged with India. By agreeing to act on their wishes, Indira Gandhi saw a permanent solution to securing India's strategic and security interests. Indian military forces stationed on the mountain heights of Sikkim would provide an effective line of defence against any Chinese attempt to threaten the vital Siliguri Corridor.

The elections that were to be held in Sikkim in 1973 asserted the popular will and came to question the position of the Chogyal, expressing anger against him and his family. A decision that was taken in March 1972 to grant the people a free hand finally came to fruition three years later, in 1975, with the merger of Sikkim with India. Around this time, the royal marriage also broke down. The Chogyal, suffering from cancer, passed away in 1982 at New York's Sloan Kettering Hospital—the last of the Namgyals to occupy the throne of Sikkim.

What was significant was that Sikkim's merger did not rouse any major protest except from the governments of China and Pakistan. This has since been, to a certain extent, overcome with China finally accepting, as part of the Tibet bargain, Sikkim's status as an integral part of India. However, it has in no way ended China's attempts to try and neutralize India's advantage of occupying strategic heights overlooking Tibet. The recent attempt by the PLA to try and gain ascendancy at Naku La in North Sikkim is part of this process.

As long as the People's Republic of China continues to occupy Tibet, the threat to India's security will remain a constant factor. Among all the areas along India's borders with Tibet that remain under constant pressure, as has happened since April 2020, the Chinese-held Chumbi Valley is the most sensitive. China has, over the years, considerably strengthened the infrastructure in the valley, specifically targeting the Siliguri Corridor. For India, this carries a message of vulnerability, especially for the North-east.

Notes

1. 'The Sikkimese Theory of Landholding and the Darjeeling Grant' in the *Bulletin of Tibetology*. This was an article that caused a degree of resentment between political Delhi and the Sikkim palace.
2. Principal Secretary P.N. Haksar's note to Prime Minister Indira Gandhi dated 14 March 1972. Cited from the Haksar Papers with the Nehru Memorial Library, New Delhi
3. Prime Minister Indira Gandhi told P.N. Dhar (former principal secretary to the prime minister) 'in very clear terms that her father had made a mistake by not heeding the Sikkimese demand for accession to India in 1947'. Mentioned in his book *Indira Gandhi: The Emergency and Indian Democracy*, P. N. Dhar, Oxford University Press, New Delhi, 2000.
4. *Tibet: An Unfinished Story*, Lezlee and Stefan Halper, Hachette India, 2014, p. 108.
5. *Ibid.*
6. *Ibid.*
7. Note recorded by P.N. Haksar, principal secretary to Prime Minister Indira Gandhi, 14 March 1972. Cited from the Haksar Papers with the Nehru Memorial Library, New Delhi.
8. *Diplomacy in Peace and War: Recollections*, T.N. Kaul, Gyan Publishing House, 2016.
9. *Ibid.*, author's emphasis.

CONCLUSION

The British never looked on Sikkim as a strategic asset that was important to the security of India. For them, Sikkim was a logistical asset serving Britain's commercial interest in Tibet. If Sikkim had been looked at in terms of its tactical significance of guarding a part of India's frontiers with Tibet, then the importance of the Chumbi Valley would have sunk in and it would not have been excised from Sikkim when the borders of Sikkim with Tibet were being delimited under the Anglo-Chinese Convention of 1890.

Sikkim's strategic importance to the defence of India really surfaced as Maoist China occupied Tibet in 1950 and the border between India and Tibet once again became a live issue, as it had been when British policies, post the Lhasa Convention of 1904, permitted the waning Manchu court of China to assert its position in Tibet. This had ended in China eyeing the Assam tribal areas (NEFA) and renewing its claims to suzerainty over Nepal, Sikkim and Bhutan.

During the entire period that India was a part of the British empire, Britain had subordinated India's strategic and security welfare in Tibet to its business interests in mainland China and to the imperatives of its European relationships with an emphasis on Russia. Lhasa had on more than one occasion exposed the myth of Chinese suzerainty by rejecting any attempts by the Chinese to impose their will over it. As this aspect became an established fact, the British launched the Younghusband invasion to arrive at a direct relationship with Lhasa.

Perhaps the biggest failure of the British was to maintain the charade of China being a nominal suzerain in Tibet, while in the same breath continuing to claim that from 1912 onwards, Tibet was 'de facto' an independent state. Whitehall in the process refused to implement the advice that it was getting from the British Indian government, that it was in India's strategic interests for London to grant diplomatic recognition to Tibet.

Unfortunately, Jawaharlal Nehru, as prime minister of a newly independent India, also failed to heed this advice. If India in 1947 had looked at Tibet as a buffer state relevant to India's strategic and security interests, it should have recognized Tibet as an independent nation by establishing diplomatic relations with it. It could have at the same time, while China was in the throes of a civil war, supported Tibet, having the protection of a membership of the United Nations. To cement its relations with a neighbouring country, India should have worked towards meeting Tibet's developmental and defence needs. Instead, Nehru permitted his romantic view of China, and the position that he had assigned to it in his vision of a resurgent Asia, to subvert the reality that a China in occupation of Tibet would pose a threat to India.

Britain had failed to keep one essential factor in mind, that China did not attach sanctity to agreements arrived with it. It had blatantly violated various agreements that it had entered into with the British on Tibet, including the Convention of 1890, the amended Convention of 1904 that it had endorsed under the Convention of 1906, and the Trade Agreement of 1908. The Chinese adhered to treaty and agreement obligations only to the point where it suited them and did not hesitate to violate the same, both in letter and spirit, when they assumed they had the upper hand.

It was only as China came to occupy Tibet and Delhi concluded that India's border with Tibet had, as in the earlier part of the twentieth century, become a live border, that India recognized Sikkim's importance to its security. This came to be reflected in the Indo-Sikkim Treaty of 1950. Unfortunately, that same logic did not carry weight with Nehru. No one in the establishment in Delhi was able to convince him that the Chumbi Valley was of vital importance to India's security and India should undertake everything possible, including the Indian Army taking it over as a defensive measure, to prevent it from falling into Chinese hands.

Thrice, the experts on the ground in Lhasa and the political office in Gangtok recommended that the Chumbi Valley be taken over. Nehru turned it down on the specious argument that India should do nothing that would 'provoke China'. He was ignoring China's past behaviour, even as he failed to take what Sardar Patel had spelt out to build up the defence of India to counter any Chinese threat to India's territorial integrity. The Chumbi Valley lay south of the Himalayan watershed and the same logic that Nehru had expressed on safeguarding the territorial integrity of the Cis-Himalayan states of Nepal, Sikkim and Bhutan could logically be extended to the valley by reclaiming it as a part of Sikkim. Moreover, the geographical structure of the valley, whose southern portion overlooking Yatung was extremely narrow, made it possible to be easily defended by a relatively small force.

Any doubts of the significance to India of the advantage that Sikkim's strategic heights provided were effectively removed as the Chinese, first during the Indo-Pak War of 1965, asked India to vacate the passes in Sikkim. China again threatened India and its position in Sikkim during the 1971 Indo-Pak War, finally attempting to dislodge India from Nathu La. Cho La was defended by a determined Indian Army in 1967. What is more, the threat the Chinese had also posed to the heights of Jelep La and Dok La had been neutralized.

One lesson that the exchanges of 1967 had driven home to the strategizing community in India was that the country had to be prepared to meet Chinese challenges that were likely to arise from time to time as they continued to upgrade their infrastructure in the Chumbi Valley. As a result, the threat to India's vulnerable Siliguri Corridor would continue to mount, with India having to build countermeasures to contain it. The actions by the PLA in 2017 at Doklam was one such challenge. The actions that they attempted at Naku La and its surrounds in North Sikkim is part of their aim to dislodge India from the strategic heights in Sikkim to reduce the effectiveness of Sikkim as a strategic asset to India's defence.

Nehru should have taken Mao's claim—that Tibet was the palm and its natural geographical reach was represented by the five fingers of Ladakh, Nepal, Sikkim, Bhutan and NEFA— seriously as it was an indication of what Mao intended to pursue as policy. Once Mao took control of China, the threat to Tibet was immediate and he did not hide his intentions. Unfortunately, what continued to prevail in Nehru's mind was a pacifist India, a country that no one would be interested in attacking—Pakistan being the only exception.

Perhaps the entire approach to Tibet that Mao and Nehru displayed can be best summed up in the following words that represent the findings of Andrew Bingham Kennedy in his study of Mao and Nehru.[1] According to him, Mao's strength lay in 'military efficacy', while Nehru's strength lay in 'moral efficacy'. One was an activist who had extensive military experience and was willing to act 'with Military boldness …' Nehru on the other hand 'remained remarkably ambitious in the diplomatic realm …' Mao acted and Nehru reacted and failed to leverage the extraterritorial rights that India had inherited as a successor state to get China to acknowledge the 1914 bilateral agreement that the British and the Tibetans, as two sovereign states, had entered into regarding India's borders with Tibet. However, Nehru's failures in this regard cannot override his considerable contributions, including the grounding of a Constitution-based democratic system of government in India.

One message that India can ignore at its own peril is that communist China is an immediate and present danger to India. China has designed a policy of containing India and has used every opportunity to put this into practice, ensuring that India is confined largely to South Asia. Prime Minister P.V. Narasimha Rao's 'Look East' policy was part of India's effort to broaden its foreign policy footprint in South East Asia and the Far East. It implied the integration of India's economic policy with those of the other major Asian economies.

It is unfortunate that the Indian political leadership has not been able to work out that China is untrustworthy and uses deceit to gain tactical advantage. Looking at all that has transpired along the Line of Actual Control since April 2020, where China has openly and with intent violated all Sino-Indian agreements to preserve peace and tranquillity along it since 1993, the Indian government should at least have learnt by now that the Chinese only bend before resolve and power. If you give them an inch, they shall see that as weakness and take their demands to insatiable limits.

Notes

1. *The International Ambitions of Mao and Nehru*, Andrew Bingham Kennedy, Cambridge University Press, 2012.

ACKNOWLEDGEMENTS

It was during the summer of 1995 when I had a long discussion with Ambassador (Retired) N.B. Menon about our days at the political office in Gangtok that he had headed and about his subsequent stint at the ministry of external affairs as the joint secretary dealing with the events that had led to the merger of Sikkim with India. I tried to persuade him to put his thoughts and views on record, but he was reluctant. This was a pity since he had liaised with China and had served twice in Nepal—the last time as the Indian ambassador—and had headed the political office, dealing intimately with both Sikkim and Bhutan. Our discussions, however, inspired me with the desire to write this book, to put across the strategic factors that lay behind India's relations with Sikkim and the fact that these were driven by events and happenings in Tibet that had come to be colonized by People's Republic of China. I would like to acknowledge the role that Ambassador Menon, his wife Aneethi and their extremely talented children played in inspiring me to write this book.

My wife Aruna, a gifted Bharata Natyam classical artiste, sacrificed her gift to participate in the adventure of diplomacy with its many ups and downs. She and my two children have been the joy of my life.

This book is also an attempt to leave something of value that my three grandchildren could identify with as it provides an insight on how I saw life as an Indian diplomat dealing with matters that were of fundamental value to India. A country that has given us a great sense of belonging, with a civilizational heritage that we can be proud of.

Last, but not least, I would like to acknowledge the support that I have received from Swati Chopra and her talented set of colleagues at HarperCollins India. They have helped in granting shape to this book that shall hopefully offer clarity and insight into the varied aspects that India has to keep in mind to ensure that its strategic and security interests are secured and preserved.

BIBLIOGRAPHY

BOOKS AND JOURNALS

Addy, Premen, *Tibet on the Imperial Chessboard*, New Delhi, 1984.

———*Tibet: Pawn and Pivot of the Great Game*, New Delhi, 2018.

Ahamd, Zehiruddin, *Sino-Tibetan Relations in the Seventeenth Century*, Rome, 1970.

———'The Historical Status of China in Tibet', *Journal of the Oriental Society of Australia,* Volume I, Numbers 1–2 of 1972–1973.

Aitchson, C.U., *A Collection of Treaties, Engagements and Sanades*, Volume 12, Leiden, 1973.

Alexandrowicz, C.H., 'India and the Tibetan Tragedy', *Foreign Affairs*, Volume 31, Number 3, 1953.

Appadorai, A. and Rajan M.S., *India's Foreign Policy and Relations*, New Delhi, 1985.

Aris, Michael and Aung San Suu Kyi, *Tibetan Studies in Honour of Hugh Richardson*, Warminister, 1980.

Aris, Michael, *Hidden Treasures and Secret Lives: A Study of Pemalingpa (1450–1521) and the Sixth Dalai Lama (1683–1706)*, Delhi, 1988.

Bajpai, S.C., *The Northern Frontier of India*, New Delhi, 1970.

Basnet, Lal Bahadur, *Sikkim: A Short Political History*, New Delhi, 1974.

Beckwith, Christopher, *The Tibetan Empire in Central Asia*, Princeton, 1987.

Bell, Charles, *Portrait of the Dalai Lama,* London, 1946.

———*Tibet: Past and Present*, Delhi, reprinted 1992.

Bhalla, Madhu, 'Nehru's Vision of Asian Identity: Implications for the Future', *South Asian Survey*, 19(2), 2012.

Bogle, George, *Bhutan and Tibet: The Travels of George Bogle and Alexander Hamilton, 1774–1777*, Roxford, 2002.

Bower, Captain H, *Some Notes on Tibet Affairs*, Calcutta, 1893.

Bushnell, Stephen W., 'The Early History ofTibet from Chinese Sources', *Journal of the Royal Asiatic Society*, 12, Number 4, 1880.

Curzon, George Nathaniel, *The Place of India in the Empire*, London, 1909.

———*Frontiers,* The Romanes Lecture of 1907.

Copeland, Ian, *The Princes of India in the Endgame of Empire, 1917–1947*, Cambridge, 1997.

Das, B.S., *The Sikkim Saga,* Delhi, 1983.

Datta-Ray, S.K., *Smash and Grab: Annexation of Sikkim*, Delhi, revised edition, 2004.

Das, Sarat Chandra, *Narrative of a Journey to Lhasa*, Calcutta, 1885.

———*Indian Pandits in the Land of Snow*, Calcutta, 1893.

Datta, Karubaki, 'Human Flows, Trade and Security: The Changing Role of the Chumbi Valley in the Himalayan Region', *Athena Journal of History*, Volume I, Issue 3.

———'Tibet Trade through the Chumbi Valley—Growth, Rupture and Reopening', *Vidyasagar University Journal of History*, 2013–14.

Dhar, P.N., *Indira Gandhi: The Emergency and Indian Democracy*, New Delhi, 2000.

Dolkar, Tsetan, *Sino-Tibetan Relations, 1990–2000: The Internationalisation of the Tibetan Issue* (dissertation), Philips University Marburg, 2008.

Duff, Andrew, *Sikkim Requiem for a Himalayan Kingdom,* Delhi, 2015.

Dutt, V.P., *India's Foreign Policy,* New Delhi, 1984.

Edgar, J.W., *Report on a Visit to Sikhim and the Thibetan Frontier*, New Delhi, 1969.

Fraser, Lovat, *India under Curzon and After*, London, 1911.

Gopal, Sarvepalli, *Jawaharlal Nehru: A Biography* in three volumes: Volume one (1889–1947) Volume two (1947–1956) and Volume three (1956–1964), Delhi, 1984.

Goldstein, Melvyn, *A History of Modern Tibet*, Volume I: 1913–1911 (1989), *Demise of the Lamaist State*, Volume II: 1951–1955 (2007), *The Calm before the Storm.*

———*The Snow Lion and the Dragon: China, Tibet and the Dalai Lama*, Berkley, 1997.

Gould, Basil J., *The Jewel in the Lotus: Recollections of an Indian Political*, London, 1957.

Gros, Stephane, *Chronology of Major Events with Particular Attention to the Sino-Tibetan Borderlands*, Amsterdam, 2019.

Grover, B., *Sikkim and India: Storm and Consolidation*, New Delhi, 1974.

Guha, Ramchandra, *Jawaharlal Nehru and China: A Study in Failure*, Harvard-Yenching Institute, 2011.

Halper, Lezlee Brown and Halper, Stefan, *Tibet: An Unfinished Story*, London, 2014.

Harrer, Heinrich, *Seven Years in Tibet*, London, 1953.

Holdich, Thomas H., *Tibet: The Mysterious*, New York, 1906.

Hopkirk, Peter, *Trespassers on the Roof of the World: The Race for Lhasa*, Oxford, 1997.

Jiang, W., *The Thirty-Strategies (Classic War Strategies, 800–300 BC).*

Lamb, Alastair, *British India and Tibet, 1776–1910*, London, 1960, 1986.

———*The China India Border: The Origins of the Disputed Boundaries*, London, 1964.

Kapur, Ashok and Wilson A. Jeyaratnam, *The Foreign Policy of India and Her Neighbours,* London and New York, 1996.

Kennedy, Andrew Bingham, *The International Ambitions of Mao and Nehru: National Efficacy Beliefs and the Making of Foreign Policy*, Cambridge, 2012.

Kirk, W., *The Inner Asian Frontier of India,* 1962.

Lau, Hon-Shiang, 'Tibet Was Never Part of China Before 1950: Examples of Authoritative Pre-1949 Chinese Documents that Prove It', *National Security*, Vol. II, Issue I.

Longer, V., *The Defence and Foreign Policies of India*, New Delhi, 1988.

Luthi, Lorenz, *Sino-Indian Relations, 1954–1962*, Hokkaido University, 2012.

Mehra, Parshotam, *Essays in Frontier History: India, China, and the Disputed Border*, New Delhi, 2007.

———*Lord Curzon's Despatch of January 8, 1903: Its Impact on His Tibetan Policy, Proceedings of the Indian History Congress*, Volume 21, 1958.

McKay, Alex (ed.), *Tibet and Her Neighbours: A History*, London, 2003.

———'A Difficult Country, a Hostile Chief, and a Still More Hostile Minister: The Anglo-Sikkim War of 1861', *Bulletin of Tibetology*, 2009/2010.

———*Tibet and the British Raj: The Frontier Cadre, 1904–1907*, London, 1997.

Mayer, Robert, *Geographical and Other Borders in the Symbolism of Padmasambhava*, New York, 2018.

Macaulay, Coleman, *Report of a Mission to Sikkim and the Tibetan Frontier: With a Memorandum.*

Markham, Sir C.R., *Narrative of the Mission of George Bogle to Tibet and the Journey of Thomas Manning to Lhasa, 1879.*

McGranahan, Carole, *From Simla to Rongbatsa: The British and the 'Modern' Boundaries of Tibet, from the Tibet Journal*, 1999.

Montgomerie, Captain T.G., 'Report of the Trans-Himalayan Explorations, during 1867', *Journal of the Royal Geographical Society*, Volume 39, 1869.

Mullard, Saul, *Tibetan and Sikkimese Relations: Preliminary Remarks on the Gam Pa Disputes and the Gam Pa—Sikkim Agreement 1867*, Namgyal Institute of Tibetology.

Mullik, B.N., *The Chinese Betrayal*, New Delhi, 1971.

Norbu Dawa, *China's Tibet Policy*, London, 2001.

Oidtmann, Max, *A 'Dog-eat-dog' World: Qinq Jurispractices and Legal Inscription of Piety in Amdo*, De l' Institut d'Asie orientale, issue edited by Jerome Bourgon.

Palace, Wendy, *The British Empire and Tibet, 1900–1922*, London, 2005.

———*Losing Face: The British Foreign Service and the Question of Tibet, 1904–1922* (dissertation), University of Durham, 1995.

Rai, Rajeev, *The State in the Colonial Periphery: A Study on Sikkim's Relations with Great Britain*, Gangtok, 2014.

Richardson, H.E., *A Short History of Tibet*, New York, 1962.

———*A Corpus of Early Tibetan Inscriptions*, Royal Asiatic Society, 1985.

Risley, H.H., *The Gazetteer of Sikhim*, Calcutta, 1894.

Sanderson, Henry, *Transgressions of the Frontier: An Analysis of Documents to the British Invasion of Tibet*, Columbia University, 2012.

Schaik, Sam Van, *Tibet: A History*, New Delhi, 2011.

Shakabpa, Tsepon, *Tibet: A Political History*, Yale, 1967.

Shakya Tsering, *The Dragon in the Land of Snows: A History of Modern Tibet since 1947*, London, 2000.

Sinha, A.C., *Himalayan Odyssey: Attempts for Federation of the Himalayan Kingdoms,* Dialogue Volume-16, No. 3.

Singh, Amar Kaur Jasbir, *Himalayan Triangle: Historical Survey of British India's Relations with Tibet, Sikkim and Bhutan, 1765–1950,* London, 1988.

Spence, Heather, *British Policy and the 'Development' of Tibet, 1912–1933* (dissertation), University of Wollongong, 1993.

Sperling, Elliot, *The Tibet-China Conflict: History and Polemics*, Washington, 2004.

Sykes, Sir Percy, *The Right Honourable Sir Mortimer Durand: A Biography*, London, 1926.

The People's Daily, 'The Revolution in Tibet and Nehru's Philosophy', 6 May 1959.

Thorat, Lt. General S.P.P., *From Reveille to Retreat*, Mumbai, 1986.

Topgyal, Tsering, *The Insecurity Dilemma and the Sino-Tibetan Conflict* (dissertation), London School of Economics and Political Science.

Vertzberger, Yaacov Y.I., *Misperceptions in Foreign Policymaking: The Sino-Indian Conflict, 1959–1962*, Boulder, 1984.

Waddell, L. Austine, *The Buddhism of Tibet or Lamaism*, London, 1897.

Walcott, Susan, 'Bordering the Eastern Himalaya: Boundaries, Passes, Power Contestations, Geopolitics', *Geopolitics*, 2010.

White, J. Claude, *Sikhim and Bhutan: Twenty-one Years on the North-East Frontier, 1887–1908*, London, 1909.

Younghusband, Francis, *India and Tibet*, Oxford, 1910.

Zhao, Yinan, *The Real Crux of Sino-Tibetan Relations*, Stanford University, 2004.

Zoe, Chen Y., 'Never Obsolescent: A Modern View of the Thirty-Six Strategies', *Global Negotiator Journal*, 2002.

INDEX

ABOUT THE AUTHOR

Preet Mohan Singh Malik has been a member of the Indian Foreign Service since 1962. He was posted in Gangtok from October 1967 to April 1970 at the political office for India to Sikkim and Bhutan. He has also served as India's ambassador to Bahrain, Cuba and Myanmar, as high commissioner to Tanzania with concurrent accreditation to the Seychelles, and Malaysia with concurrent accreditation to Brunei. He has worked at the permanent missions of India to the European office of the United Nations (UN) in Geneva where he was also a delegate to the Disarmament Conference and on the governing body of the International Labour Organization. He was a deputy permanent representative at the UN Mission in New York. He specialized in economic diplomacy, covering both bilateral and multilateral areas. He was a member representing the ministry of external affairs, of both the Foreign Investment Promotion Board and the steering committee on economic reforms chaired by the principal secretary to the prime minister (1992–95).